EVERYDAY WAR

EVERYDAY WAR

The Conflict over Donbas, Ukraine

Greta Lynn Uehling

CORNELL UNIVERSITY PRESS   ITHACA AND LONDON

First published 2023 by Cornell University Press

Printed in the United States of America

Library of Congress Cataloging-in-Publication Data
Names: Uehling, Greta Lynn, author.
Title: Everyday war : the conflict over Donbas, Ukraine / Greta Lynn Uehling.
Description: Ithaca : Cornell University Press, 2023. | Includes bibliographical
    references and index.
Identifiers: LCCN 2022016914 (print) | LCCN 2022016915 (ebook) |
    ISBN 9781501767593 (hardcover) | ISBN 9781501768484 (paperback) |
    ISBN 9781501767609 (pdf) | ISBN 9781501767616 (epub)
Subjects: LCSH: Ukraine Conflict, 2014—Social aspects. | War and society—
    Ukraine—History—21st century. | Donetsʹka oblastʹ (Ukraine)—Social
    conditions—21st century. | Luhansʹka oblastʹ (Ukraine)—Social conditions—
    21st century. | Russia (Federation)—Foreign relations—Ukraine. |
    Ukraine—Foreign relations—Russia (Federation)
Classification: LCC DK508.852 .U33 2023 (print) | LCC DK508.852 (ebook) |
    DDC 947.7086—dc23/eng/20220527
LC record available at https://lccn.loc.gov/2022016914
LC ebook record available at https://lccn.loc.gov/2022016915

This book is dedicated to my students at the
University of Michigan: past, present, and future.

When the rich wage war, it's the poor who die.
—Jean-Paul Sartre, *Le diable et le bon dieu*

Contents

Preface

This book explores the conflict over the eastern Ukrainian provinces of Donetsk and Luhansk. The chapters that follow are part of a larger effort to understand the subjective experience of war and forced displacement. I aim to bring these experiences, which are not incidentally the experiences of an increasing percentage of the world's population, to my undergraduate students as well as other readers. The book is intended to provide an accessible lens through which to grasp something of what noncombatant civilians go through in a war zone: for as long as there are armed conflicts, we need to grasp more concretely and realistically what they are all about.

I carried out the research for this book as a Fulbright scholar in Ukraine between the years of 2015 and 2017. As a Fulbright scholar, I was fortunate to have a grant that enabled me to fulfill my teaching obligations at the University of Michigan during the academic school year and do fieldwork in the summer months. On three consecutive trips of two months each, I visited shelters for the internally displaced, attended workshops intended to help forced migrants adjust to their new circumstances, and completed many interviews, crossing the country repeatedly to talk to as many people as I could.

This project almost did not get off the ground. My proposal to the Fulbright foundation had laid out a plan to investigate the relationship between public commemoration of the past and ethnic tolerance in Crimea. That book will have to wait because while my proposal was being considered by the Fulbright foundation, something my Crimean Tatar friends had been warning me about since the mid-1990s happened: Crimea was occupied by the Russian Federation. This prevented me and most other foreigners from traveling to Crimea. The Fulbright foundation generously suggested I carry out research anyway. With many of my Crimean Tatar friends and colleagues having fled the peninsula for their safety, and having carried out multiple research projects on forced migration in a variety of settings in the past, it made sense to shift my focus to the forced migration resulting from the 2014 attempted annexation of the Crimean peninsula and the population displacement from the eastern provinces of Donetsk and Luhansk.

I embarked on this project, then, having previously completed other ethnographic fieldwork in former Soviet republics. In the late 1990s, my dissertation research was concerned with the repatriation of the Crimean Tatars, who were deported from their historic homeland in Crimea to the Urals and Soviet Central

Asia in 1944 according to an order by Josef Stalin. For that project, I lived in Crimea and the Central Asian republic of Uzbekistan, traveling to the Russian Federation for archival research and to Tajikistan and Kazakhstan for interviewing purposes. In the intervening years between the book that emerged from my dissertation, *Beyond Memory*, and this one, I benefitted from opportunities to work with intergovernmental organizations like UNHCR on issues of migration. I also expanded my knowledge by working with nongovernmental organizations that were providing services to undocumented migrants, survivors of human trafficking, and refugees.

My interest in what was happening in the Donetsk and Luhansk provinces of Ukraine solidified when I spoke with Mikaela. She had been forcibly displaced from Donetsk at the beginning of the military conflict. Active in politics, she had voiced her opinion that Donetsk remain part of Ukraine. Her name was placed on a ledger of people to be killed. A mid-morning phone call in March 2014 tipped her off that people known to be pro-Russian separatists were driving toward her rural home. Expecting such a day, her political allies had been keeping their eyes on the roads and estimated that she had about twenty minutes until they arrived. Following a preestablished plan, she stepped out to her neighbor's house with nothing more than her wallet, phone, and a change of clothes in her purse. She and her neighbor got into his car and, without any need for discussion, drove to Kyiv. On the surface, Mikaela confirms what we have learned to expect from wartime displacement: loss. In just a few minutes, she had lost her comfortable home, her career in metallurgy, and the ability to care for her young children, who went to live with their grandparents. Mikaela's story, however, also illuminates how some of the conflict's dynamics were far less chaotic than one might imagine. Her departure was finely calibrated by cellular phone. And in one of the most wrenching moments of her life, she had support: her neighbor was willing to undertake this risky drive even though he was under no obligation. To what extent did Mikaela's experience exemplify a broader, national experience? I wanted to know so much more.

The topic of conflict in eastern Ukraine resonated with me not only because of these scholarly and professional experiences, however, but my personal experiences growing up. When the Vietnam War was winding down in the mid-1970s, I was still a girl. I remember the black-and-white images of beleaguered American soldiers flickering across my parents' twelve-inch black-and-white television screen. From the perspective of my perch at the foot of my parents' bed, the war was very perplexing. When the photo of a naked girl, Kim Phuc, fleeing her village after an aerial napalm attack appeared on the cover of *Life* magazine, I was troubled by the sight of a girl about my own size in such a public display of agony. Why were she and people like her—nonparticipants in the military conflict—not more protected? The Pulitzer Prize–winning image haunted me from the coffee table in our living room. It did not make sense to me, even after it became iconic of the war itself. Perhaps this is the way stories of war get told: we create icons of violence that come to stand for a multiplicity of experiences. This book is an invitation to think about war in a more complex and personal way.

The work I have done on the conflict over the Donetsk and Luhansk provinces related in the chapters ahead brought me full circle. Fieldwork offers ethnographers unique opportunities to reflect on assumptions that have previously been taken for granted. In particular, I revisited and revised the sense that—to phrase it perhaps too simplistically—we are all fundamentally alone and must fend for ourselves. Everywhere I turned while doing fieldwork, it seemed, were examples to the contrary. Maybe Pasha, a man who fled Luhansk to put down stakes on the outskirts of Kyiv said it best when he asked rhetorically, "You know that feeling that you could be left without anything? It's gone." In writing about individuals seeking peace and protection amid indiscriminate violence, I often reached back to the thoughts of that girl at the foot of her parents' bed who wondered how the authorities in charge could abandon the victims and survivors of war. This is a book about the human capacity to deliver comfort and care in spite or perhaps because of military conflict.

Acknowledgments

Foremost, I am indebted to the many people in Ukraine who shared their thoughts with me. This book would simply not have come to fruition without your willingness to speak about the painful subject of the military conflict tearing your country apart. The thoughtfulness with which you engaged my questions deepened my study immeasurably. In addition to the internally displaced persons who shared their remarkable stories, I want to thank the humanitarians and other professionals who, as a result of their aid and mental health work, helped me to see both the themes and their variations. A special thanks go to humanitarians "Kyrylo," "Taras," and "Sergei" for so generously sharing their extensive knowledge with me. Without them, this book would have been very different.

My work in Ukraine was greatly advanced by nongovernmental organizations KrimSOS (multiple branches), VostokSOS (Kyiv), Country of Free People, and Crimean Diaspora. With laudable professionalism, these organizations introduced me to many of the internally displaced persons we hear from in the pages ahead. On some occasions, they also provided me with a quiet place to converse, eliminating the need to choose between the shrill scream of espresso machines in coffeeshops or dizzying exhaust fumes wafting through public city parks I had otherwise to contend with. A special thanks go to professionals Tamila Tasheva, Alim Aliev, Anatolii Zasoba, Vitalii Zakharchuk, Elena Shlyapentokk, Olexandr Danylov, and "Natasha," who were all immensely helpful to the completion of this project. Martin Kisley, in a category of his own, was always ready with all kinds of help and advice.

I am very grateful to Fulbright Ukraine for funding the research on which this book is based, and having confidence in me as a scholar when the project I proposed was no longer viable due to political events. I owe a special debt to the wonderful, caring, and intelligent Marta Kolomayets, then director of the Fulbright program in Ukraine, who passed away while this book was under review. Our conversations sparked the idea for the draft title of this book: *PTSD Land*. Natalia Zalutska provided magnificent and indeed multifaceted support from crisis mapping and suitcase storage to introducing me to other scholars in Ukraine.

In Kyiv, I benefitted greatly from Taras Shevchenko National University, which provided an institutional home base while I was in Ukraine. At Taras Shevchenko National University, I would like to thank Olga Pyshnokha, head of the newly formed Department of Crimean Tatar Studies (under the auspices of the Department of Turkish Studies) and Irina Ka for hosting me. They included me in all manner of cultural events, provided tireless support on complicated visa issues, and made my time in the capital much more enjoyable than it otherwise would have been.

Many classes, conferences, and symposia afforded me the opportunity to obtain valuable feedback on this work. During the period in which I was writing, I presented at the Center for Russian, East European, and Eurasian Studies (CREES) at the University of Michigan, the International Studies Association (ISA), the Council for European Studies, Soyuz: The Research Network for Post-socialist Cultural Studies, the University of Indiana symposium "Population Displacement in Eurasia" held by the Department of Anthropology, and the Temerty Contemporary Ukraine Program at Harvard University. The 2015 Danyliw Seminar hosted by the Chair of Ukrainian Studies at the University of Ottawa provided an especially rich and sustained forum for discussion. Another opportunity for which I am particularly grateful was presenting this work at the "Rewriting the Paradigm of Foreign Affairs" symposium held by the *Tulane Journal of Policy and Political Economy*. And speaking of undergraduates, my life and the life of this book have been enriched by my interaction with students in the Program in International and Comparative Studies at the University of Michigan. Their intellectual curiosity and energy are in many ways the "special sauce" that sustained me over the long process of book writing.

During the summer of 2018, I was a fellow at the Institute for the Humanities at the University of Michigan. The eight-week position provided a safe harbor for thinking and most importantly rethinking the overall trajectory of the book. Many thanks are due to Peggy McCracken, Philip D'Anieri, Jeremiah Chamberlain, Ashley Lucas, Scott Spector, Victor Fanucchi, and David Gold (in no particular order) for reading and discussing drafts of chapters both during and long after the fellowship ended. I feel especially indebted to Peggy McCracken, the Institute's director, for her many insightful comments. I learned a great deal from our exchanges, which determined the order of the chapters and informed the shape this book eventually took.

To my daughter Thea, thank you for your patience. In addition to cheerfully caring for the full menagerie of pets and plants during my absences, your "beginner's mind" questions over meals were enormously helpful, enabling me to sharpen my thoughts and renew my purpose. Perhaps someday we will be able to travel through eastern Europe together.

Any errors or omissions in the manuscript are of course my own.

Abbreviations

ATO	Antiterrorist operation
DNR	Donetsk People's Republic
ERW	Explosive remnants of war
GCA	Government-controlled area
ICC	International Criminal Court
ICRC	International Committee for the Red Cross
IDP	Internally Displaced Person
LNR	Luhansk People's Republic
NATO	North Atlantic Treaty Organization
NGCA	Nongovernment-controlled area
NGO	Nongovernment organization
OCHA	Office for the Coordination of Humanitarian Affairs
OHCHR	Office of the High Commissioner for Human Rights
PTSD	Posttraumatic stress disorder
CIMIC	Office of Civil-Military Cooperation of the Armed Forces of Ukraine
SBU	Security Service of Ukraine
UN	United Nations

Note on Transliteration

This transliteration of Russian and Ukrainian names used in this book conforms to the Library of Congress transliteration system, without the diacritical marks. Geographical place names are given according to the official form accepted in Ukraine at the time of the book's writing. In the bibliography, however, I follow the Russian spelling of "Kiev" as a place if it was the spelling used in the original. Unless otherwise indicated, all translations of quotations from Russian into English are my own. Translations of quotations in Ukrainian were made by the author's research assistant.

EVERYDAY WAR

EVERYDAY WAR

"Do you want to go to the green, yellow, or red zone?" Kyrylo bellowed enthusiastically. He was gripping the wheel of his probably mufflerless SUV and we were barreling down a superhighway outside of Kyiv, Ukraine. It was 2015, and Kyrylo lived on the other side of the country in the nongovernment-controlled part of Donetsk, but traveled to the capital city regularly to gather supplies and meet with colleagues about his humanitarian work. His color-coded levels of risk, brilliantly calibrated to the universal language of the stop light, were intended to help manage the perils of working in close proximity to military violence. For the red zone where sniper fire was common, I would need a helmet, Kevlar, and exhaustive knowledge of where to take cover at any moment. In the yellow zone where there could be heavy artillery fire, I would need to be connected to the flow of information at a granular level: knowing the forecast in the military microclimate was essential to survival. In the green zone, I might see plumes of smoke or be awakened by the grumbling of artillery fire, but there would not be life-threatening dangers, he told me. Kyrylo's stoplight metaphor challenged my previous way of thinking about war as chaos. He showed me the side of military conflict that entails planned destruction. But the simplicity of this mental mapping stands out against another reality, which was the complexity of who was fighting whom, and why. And while it might seem surprising, people, including families with small children, lived in the red zone, vividly demonstrating that contemporary conflicts threaten life's very ongoingness: one could be shot and killed while stepping out to buy bread.

Between 2014 and 2017 alone, the conflict over the Ukrainian provinces of Donetsk and Luhansk extinguished well over 13,000 lives (many of which were

FIGURE 1.   Map of Ukraine. Cartography by Bill Nelson

civilian) and injured at least 24,000 people (OHCHR 2017, 1). Tens of thousands were missing and presumed dead. Over two million people had been forcibly displaced (OHCHR 2017, 1; Mukomel 2017, 105), and the United Nations Office for the Coordination of Humanitarian Affairs (OCHA) estimated the population of humanitarian concern to be five million (OCHA 2020, 1). The scars of the conflict marked the earth itself: by 2017 Ukrainian soil had one of the highest concentrations of landmines in the world (OCHA 2020). Unless removed, these mines will shift over time and take lives and limbs for decades to come. Eight years on at this writing, and despite multiple efforts to end the conflict, peace remains elusive.

This book is less concerned with the statistics, however, than the subjective experience of military conflict. The chapters seek to expand the boundaries of what we take to be war. Contemporary military conflicts are increasingly being fought in residential areas, and the protagonists have changed. We therefore need to stop thinking about military conflict as something that is primarily waged between the trained soldiers of states. Theories of "new wars" and "hybrid wars" (Kaldor 2013; 2006; Hoffman 200) postulate that cyber-technologies, Jihadists, mercenaries, disinformation, election interference, and forcible population displacement characterize contemporary military conflicts. But these concepts still implicitly treat states as the most important actors. If today's wars are increasingly fought in civilian areas, it is all the more imperative to study (as this book aims to do) what happens among the noncombatants who live in areas where conflict and combat occur.

The Conflict over Donbas and this Book

The military conflict began in the wake of the 2013–2014 revolution, also known as the Revolution of Dignity or the Maidan movement. The revolution initially sought to bring about greater integration with the European Union, an objective that aroused sharp controversy in the eastern provinces of Donetsk and Luhansk, Ukraine. Protestors took to the streets and while some supported the political transition going on in Kyiv, others were against it. In March 2014, insurgents in the city of Sloviansk seized administrative buildings as well as the police station, and the first shots were fired. It was the beginning of a bloody armed conflict, sometimes called a hybrid war because of Russia's covert intervention using multiple modalities on behalf of the insurgents. The conflict therefore had both domestic and international dimensions that are elaborated on in the next chapter.

For now, suffice it to say that Ukraine's aspirations to be more integrated with the West, aspirations that the United States and the European Union encouraged, hardly played well in Moscow, and helped inspire the occupation of Crimea. The "success" of the Crimean operation is believed to have helped embolden President Vladimir Putin to support the anti-Maidan insurgency in eastern Ukraine. In the beginning, mercenaries paid by the Russian Federation were important actors in the conflict. At the battle of Ilovaisk, that began in August 2014, Russian military forces became more identifiably involved. Owing to how weak the Ukrainian military was at this time, it was up to battalions of volunteer fighters, coming from all walks of life, to limit this advance. The United States also provided support, including technical advice, training, and eventually the transfer of advanced military equipment like surface-to-air missile launchers. This was on top of the United States Department of State having advised the Ukrainian government to have its troops stand down when Crimea was occupied. A great deal of debate has centered on who is to blame: kto vinovat? Ukraine's territorial integrity and the social identities, political rights, and economic livelihoods of people across this region, not to mention respect for state sovereignty more generally, are at stake.

The first half of the book takes place in government-controlled parts of Ukraine. These chapters are organized around friend, family, and romantic partner relationships to illuminate the specific ways in which war can reconfigure intimacy while intimate relationships are the site of a different, everyday kind of war. The second half of the book is focused on life in and around the Donetsk and Luhansk provinces, where residents in close proximity to the military conflict were left, for the most part, to fend for themselves. Based on my interlocutors' descriptions, a place with mercenary gunmen, criminal gangs, and political chaos was, paradoxically, also a place where ethics thrived.

In fact, what I found throughout was a constellation of social practices demonstrating care. I understand care here as the practices directed toward repairing and maintaining a livable world (Puig de la Bellacasa 2017, 3). Practices of care give rise to moral thinking based on the "existential fact of human vulnerability and relatedness, and the capacity to recognize and respond to the needs of others" (Vaittinen et al. 2019, 197). Not just any others of course, but specific others, both dead and alive. Each person navigated choices about when and where to care, and oftentimes, priorities changed. They affirmed what philosopher Emmanuel Levinas claimed about our ethical obligations extending beyond already established relationships and communities. Each chapter considers a different site where care can produce interpersonal peace or its antipode, everyday war. The overarching question is: how did people create care and forge peace in the face of indiscriminate violence, and what kind of peace was it? I traversed Ukraine from north to south and east to west to find out.

I have often been asked why the chapters of this book are so concerned with interpersonal relationships. Why not NGOs, for example? As one reader pointed out, they too were involved in caring for people, and perhaps on a much larger scale. The answer is hidden in plain sight. As an anthropologist, I have always hewed closely to an inductive approach. With an inductive approach, a researcher begins with as few preconceptions and intellectual agendas as possible, allowing the theory to emerge from the data. This can be contrasted with a deductive approach, in which a hypothesis is generated from existing theory, and data are collected to test the hypothesis. The people I spoke with across Ukraine told me repeatedly and in no uncertain terms that they were most troubled by the effect of the military conflict on intimate relationships. When I consulted the anthropological literature on armed conflict, I found that this subject was typically addressed tangentially. Most often, the focus is particular categories of people (e.g., child soldiers, survivors of rape, etc.). When relationships are addressed, it seems the main concern is with instances of unexpected violence between people who had amiable relationships in the past. Titles like *We Wish to Inform You That Tomorrow We Will be Killed with Our Families* (Gourevitch 1998) and *Intimate Enemies: Landowners, Power, and Violence in Chiapas* (Bobrow-Strain 2007) provide rich insights into this topic. With utmost respect for the value of these works, I found the instances when violence did not occur—and examples will be provided in the pages ahead—to be productive sites of inquiry.

The inductive approach that led me to relationships also suggests a departure from the larger trajectory of military memoires over time. After thousands of years in which the dominant literary paradigm was to valorize the "guts-and-glory" of war, the last one hundred years has seen a dramatic shift to the idea that "war is hell," argues Yuval Harari (2004, 19). Military memoirs have concomitantly gone from emphasizing collective campaigns for victory to personal journeys. Many of the best written accounts in Harari's estimation argue war is not what you see in the movies. Ironically, the most popular movies try to show that war is not what you see in the movies (Harari 2004, 20). But what kind of "hell" is this? My research provides a new angle on this question by considering relationships. I show how in Donbas, it was an interpersonal "hell" in which you cannot call home because you mother (or sister, father, brother, or lover) is on the opposite political side.

The "subjects" in this ethnography, then, are not so much individuals, although individuals do figure prominently, as the relationships between them. This is to say the book is concerned with the interstitial social spaces of human relationships. People who ended friendships as a result of the conflict, for example, expressed the salient political divisions microcosmically in a quotidian cold war. The extent to which this served any macropolitical outcome is difficult to calculate. What most interests me here is that relationships became another site for working out the conflict's tensions. This is the underbelly of war that, if illuminated, could stand to transform how we understand the beast.

The main weakness of the inductive approach is that it is incomplete. Most frustrating at the time I did my research was just how difficult it was to find people willing to articulate a pro-Russian position. I know they existed. On one occasion, for example, a friend suggested I meet Liuba because she would "blow my mind" with her favorable outlook on the Donetsk People's Republic or DNR. The three of us met but Liuba did not say anything in favor of the DNR or Russia. Even when probed, she shrugged and disavowed any favorable thoughts on the regime set up by the de facto authorities there. Over time I came to better appreciate how she could not have affirmed the delegitimized proto-states without also taking an enormous risk. So important was it to keep her Donbas origins and her political opinions private that she told people she was from Crimea to "keep things simple." Just coming from Donetsk jeopardized her prospects for housing and employment in the government-controlled parts of the country. In this politicized atmosphere, pro-Russian speech was considered tantamount to treason. This, too, is part of the story of war.

Methodology for a Country at War 2015–2017

The chapters that follow are based, as I have mentioned, on ethnographic field-work carried out in Ukraine over the summers of 2015, 2016, and 2017. To understand how the conflict was affecting people, I spent time in shelters for the internally displaced. These dwellings took a variety of forms because schools, hospitals, hotels, homes, and even the servants' quarters of the former president's estate were all repurposed to accommodate the displaced in the early days of the conflict. With internally displaced persons (IDPs) I attended barbecues, went on day trips, and participated in workshops. Long and unstructured periods of time spent at the homes of the internally displaced allowed me to become more deeply familiar with what daily life in a situation of forced displacement was like. I also went to veterans' centers, attended church services in former conflict zones, and spoke with the families of deceased soldiers. Conversations over coffee with social workers, humanitarians, psychologists, and the staff of social service agencies helped me get my bearings in this terrain. In trips lasting approximately two months each, I taped sixty-five interviews pertaining to the war in Donbas.

Like a fellow itinerant, I spent a great deal of time on the Ukrainian railroad: in summer 2016 alone, I covered 2,974 miles. The extensive travel during my research made it clear that perceptions of the conflict transpiring in the Donetsk and Luhansk provinces varied greatly in different parts of the country. Near to the fronts, such as in Kramotorsk, the atmosphere was bleak. Especially in towns where combat had occurred, schools, health clinics, and stores lay in rubble, the road signs still pockmarked with bullet holes. In the western part of the country in contrast, the cheerful flowerboxes and bustling restaurants betrayed no signs of the fighting. The picture also changed over the time I was there. In the beginning there was a profusion of men in uniform displaying a dizzying array of shoulder sleeve insignia, epaulets, and pins to identify their volunteer battalions. In time, the conflict became less visible. In short, these contrasts are part of the story of the war, which is not a homogenous experience.

Throughout, I carried out two main kinds of interviews: semistructured sessions with internally displaced persons based on a series of questions that was held constant, with only minor variations over the three summers; and conversations with people who were best engaged in a much less structured way because of their professional work. All interviews were carried out face-to-face and in a language of the interviewees' choosing. The majority chose Russian, having recently left a predominantly Russian-speaking area. This is a language I am fluent in. Others chose English or Ukrainian. Since I understand but do not fluently speak the latter, I employed the services of a native Ukrainian speaker for the interviews in Ukrainian. Of the sixty-five taped interviews pertaining to Donbas, forty-five interviews were carried out with displaced people using the semi-structured interview format, and twenty were carried out using questions tailored to the individuals' expertise as social workers, mental health providers or humanitarian workers.

The forty-five respondents for the semistructured interviews were selected with an eye to balancing age and gender in the selection process through quota sampling. Demographic information pertaining to level of education, marital status, employment status, type of housing, and perceived economic well-being was also collected. As for ethnicity, the majority of the people I spoke with had mixed Russian and Ukrainian heritage. The shifts taking place in ethnic and national identity present a complex subject dealt with in the pages ahead.[1] For logistical help in locating internally displaced persons to interview, I partly relied on the "hubs" (khabs), nongovernmental organizations where IDPs congregated for advice, training, and social support. I also used what has been called "opportunistic sampling" by inviting people I met at social events over the three-year period to speak with me privately about their experiences.

Since the conflict dispersed people across Ukraine, I traveled to multiple cities and villages to speak with as wide a spectrum of people as possible. Several cities proved especially advantageous to research. Of the places I stayed each year, Kyiv has the largest concentration of IDPs and was commonly described, by IDPs at least, as the best location for their employment and political engagement. Lviv, considered the cultural capital of the country, was attractive to people who identified as entrepreneurial or creative. As one of the most western cities in Ukraine, it also appealed to people who were considering onward migration to western Europe. In the east, I spent time in Sloviansk, where the fighting initially started, and Kramatorsk, which had undergone an intense siege. IDPs who hoped to return to Donbas or had relatives in the nearby NGCA congregated in these cities. In the southeast, Kherson proved to be a magnet for people who wanted a safer distance than Sloviansk or Kramatorsk could provide. As a port city with a concentration of professionals concerned with IDP issues, it also boasted a robust support network.

Upon my return to the United States each year, I transcribed the recordings with the help of an assistant. I then coded and analyzed the transcripts thematically. I elected to code with an "emergent" or iterative approach to be as sensitive to what people were telling me as possible, rather than code according to a predefined scheme. Once the material was coded, queries were carried out to understand

FIGURE 2. Damaged mill and bicyclist

FIGURE 3. Store damaged by military conflict

the density of each theme and how the themes that emerged were related to one another. In the final structure, relationality, subjectivity, and governance were umbrella or "parent" codes for more granular themes, including changes to friends and family, values, and attitudes toward the violent conflict.

As many before me have attested, the violence propagated by war is difficult—some argue impossible—to render into language. Unless careful, researchers risk causing immense harm. I navigated this metaphorical minefield in a number of ways. As a matter of professional ethics, I avoided interviewing individuals I knew to be experiencing serious or debilitating mental health issues as a result of their experiences. In this regard, the help of NGOs (nongovernmental organizations) was especially valuable because they introduced me to those internally displaced persons who they felt were ready to talk about their experiences.

With some qualifications that I will elaborate on in a moment, I found the people I spoke with eager to share their experiences. They told me that they valued speaking with someone who had not experienced the military conflict in the ways they had. In this respect, my identity as an outsider was useful. This sentiment was perhaps most succinctly stated by Yuliya, who thanked me for our conversation by stating it was like her "pill for the day." Noting the empathy that she felt during our encounter, she expressed gratitude for the opportunity to talk. I do not think she was being polite because other people also said it was cathartic—in a good way—to tell their stories to someone who had not gone through what they had. To them I represented something of a blank slate: I had no Ukrainian political party affiliation to quarrel about or personal experience of forced displacement that would render their account redundant. But I was uncomfortable with the idea that my work was construed as therapeutic because I am not a mental health professional. Given the vulnerability of my interlocutors, and in keeping with the ethical considerations described above, I began each interview by clarifying that my interlocutor could at any time opt out of answering any question, take a break, or end the conversation for any reason at any time.

I hoped that allowing respondents to opt out of any question would remind people who had been forcibly displaced that they still had a choice when it came to speaking with me. I also intended these measures to create a sense of emotional safety. Since politics were at the nucleus of the military conflict, many people were skittish about discussing politics, and some agreed to be interviewed only on the condition that they would not have to answer questions construed as political. I did speak with people who worked with the de facto authorities of the DNR and LNR and who would have preferred to go to Russia. They were especially circumspect about discussing politics because when I was carrying out my fieldwork; the only politically correct stance in government-controlled Ukraine was to be pro-Ukrainian. This shaped the text in front of you. I came to understand the political dimensions of the conflict through its impact on interpersonal relationships, and the chapters of this book reflect this epistemology.

To protect the identities of the people I spoke with, all interviewees were given anonymity. In fact, I did not ask my subjects' last names when I carried out the interviews. This too seemed to help put people at ease. All of the people quoted in this book have been given pseudonyms. In some cases, I have changed the names of cities to protect individuals' identities. I have also imposed pseudonyms on top of the pseudonyms humanitarian workers were already using to avoid identifying them inadvertently. This was prudent because humanitarians were sometimes vilified as Ukrainian "spies" in the noncontrolled territory and feared to be separatist "terrorists" when they returned to government-controlled areas.

In a way, being American was advantageous. Although people did occasionally entertain the possibility that I might be running an intelligence operation, they did not seem troubled by the prospect. More important to them was that I did not have Ukrainian political allegiances. It would have complicated my work immeasurably had I been from Russia.

In a few instances, people were not interested in speaking with me. I felt it most acutely the time when an acquaintance, Fiona, offered to organize a number of interviews in a village that was densely settled by IDPs. I was enthusiastic about the prospect, but by the time I got there the other internally displaced people had changed their minds, deciding that without payment or humanitarian aid, they would not speak with me. Their reaction was part of what humanitarian Kyrylo would later call a dependency syndrome in his attempt to develop "smart help," but this type of reaction was something I only encountered a few times.

Throughout my research, I had more access to women than men. This is primarily because the displaced population is disproportionately female. A common pattern was for mothers to leave with the family's children while the father stayed in the nongovernment-controlled area (NGCA) to watch over the family's property or elderly parents. Women also seemed to be more eager to converse with me. I suspect the stakes associated with sharing were higher for men, who may have felt a need to project a particular image. As we will explore in chapter 2, militarized masculinity plays an important if often misunderstood role in the way that conflicts advance.

A group with which I had only very limited contact comprised the uber-wealthy political and economic elite, many of whom left the country before I arrived. Like all ethnographic work, then, mine is based upon what ethnographers call "situated" knowledge. I cannot claim that the book is representative of Ukraine or Ukrainians as a whole. Creating such a picture would lie far beyond the abilities of an ethnographer working alone.

According to the terms of my funding, I was strictly prohibited from entering rebel-held territory (Kyrylo's red zone). This, combined with the constraints placed on pro-Russian speech I mentioned above, meant it was difficult to engage with people who supported the separatists directly. Some may hastily conclude the book in front of them is therefore one-sided. To them, I suggest that it is precisely this apparent one-sidedness that opens up an insight into what political conflict is all about. Even though one might want to listen, listening can be perceived as legitimizing, and legitimizing both sides of the conflict would have undermined the trust of both sides, thereby jeopardizing the entire project. Here lies a lesson about the ethnography of war. There are, however, ways to work around the epistemological barriers political conflicts set up. As we see in the next chapter, for example, internally displaced people I spoke with presented evidence of popular support for secessionist politics in 2014, even as they simultaneously sought to delegitimize that support by labeling it "foreign" or supplied by brainwashed "zombies." And there are also physical limitations. Had neither the safety precautions imposed by the funding agency nor the issue of establishing trust and rapport existed, working alone and unarmed as a female researcher imposed its own constraints. Here too, reality sets in. Neither drone with a bird's eye view nor a Rambo-like figure, I worked with what I had: my ability to connect to the survivors of the conflict.

Fieldwork in a Country at War: Vicarious PTSD

One of the most powerful tools an ethnographer can use is their own embodied experience. A good illustration of the impact of embodied experience on my work as an ethnographer occurred toward the end of my first summer of fieldwork. As I was falling asleep in my rented apartment one night, I noticed that it had begun to rain. For what seemed like a long time, I listened to soft bursts of wind and rustling leaves outside the window, along with the steady patter of raindrops on the corrugated metal awning just under my window. Then, as I was dozing off, I heard . . . Grad rockets? Gunfire? I was jolted awake by the sound of car alarms sounding off on the street outside. With my heart pounding, I leapt out of bed and started to climb under it. No, I do not want to die in a pile of rubble here, I thought. I grabbed my rumpled clothes from the day before and threw them on, picked up my wallet and passport, and stumbled around the room trying to decide, with my sleep-addled brain, what to take with me. The computer? Yes. The suitcase? No. Then, breathing rapidly and turning the key in the heavy metal deadbolt to get out, it finally registered what I was hearing. Thunder.

Even though I was far from the conflict itself at the time, I interpreted rain and thunder as military conflict because I had been listening carefully to people who had escaped the fighting and told me harrowing stories about their experiences. In the language of psychology, this is called "vicarious posttraumatic stress disorder." In the discourse of anthropology, it's called "participant observation." It was at this moment that I realized I had not only heard what people were telling me, but had also internalized the information.[2] My position as an observer had given way to that of an ethnographer with an embodied sense of my suroundings.

Ethically Motivated Care

Throughout my fieldwork, one thing was clear. The conflict that had upended lives had also led people to express levels of responsibility and care for one another that they characterized as unprecedented. The military conflict also opened people to all kinds of emotional experiences. A good example of what this meant on a concrete level was supplied by Pasha. His home was destroyed in a mortar attack. Having fled to a small town not too far from Kyiv, he and his wife began rebuilding an abandoned house by using the materials they could scrounge up. Pasha observed that the neighbors started to show up and ask what they needed. Slowly but surely, everything from spare doors and windows to canned tomatoes and pickles started to be dropped off. Because of receiving care he did not expect, Pasha's experience of dispossession paradoxically relieved rather than aggravated fears about finding himself bereft of support. Fears like his are deeply human. Only the most cloistered among us have never worried "what if" (I lose my job, my house burns down, etc.). Pasha communicated a profound sense of ontological security when he stated his previous fears and anxieties about abandonment dissipated with the conflict: "You know that feeling that you could be left without anything? It's gone." Statements like his underscore the capacity for demonstrations of care to mitigate the effects of violence. This is especially meaningful in a situation of new or hybrid wars in which targets may include hospitals, residential neighborhoods, and marketplaces, despite humanitarian laws and principles that forbid warfare against civilians. I therefore suggest extreme harm and intense care coexist in a symbiotic relationship.

In listening to stories of the conflict I discerned a pattern in which many decisions were based on safeguarding others or tending to their emotional well-being. This pattern supports what feminist ethicists of care have been arguing for some time, which is that the kind of morality that has been valued in the Western tradition is only one kind (Hekman 1995). Carol Gilligan was among the first to formulate care ethics as different from justice ethics by considering how people (in her case, young women) actually reasoned through what was "right" and what was not, rather than relying on (supposedly) universal moral rules. Gilligan was especially interested in the kinds of moral "voices" not usually acknowledged *as* moral (1983). While Gilligan was studying peacetime America, her thinking and that of subsequent philosophers of care ethics is especially apt for how the people I spoke with justified their actions in relation to one another when rules and justice appeared to have been trampled.[3] Peace and conflict researchers have directly linked this moral voice or way of thinking about the world to peace-building.[4]

There is also a significant surge of interest in ethics among anthropologists (Lambek 2010; Fassin 2012; Keane 2014, 2015). Veena Das' work along these lines is inspiring because she advocates thinking of the ethical as a dimension of everyday life in which there is no need to rise above the ordinary (2007; 2012, 134). To her way of thinking, the ethical happens not so much by orienting oneself to formal principles or transcendental laws, as immersing oneself in local, quotidian, and seemingly small choices. The impulse behind this work is to hold the "profundity of philosophy" and the mundane as together expressive of ethics (2012, 139). As philosopher Paul Ricoeur suggested, ethics is about how one lives well *with* and *for* others (1994).

Care and Death

The ethically motivated caring I am describing extended to the dead. As I explore more fully in chapter 8, for the first four years of the war, the bodies of soldiers were not retrieved by the Ukrainian military. Surmounting obstacles that ranged from landmines to armed separatists, volunteer body collectors began filling the gap left by the state military. Imagine for a moment what it took to negotiate with armed separatists and then retrieve someone's dead and partially eaten husband, with little more than a shovel, a mask, and a bag. What people deemed the right course of action, it seemed to me, had to be improvised rather than based on already established norms and rules.

To mark the social innovation surrounding death, this book uses necrosociality (Marr 2019) to describe and understand the existence of volunteers carrying out the body collection. Volunteer body collectors vividly demonstrate how ethically motivated care proliferated in a situation characterized by state weakness and corruption. All kinds of bonds between diverse and even competing groups were forged in the linking of death and care, and these bonds were sustained over time. In addition to necrosociality, there was activism to challenge the death toll and hold the military more accountable. The larger significance of these relationships is that they compensate for the failure of social safety nets resulting from the conflict. Part of what is at stake here is whether the fatalism that attends most studies of war, conflict, and population displacement can be pushed back for long enough to capture the reassertion of human dignity.

Everyday War

Ultimately, what care produced was "micro" practices of peace. The field of peace and conflict studies has developed the concept of "everyday peace" to more carefully consider the significance of nonelite actors like the people I came to know in Ukraine. The term everyday peace refers to "the practices and norms deployed by individuals in deeply divided societies to avoid and minimize conflict and awkward situations at both inter- and intragroup levels" (Mac Ginty 2008, 553). This requires a preliminary step of shifting to bottom-up perspectives that can reveal how peace (and conflict) are enacted on multiple societal levels simultaneously (Richmond 2010, 676; Mac Ginty and Firchow 2016). To discount any level, except for heuristic purposes, they argue, is to overlook informative sites of inquiry (Ring 2006, 3; Sylvester 2011; 2013; Williams 2015).

While scholars of everyday peace track the multiple and everyday sites of peace-building so as not to miss potential ways to build peace writ large, I disagree with this approach. Even when peace accords moved forward in Ukraine, large numbers of Ukrainians were against them (Sorokin 2019). What my research suggests is that it may not be possible to scale up everyday or interpersonal peace in a way that makes intractable conflicts any less intractable. My point is that valuing so-called everyday peace efforts for what they might contribute to geopolitical peace misses the essential point that these small practices of peace hold value in and of themselves for the actors concerned. Reducing these efforts to building blocks for broader peace minimizes their significance and returns the primary emphasis back to the state. The notion of bottom-up, then, betrays its ideological commitment to the very hierarchies it purports to dismantle.

I go further to propose everyday peace has a B-side in "everyday war," a term I develop in critical dialogue with the scholarship on everyday peace. I use everyday war to refer to the conscious and deliberate practices people used to participate in the conflict. From many locations in the patchwork quilt of conflict, forging peace was a luxury people could not afford. Civilians therefore engaged war through mundane activities such as sending appropriate footwear to the front or driving there in private cars with bread, meat, or antiseptic they purchased themselves when the Ukrainian military was unable to provide these things in sufficient quantities. Everyday war can be distinguished from everyday peace (and war itself) by its objective. The people engaged in what could be called everyday war were not interested in killing, but rather achieving and maintaining a greater sense of connection. They did what they did not to crush the enemy, but to nourish relationships and national belonging. Everyday war can also be distinguished from "negative peace," conceived by peace researcher Johannes Galtung (1996) as the mere absence of fighting. Everyday war is what transpires at an intersubjective or relational level when countries are actively at war.

A few words are in order to explain the word "everyday" in this context. Historians and geographers have used the term to acknowledge happenings outside the spectacular events of history. Philosopher Michel De Certeau (1984) advanced this inquiry by writing about how lived routines establish the unstated "practical knowledge" that governs social experience. Even though it typically fades into the background of consciousness and social life, Erving Goffman (1959) showed our everyday "presentation of self" actually takes a great deal of effort to maintain. The everyday has been an especially fertile source of insights for scholars in the fields of international relations and peace and conflict studies (Sylvester 2011, 2013; Åhäll 2018; Bjorkdahl et. al 2019) striving to work beyond an exclusively state-centered approach.

People Were Like Bombs

As I have described, one of the most disturbing elements of the conflict over Donbas was that it reconfigured relationships: people renegotiated relationships in a context of political disagreement, physical separation, and forced migration. As a woman I met with during each of my three periods of fieldwork, Yuliya, phrased it: "People are like bombs, so a phrase can easily explode into conflict." She was referring to a pro-Ukrainian statement that had sparked hostility between longtime friends. This type of situation is far from unique in the world and this exploration therefore stands to potentially illuminate aspects of other divided societies. Just as relationships were disrupted over the issue of whether Great Britain would leave the European Union in the "Brexit" referendum, and friendships in Hong Kong were reconfigured as a result of ongoing protests in 2020, people in Ukraine found that the questions over the territorial integrity of Ukraine could make people, metaphorically speaking, explode. The suggestion that personal relationships can "blow up" as a result of military conflict invites curiosity about the specific materials, fuel, scenarios, and outcomes.

Chapter Overview

The first chapter provides a foundation for understanding the outbreak of hostilities and the humanitarian needs that resulted from the Donbas conflict. I contend that multiple gaps in the protection of civilians led to massive forced displacement and amounted to politics of neglect and death. The ethics of care that arose in this landscape, explored in the remaining chapters, are especially significant against the background of forced migration and state neglect.

Chapter 2 brings readers to a military-themed café. Although the literature on militarization emphasizes the unconscious ways in which militarization infects and spreads through a society, I demonstrate how the café's proprietors, themselves war veterans, aimed to heighten conscious awareness of military conflict. Their goal was to have an "antidepressive" effect on fighters and to provoke critical thinking about war among noncombatant patrons. The strategic way in which they elevated the position of veterans exemplifies everyday war.

The third chapter serves as a continuation of the second by metaphorically following the patrons of the café home to understand what transpires in the intimate spaces of living rooms and kitchens where the intersecting forces of military conflict and national propaganda reconfigured relationships. I show how the care at the center of this book produced an interpersonal, everyday kind of peace. Svetlana provides a good example because her friends from opposing militaries—people who may one day kill each other—shared tea at her kitchen table in the evenings. This everyday peace, however, came at a cost and was sufficiently flawed that it prompted me to start thinking about everyday war.

Like friendships, romantic partnerships sometimes became casualties to the conflict. In Chapter 4, I advance the argument that an innovative way to think about the catastrophic effect of war on relationships is that it upsets the established relationships between relationships. People were torn by decisions like whether to volunteer at shelters for internally displaced strangers or cook for their spouse. In line with the thesis that interpersonal relationships provide valuable insight into war, the intersectionality that interests us in this chapter is between different kinds of attachments.

Chapter 5 exposes the continuation of war in the places one might least expect: family. Specifically, the chapter uses the cases of two women to show how kinship can become "tactical." Oleksandra provisioned her father who fought as a volunteer sniper killing (pro-Russian) former neighbors. Larysa redoubled her commitment to country after her son was shot by separatists that her mother and sister funded. In their stories, we find vivid examples of everyday war.

In addition to being divided by a political line of demarcation, Ukraine was characterized by two very different ways of coping with the military violence emotionally. In Chapter 6, we consider how individuals concerned about the desensitization to violence made it their work to care for the individuals who seemed to have stopped caring for themselves. The other way of emotionally being in this world rejected "working through" or "getting beyond" trauma. The descent into everyday war sometimes meant choosing to die with one's children rather than be evacuated, or praying to be killed at once rather than being maimed or having to suffer.

The sense that the world—including pets, neighbors, schoolmates, teachers, shop clerks, police, and so on—had become strange was pivotal in the decision to leave the nongovernment-controlled territory, and added impetus to the military conflict itself. Chapter 7 adopts the term "everyday sci-fi" to describe how people saw their lives as similar to living in a science fiction drama. Viewing people in the separatist controlled territories as "zombies" might be viewed as a tactic for absolving people of wrongdoing and thereby maintaining everyday peace, but I contend it is more aptly described as everyday war. The fantastical language of human "herds," mysterious "waves," and gender mutants formed the basis of an embodied and practical orientalism that divided the social world into us and them. This would intensify later, with the 2022 invasion of Ukraine.

In Chapter 8, we follow the Black Tulips, a group of volunteer body collectors. The group's strict neutrality enabled them to operationalize everyday peace with the separatists face-to-face. And body collection was only half the equation. The other half was supplying life-saving medicines for children by smuggling insulin into the noncontrolled territory in the very same trucks bringing bodies out. Like a massive Kula ring, the flow of insulin to, and bodies from, the separatist-controlled territories illuminates the dialectic between violent conflict and ethics of care. Perhaps nowhere is it clearer that adversity in combination with the state's inattention to people elicited ethically motivated caring.

"NOW WE HAVE FUNERAL AFTER FUNERAL"

The Conflict over the Conflict in Donbas

The military conflict over Donbas that began in 2014 was described in such wildly different ways by the parties concerned that it would have been easy to think people were talking about different conflicts. Russian sources long referred to the fighting as a Ukrainian "civil war." Especially in the first six months of military engagement, Russian authorities disavowed any involvement whatsoever. By contrast, Ukrainian sources typically insisted that the conflict was best described as "Russian aggression." With various shadings and emphases, and utilizing diverse theoretical frameworks, American and European sources most often echoed the Ukrainian position. The gaping disparity between Russian and Ukrainian perspectives revealed a very real discursive conflict over the military conflict. And while the violence in Donbas had extinguished well over 13,000 lives, injured tens of thousands, displaced over two million people, and led to the largest population of humanitarian concern in Europe since World War II, it was never officially declared a war during my research. Only with the February 2022 invasion of Ukraine by Russia was broad and international consensus reached that Russia was waging war on Ukraine. How best to understand the start of the conflict over Donbas?

A good place to begin is with the 2013–2014 revolution. When former Ukrainian president Victor Yanukovych declined to sign a long-awaited association agreement with the European Union in 2013, protesters hit the streets. Demonstrations on Kyiv's Maidan Nezhalezhnosti, or Independence Square, coalesced into a full-blown revolution, and protests sprang up all over Ukraine. People came out to express their discontent with the authoritarian policies of President Yanukovych and his party, along with the corruption and rising social inequalities that characterized his administration. Stated succinctly, the protestors in Kyiv were keen to pursue European integration, even if it would damage Ukraine's relationship with Russia.

For many people in Donbas, however, the revolution represented an existential threat. Not only did they hear about proposals to demote the status of the Russian language, but the trade deal, they thought, would be disastrous for their region's economy, which was reliant on trade with Russia. After President Yanukovych fled the capital, they viewed the acting authorities in Kyiv as illegitimate and sought greater autonomy for their respective regions. Waving Russian flags, they took to the streets, referring to the authorities in Kyiv as "fascists" and a "junta." From their perspective, a whole way of life was at stake.

Of course, not everyone viewed the 2013–2014 revolution this way. Some residents of Donbas supported the transformations underway in the capital city of Kyiv. Although the divisions within Donbas fomented both pro- and anti-Maidan protests, the later gained the most momentum and led to referendums on independence for both Donetsk and Luhansk provinces. Within months, separatist leaders declared two autonomous people's republics, the Luhansk People's Republic (LNR) and the Donetsk People's Republic (DNR), respectively. To regain control over the territory declared by the self-proclaimed republics, Ukraine launched a military counteroffensive called the Antiterrorist Operation (ATO) in April 2014.

This chapter supplies a foundation for understanding what happened next in the lives of civilians, the main subject of the book as a whole. Readers will find more depth and detail on the region's history, culture, politics, and the military conflict itself in the many articles, books, and films that are emerging on these topics. In what follows, we start in Donbas with the role played by regional identity. Moving outward, the chapter then turns to the region's political economy and the linguistic issues that were confronting Ukraine at the time. A crucial question has been the extent to which it was forces external to Donbas versus homegrown protests that led to military violence. We therefore consider the international influences that contributed to the initial outbreak of hostilities next. After briefly considering the hostilities themselves, we turn to the humanitarian crisis. In this section, I contend that multiple gaps in the protection of civilians amounted to politics of neglect and death. The ethics of care that arose in this landscape, explored in the remaining chapters, are especially significant against this foundation.

Regional Identity

Ukraine became an independent country in 1991. But strong regional identities, ethnolinguistic differences, the operation of powerful political parties, and wealthy oligarchs complicated the process of national identity formation (Kubicek 2000; Barrington and Herron 2004). Donbas has a unique regional identity that is said to have coalesced around the process of industrialization (Stebelsky 2018). At least official discourse long portrayed Donbas as the leading industrial area in the Soviet Union and valorized the workers in the factories and mines (Kuromiya 1998, Zhukov 2016). Even the word Donbas, short for Donetsk Coal Basin, points to the centrality of industry.

Looking at a map, one can see that the two constituent provinces, Donetsk and Luhansk, are stacked on top of each other with Luhansk to the north and Donetsk to the south. One might think about the Donbas "core" as a band of industrial cities and mining towns running down the middle of both provinces. The northern part of Luhansk and the southern part of Donetsk Oblast, however, are mainly rural. This, too, is an important part of Donbas that prides itself on its Zaporozhian Cossack heritage and is suspicious of Russian encroachment on Ukrainian Cossack values and culture. The Zaporozhian Cossacks were a military and political organization that arose in the sixteenth century and prided itself on its warrior skills. They were "free men" who created farming and raiding-based communities independent of the powers at that time, having avoided serfdom and circumvented the pressures of religious societies (Wilson 2000, 58). Donbas has a dense concentration of prisons, high rates of violent crime, and its political parties are associated with organized crime. Combined, these features are believed to have shaped a "Wild West" or frontier mentality that distinguishes Donbas from other parts of Ukraine (Kuzio 2017). Those native to Donbas would likely add that their abundant universities, higher-than-average salaries, state-of-the-art stadium (now destroyed), new international airport (now destroyed), and fragrant rose gardens are a few of the hallmarks of their development and civility.

Given the differing views of the 2013–2014 revolution, it should not be surprising that residents of Donbas were invested in different historical narratives, each with a unique image for the future. Yakubova suggests there was both a "Soviet Donbas" narrative forged in the urban industrial core and an opposing "Ukrainian Donbas" narrative built around opposition to Soviet collectivization of agriculture, the state-imposed Holodomor famine, and the persecution of intellectual dissent that had gone on under Soviet rule (Yakubova 2015). A third narrative, promoted by Moscow, was that Donbas was part of a new Russia or Novorossiya with a heritage in imperial Russia (Stebelsky 2018).

While authorities in Kyiv have consistently portrayed the leaders of the DNR and LNR as illegitimate, leaders of the DNR and LNR saw it the other way round. The leader of the self-proclaimed LNR turned Kyiv's standard narrative on its head in a newspaper article as follows: "Residents of Donbas went to peaceful rallies to achieve compliance with their constitutional rights. Instead of engaging in dialogue with a significant part of its citizens, however, Kyiv unleashed an antiterrorist operation against us, the 'Antipeople's Terrorist Operation.' We had to take up arms to overcome the bombing, shelling, blockade, lack of light and water. The price was high but we defended our freedom, our legal right to be masters in our native land, not slaves."[1] While the official Ukrainian narrative figured the people taking control of territory in the east as the aggressors, people who wanted greater autonomy for Donbas saw Kyiv as the threat. This speaker underscores his critique of the central authorities by referring to what the government called an "anti-terrorist" operation as anti-people.

Many people I spoke with who fled to government-controlled Ukraine told me they had initially sided with the separatist authorities but eventually found themselves disillusioned. As Natasha, a middle-aged IDP, put it: "It all started one way and ended another. People went to the referendum with pleasure, they brought tea and cookies and candies for everyone. They were so happy. They went with hope that things would be different in Donbas. What they wanted was for the money made in Donbas to stay in Donbas, rather than being sent to Kyiv and returned after a percentage had been taken out. What they thought they were voting for was a "federation," meaning more independence from Kyiv. They voted and it quickly turned into killing, bombing, and shelling." The Novorossiya idea did not gain sustainable traction. A woman I will call Zoya, who identified herself as apolitical told me the idea was not only strange to her, but imposed from outside, violently: "When the war started, they came with machine guns, shirtfronted [confronted] us and said: 'Do you want to live in Novorossiya?' I said, 'No, I do not. I've been living in Ukraine for more than 50 years now. What Novorossiya?' They said, 'We'll rescue you, and we'll make Novorossiya exist.' They started taking food and threatening us. It was simply horrible." It makes sense, then, to think of the unique regional identity as a contributing factor that was necessary but not sufficient (Wilson 2016, 631) to cause the beginning of the military hostilities. As Wilson points out, up until the outbreak of hostilities, there was a broad scholarly consensus that Donbas operated with a distinctive regional and borderland identity (sandwiched between Russia and Ukraine), not an irredentist one (2016, 638). Given the strong regional identity, what role did language play?

Language Policy

Donbas is predominantly Russian speaking. According to the State Committee on Statistics, 74.9 percent of those living in Donbas listed Russian as their native language in the most recent census (State Committee on Statistics 2001).

Donbas also had the highest share of ethnic Russians in Ukraine and the highest proportion of Russian-speaking Ukrainians (Stebelsky 2018, 45). Of ethnic Ukrainians, 58.7 percent claimed Russian as their native language. Residents of Donbas had one of the lowest rates of identification with independent Ukraine and the highest rates of identification with the Soviet Union (Stebelsky 2018, 45).

When Ukraine became independent in 1991, Ukrainian was deemed the only official language. Many people (especially in Donbas) did not speak Ukrainian with any fluency and official documents were still in Russian, creating enormous problems for courts, schools, hospitals, local governance, and other state institutions. When Victor Yanukovych (who hails from Donbas) was elected president in 2010, he sought to ease the difficulties by signing a law giving official status to any language spoken by 10 percent of the population or more in any given oblast. Outside Donbas the bill was unpopular because in most other areas, promoting the Ukrainian language was seen as crucial for strengthening national identity.

Inspired by the 2013–2014 revolution, the Ukrainian parliament or Verkhovna Rada passed a bill attempting to overturn the law that accommodated Russian speakers. On the same day that President Yanukovych was overthrown by revolutionaries, February 23, 2014, parliament moved to make Ukrainian the sole state language again. The idea was so controversial that the debate in the Verkhovna Rada was accompanied by now legendary fistfights and public demonstrations. There was a great deal of public debate about the language issue, and the bill never became law. Language politics nevertheless provided fuel for protests in Russian-speaking regions like the Donetsk and Luhansk provinces, where media outlets played up the issue as evidence the authorities in Kyiv were insensitive to residents in the east (Jaitner 2015). The way the question of the official state language was handled by government and press eroded hopes that the Russian language would be respected by the postrevolutionary government in Kyiv. The issue of language is also believed to have helped inspire pro-Russian nationalists from areas of Russia that neighbored Donbas to come and help residents of Donbas in their struggle against Kyiv.

To be clear, linguistic identification does not map very neatly onto either ethnic identity or political orientation in Ukraine (Harris 2020). What is more, the Ukrainian military conducts its operations more in the Russian language than in Ukrainian, and some of the top leaders in the pro-Russian breakaway republics are ethnic Ukrainians (Grossman 2018). Many citizens have mixed Ukrainian and Russian ethic heritage, and mixed marriages are common. Thus, while language policy may have inflamed tensions between various publics, we must be very careful not to overinflate its role in the military conflict. If neither regional identity nor linguistic factors were sufficient to engage militarily, what else was at play?

Political Economics: "Someone Needed this War"

In the midst of the 2013–2014 revolution, the Russian Federation implemented preemptive trade measures such as blocking some of the Donbas region's exports and imposing tariffs. This sent a clear signal that Russia disapproved of Ukraine's expanding relationship with the European Union. Additionally, the favorable trading relationship with the European Union was projected to result in cheap European imports that would present unfair competition with products made in Donbas. There would be exorbitant costs associated with the European Union association agreement because it stipulated adopting European Union production standards. The three main industries—coal, metals, and machine-building—were ill-suited for the European course adopted by the new authorities. Anti-Kyiv resistance was the strongest in areas of machine-building, which was the most vulnerable to disruption (Zhukov 2016). Zhukov's research suggests that at this stage, a municipality's prewar employment profile was a better predictor of conflict than the ethnolinguistic composition of the local population (2015, 13). He argues the pro-Russian demographic in Donbas favored Russian-backed rule *not* because of ethnicity or language but because their economic stability and prosperity depended on trade with Russia that was jeopardized by agreements authorities in Kyiv were signing with the Europe Union in the wake of the revolution.

Although Donbas was heralded as a heavily industrialized area collectively responsible for a sixth of the country's GDP, the area had long been falling into decline, and productive output relied on robust state subsidies from the central authorities. What was to be done with the old industrial infrastructure? This brings us to the role of the oligarchs. The industrial infrastructure is largely owned by oligarchs who occupy positions of political authority and wield enormous power.

Seeking to protect their interests, some oligarchs opposed the transformation and backed former President Yanukovych, some sided more with the Maidan protestors, and others operated on both sides (Wilson 2014, 130–131). Once the conflict escalated to a full military confrontation, oligarchs became parties to the conflict itself with some funding the separatist forces and others funding the volunteer battalions seeking to protect Ukraine's territorial integrity. Many accounts of the conflict over Donbas go further to assert that until the oligarchs' criminal behavior is fully accounted for, the conflict will remain poorly understood (Galeotti 2016a; Galeotti 2016b; Kuzio 2017; Herron 2020).

In short, the oligarchs stood to be profoundly affected by whether Ukraine proceeded in a European direction or remained closely linked to the Russian economy. This seemed to be fairly transparent to civilians on the ground at the time. As

Mykola put it: "Well, about war in itself—there is a war, and at the same time there's, like, no war, you know? People die, that's true. But basically, everything has to do with men in power—it's a deceptive maneuver that covers a huge theft." Eyewitnesses to the conflict point to selective bombardment that left some oligarch's investments intact as further evidence that a contest for oligarchic power was a significant political-economic component shaping the conflict.

Oligarchs were not uniform in their level of influence, of course. The Yanukovych clan or "family" was quite central in providing money and banking services to the separatists (Umland 2014). They were protected by the police and security services that prioritized "the family" over the law (Umland 2014). In this regard, and adding depth and detail to the regional identity, Taras Kuzio has argued that Donbas operated under the "law of the jungle" (*zakon dzhunhliv*) in which various criminal strata were imbricated with regional and national governance (Kuzio 2017, 156).

So far, we have considered how a strong regional identity, a controversial language policy, and a vulnerable economy all contributed to the conflict. It was factors outside Donbas, however, that appear to have proved decisive in turning the matter of civil unrest into outright military conflict (Wilson 2016; Mykhnenko 2020) with strong oligarchic (especially Yanukovych) overtones (Kudelia 2014; Malyarenko & Wolff 2018).

Outside Factors and the Geopolitical Context

Ukraine's postrevolutionary ties with the United States and European Union were viewed as a threat by the Russian Federation. President Vladimir Putin and the Russian political elite saw the 2013–2014 revolution as a coup that was orchestrated by Western countries like the United States. As such, it represented a threat to Russian national security interests. With the historic alliance with Ukraine in jeopardy, Russia had to even more seriously evaluate the expansion of NATO to its own border. The Russian response to that threat was robust and came in the form of a hybrid war. The first step was the occupation and attempted annexation of the southern province of Crimea. The next was supporting the separatists in Donbas with intelligence, materiel, and armed forces. Both territorial incursions were intended to bring Ukraine's integration with the European Union to a halt (Dragneva and Wolczuk 2015).

Control of information was also important to the military conflict over Donbas. In new (Kaldor 2013; 2006) and hybrid (Hoffman 2007) wars, cyber technology is central and information is paramount among the weapons. State-sponsored

Russian media in eastern Ukraine sought to persuade the population that their safety, freedom, and prosperity could only be guaranteed by the Russian Federation (Jaitner 2015; Polyakova 2018). In a conflict like this one, territory is won not only by engaging in combat but also by influencing how people think (Polyakova 2018). The debates about the significance of information wars in this conflict are far from over (Bauman 2020). What can be stated without reservation is that information was used strategically to advance the conflict from the first days.

Another way Russia influenced the conflict in Donbas was by infiltrating local governance structures with Russian cadres. As Mila told me: "I got curious about the mayor of my city himself and did some research on government websites. The website said that he studied at my secondary school. It turned out he graduated from my school. And it turns out he was in my graduating class. Hmm. Interesting. I looked at the school yearbook and he was nowhere to be found." In other words, the ostensibly local support was in many cases a fiction that had been curated by elites.

These elite cadres had the support of local authorities. As Konstantin described: "It happened before my eyes. And along with this, I want to say that it happened with the full support of the local authorities, at that time they were Ukrainian, the existing regional authorities. And so I probably should not tell you about that moment when Shepa in Sloviansk led that band in the capture of that building. And then it continued on, they turned their fighters on Sloviansk. All the while this is still happening under the action of the Ukrainian authorities of the Party of Regions, the local authorities." Thus my interlocutors presented evidence of popular support for secessionist politics, even as they sought to delegitimize that support through various discursive strategies. The cognitive dissonance was resolved by making a sharp distinction between "the people" of Ukraine who were ostensibly innocent and peaceful and the country's elites who were waging war in their own self-interest.

All of this transpired at a time when Ukraine was militarily weak. Ukraine had agreed to give up its nuclear weapons after the disintegration of the Soviet Union. As part of the USSR, Ukraine had the third largest nuclear arsenal in the world, and its intercontinental ballistic missiles and strategic bombers were directed primarily toward the United States (Pifer 2019). Under the Budapest Memorandum on Security Assurances signed in 1994, Ukraine promised to accede to the Treaty on the Non-Proliferation of Nuclear Weapons and give up these nuclear weapons in exchange for assurances that the country's territorial integrity and political independence would not be violated (Synovitz 2014). As a result of the Budapest Memorandum, the Ukrainian military was downsized (Wezeman and Kuimova 2018; Sanders 2017). There were big plans to reform the military so Ukraine could one day join NATO, but in the aftermath of the memorandum, conventional military hardware gradually became outdated and military conscription ceased in preparation for the formation of a professional army (Käihkö 2018).

The Military Conflict

The first shots were fired in April 2014, when insurgents entered the city of Sloviansk and took over its administrative buildings. In this phase, Russian special forces, or *spetsnaz*, and secret service officials worked with local Donbas criminals and Russian nationalists coming in from Russia (Mitrokhin 2015). Between 25 and 30 percent of police and security forces in Donbas switched to the separatist side once the conflict erupted (Gorenburg 2014, n.p.). In the beginning stages of the conflict, Russia relied on proxies, keeping soldiers who were obviously Russian far behind the front lines (Grossman 2018). These proxies helped create strategic confusion about what was going on and were helpful in taking control of key cities. At the battle of Ilovaisk in August 2014, the Russian military became more explicitly involved. As that conflict progressed, the Russian Federation adjusted its narrative, admitting that it was assisting newly formed entities in achieving their objectives while protecting its own national security in the process.

Volunteer battalions rose to the Ukraine's defense. Between April and May 2014, units called hundreds, or sotnia, which were created during the Maidan regrouped themselves into battalions. Inspired by revolution, the volunteer battalions rode a patriotic wave. The battalions were especially crucial in spring and summer 2014, when they prevented the separatists from advancing appreciably. Military leaders speculate that had it not been for the volunteers, the line of demarcation would have been drawn closer to the middle of Ukraine, along the Dnipro River, instead of where stabilized until 2022, down the middle of what were formerly the Donetsk and Luhansk provinces.[2] Many of these battalions operated on crowdsourced funds and what they could generate from activities like bake sales. Ultimately, however, the battalions proved to be uncontrollable from Kyiv and, accused of crimes that will be discussed in the next chapter, were either dismantled or incorporated into official forces (Amnesty 2014; Klein 2015; Puglisi 2015).

The line of demarcation that separated Ukrainian government-controlled territory and the separatist-controlled areas was monitored at check points, or "block posts." They were intended to prevent the separatists (terrorists, in the eyes of the government in Kyiv) from infiltrating the government-controlled areas of Ukraine. They were also significant because of how strictly they regulated the passage of civilians in need of basic public goods. Permits were difficult to obtain:

FIGURE 4.   Cake at the Azov battalion bake sale to raise funds

in the early years of the conflict, one had to apply in person and wait two weeks to receive a paper permit to cross the line of demarcation. Then an online system was inaugurated, plagued with glitches and down time, according to professionals I consulted on this topic. Even with a permit it could take days to reach the head of the line of cars waiting to cross. People made do by sleeping in their cars, which could be difficult for anyone but impossible for the elderly and those with certain medical conditions. In addition to disadvantaging some of the most vulnerable people, the efficacy of these block posts was questioned because anyone with financial means could bribe their way through or find a detour. Inevitably, then, those suffering most acutely from the restrictions were pensioners and the region's more economically disadvantaged men, women, and children.

Forced Displacement in PTSD Land

The military conflict, fought in large part in residential areas, forcibly displaced millions. A primary focus of this book is therefore the experiences of the people forcibly displaced within Ukraine. According to the United Nations Guiding Principles on Internal Displacement, IDPs are "persons forcibly uprooted from their homes by violent conflicts, gross violations of human rights and other traumatic events, but who remain within the borders of their own country" (United Nations 1998, 5). Unlike "refugees," who are eligible for international protection, IDPs are only entitled to the protection of the states where they live. Although the Guiding Principles stipulate that internally displaced persons should be able to enjoy the same rights as citizens, the people displaced within Ukraine lacked certain voting rights (Krakhmalova 2019), faced limited employment opportunities (Semenenko 2018), were for extended periods denied access to their pensions and other benefits (Kuznetsova et al. 2018), could not enjoy freedom of movement (OCHA 2020), and suffered from discrimination (Bulakh 2017). Benefits for the forcibly displaced in government-controlled areas were so low that some people did not bother to register as displaced. Many of those who fled were forced to return to the conflict zone when they could not afford to live in government-controlled parts of the country.

An important conceptual anchor for the literature that explores the effects of armed conflict and forced displacement is trauma. "PTSD Land" was my study's working title and still provides a rubric for thinking about trauma in Ukraine, where trauma is multigenerational and complex. Anthropologists have justifiably argued, however, that the concept of this disorder places too much emphasis on individual experience (Hautzinger and Scandlyn 2013). Focusing too much on PTSD has a way of casting survivors of war and conflict as innocent and helpless victims, glossing over the complexities of situations in which the distinction between combatants and noncombatants might not be clean, such as in Donbas. This book goes further, following noninnocent and far-from-helpless civilians' participation in the conflict, which tended to be motivated not by heroism or even patriotism but by their caring relationships.

Some of the limitations of relying on PTSD as a framework for analysis can be avoided by turning to the concept of social suffering, which considers how policy decisions cause human misery (Kleinman, Das, and Lock 1997; Kleinman 2006; Willen 2007; Skoggard and Waterston 2015).[3] At the same time, social suffering and closely related work on "narratives of vulnerability" and "abjectivity" (Butler 1999; Gonzales and Chavez 2012; Schweitzer et al. 2011) have a way of underlining what is done to people, often losing sight of what I want to emphasize in this book, which is once again how people act on their own and, even more importantly, others' behalf. The shortcomings of relying on a "suffering slot" require us to develop a still better conceptual vocabulary for describing the experiences of forced migrants (Trouillot 2003; Robbins 2013; Dunn 2017, 17). In this book, we track the experience of war using an intersubjective perspective to discover how the care I described above produced a space of tolerance, but also a conscious and strategic, everyday kind of war.

Life in a World of Death: A Humanitarian Crisis

In thinking through the dynamics surrounding contemporary conflicts like this one, philosophers and social theorists have sought to understand how it is possible that so many people are so consistently politically disenfranchised and subjected to hazardous living conditions. Traditional concepts of sovereignty seem ill-equipped to encompass these dynamics. Philosopher Giorgio Agamben used the term "state of exception" to explain the deep structures organizing the political cultures in which executive privilege, social exclusion, and the reliance on discourses of emergency are used to justify extreme measures (2005). He uses the figure of *homo sacer* who lives what has been called "bare life," as the exemplar of life under these conditions (1998). The concept has been helpful in exposing how vulnerable populations like those in Donbas find themselves in situations in which the normal rights and freedoms of citizenship have been suspended.

Engaging with notions of bare life and the state of exception, philosopher Achille Mbembe introduced the idea of necropolitics to communicate his view that politics are not only involved in sustaining a population's life but also work to systematically expose people to structural and political violence that leads to death. For Mbembe, conditions are such that people become like living dead (2003, 40). Mbembe directs our attention to the ways in which state authorities deliberately produce abject conditions resulting in a "morbid spectacle" of suffering (2003, 35) and death world. This is important context for the argument in this book, which is about what happened *between* people in response to these conditions. Some resisted by practicing scaled down micro- or interpersonal peace. Others found themselves playing support roles in the conflict itself and engaging in everyday forms of war.

Humanitarian Needs

The military conflict led to deplorable conditions. A major problem was accessing survivors. The security situation was often too dangerous, and hostilities continued in spite of cease-fire agreements. Furthermore, the authorities of the DNR and LNR required humanitarian organizations to register in order to operate in the territory they controlled, and they restricted the movement of humanitarians and their goods in ways that were often inconsistent and therefore difficult to predict beginning in July 2015. Other markers of precarity included the restrictions on leaving the zone of conflict, and the military activity itself when there was indiscriminate shelling of civilian areas. Overall, multiple gaps in the protection of civilians amounted to politics of neglect and death.

FIGURE 5. Map of Buffer Zone. Cartography by Bill Nelson

The humanitarian needs varied across government-controlled (GCA), non-government controlled (NGCA), and the so-called buffer zone between them. The needs were most intense in the buffer, where 3.2 million of the approximately five million in need of humanitarian assistance resided (OCHA 2020). Women constituted an especially vulnerable group, and a full 70 percent of the households within the buffer zone were prone to food insecurity (OCHA 2020, 18). The population was also disproportionately elderly: the elderly comprised 41 percent of those in need in the buffer area (OCHA 2020, 18).

The cumulative effect of the hostilities had a wrap-around quality that threatened life's very ongoing-ness. The presence of landmines, which can shift over time once implanted in the earth, shackled people from accessing social benefits, services, and even their own farmland. According to the 2019 Landmine Monitor Annual Report, Ukraine ranked fifth in the world for casualties due to landmines and other explosive remnants of war (ERW).[4] The indiscriminate shelling of civilian infrastructure affected water, electricity, central heating facilities, and even schools. Some two-thirds of the health facilities along the line of contact were damaged, meaning many people lacked access to basic health care. When residences were damaged by the conflict, their occupants often lacked the ability (if elderly and infirm) or the means (if unemployed or poor) to repair. Ukraine's frigid winters made this a terrible situation. Loss of income and lack of employment opportunities were correlated with increased alcohol and drug use as well as intimate partner violence and survival sex. Whatever its causes, the conflict over Donbas profoundly affected life in eastern Ukraine.

This chapter has offered a baseline for understanding the conflict over Donbas, in which even the words used to describe the events are contested. This book follows the United Nations in referring the military hostilities between 2014 and 2017 as "a conflict between Ukrainian government forces and separatist militias," but I also refer to the conflict as a "war" as an abbreviation for "undeclared war." Even the term "breakaway republic" was contested by Ukrainians who preferred to think of their territory as "temporarily occupied" by a "foreign aggressor." The Office of the Prosecutor of the International Criminal Court referred to the conflict as a noninternational armed conflict when referring to the siege of Sloviansk and an international conflict involving the armed forces of the Russian Federation and Ukraine from July 2014 onward (ICC 2018). In this book, I place the most contested words such as "terrorists," in scare quotes.

Outside of the discursive battlefield, the beginning of the conflict, at least, defied simplistic characterizations as "civil war" or "Russian aggression." Residents of Donbas were genuinely divided by the 2013–2014 revolution. Many saw the resulting political transition in Kyiv as an existential threat: their language rights, autonomy, and incomes were all at stake. One can certainly understand why they went to rallies to leverage their constitutional rights. Unfortunately, what happened next was full-scale military conflict. Like other contemporary conflicts, it has a protracted quality, utilizes information as a weapon, and draws upon many different kinds of both state and non-state actors. Just as with other contemporary military conflicts, it is the civilian population that unjustifiably suffers. Although in conversations they often referred to themselves as "ordinary people" (*obychnyye lyudi*), I think readers will come to agree they are anything but.

WELCOME TO CAFÉ PATRIOT! MILITARIZATION AND A THEMED CAFÉ

"Welcome to Café Patriot!" was the caption beneath the life-size image of a tank that caught my eye as I powered up Petro Doroshenko Street in Lviv, Ukraine. When I crossed the bright green AstroTurf landscaping toward the entrance, the smell of grilling meat wafted toward me. The railings of the stairs down to the doorway were covered with camouflage-colored nets brought back from the front in eastern Ukraine, where they had been used to disguise combatants' positions. Yuri Antonov, one of the owners, was waiting for me. As I descended, I noticed a crate filled with bullet casings next to the handrail. I paused and, encouraged by Yuri, ran my hand through them. He invited me to pocket some casings as a "souvenir," noting with sarcasm that with no end to the conflict in sight, the supply was unlikely to run out. That was in 2017. Once I was standing in the doorway of the subterranean restaurant, I was confronted at eye level by enormous bazookas hanging from the ceiling like Christmas decorations. Some were painted with delicate flowers, others remained scratched and dented from battle. The atmosphere was menacing yet also cheerful, bringing up multiple emotional valences simultaneously.

Yuri Antonov, Ostap Prets, and chef and manager Eduard Krokhmalyuk (hereafter referred to collectively as the owners) designed the café to be the epitome of interactive: at one table, the bulletproof vest Yuri wore in combat hung on the back of a chair, available to pick up and try on. When a family came in with two young children, Yuri helped the little boy into the vest, then showed him how to hold the real Kalashnikov lying on the table. His mother snapped a number of pictures as Yuri coached the boy, who appeared thrilled. Later, I tried

FIGURE 6. Interior of Café Patriot

on the vest. For a moment, war was play. But the vest also weighed heavily on my shoulders, and when Yuri handed me a bazooka, I began to imagine soldiering in a more visceral way. Later, I felt apprehensive when I had to pick up a de-activated landmine to reach a paper napkin. This was part of the experience: on a subsequent visit, Yuri brought vodka in shot glasses in holders made of mortar casings. It would be impossible to patronize the café and not touch, feel, see, and interact with the detritus of war.

Until March 2018, when it closed, the café offered an opportunity to interact with military paraphernalia and veterans themselves while relaxing over coffee or savoring a pizza. Does that make Café Patriot an example of militarization in which ex-fighters capitalize on their aura of military prowess while popularizing war for civilian patrons? Through processes of militarization, people, companies, organizations, and institutions gradually come to depend on the military for their well-being (Enloe 2000, 3). As a result, the military shapes popular culture, economic priorities, gender identities, and even the metaphors used to describe reality (Enloe 2000, 2). The more militarization infuses a society, according to this theory, the more military assumptions are generally adopted. This is advantageous to achieving military objectives, according to feminist thinking on the topic, because it naturalizes war itself.

On the surface, the café appeared to be a prime example of militarization. Fighters in camouflage smiled heroically from pictures on the walls; the real Ka-

FIGURE 7.   Landmine napkin weight, interior of Café Patriot

lashnikov offered the fantasy of having the power to kill; and the name, Café Patriot, tied nourishment to national identity. In fact, the kitschy, interactive elements directly recall the "Disneyfication" of war in the United States (Smiley 2016). But the mix of quotidian and macabre objects, and the juxtaposition of smiling hospitality and evidence of war's destruction, invite us to think again about the purpose of Café Patriot. I show how the café owners used the objects transported from the conflict zone for two very different objectives: soothing de-mobilized soldiers, on one hand, and provoking citizens to become more aware of veterans—and the war itself—on the other. Because of the highly conscious and indeed double effort the owners make, the café, I argue, does not represent a conventional case of militarization but is better described as a manifestation of everyday war.

Café Patriot is more nuanced than might initially be imagined, because in ad-dition to contesting the reasoning behind the war, the owners hoped to regain their good standing. They wanted societal acceptance of their voluntary service (at a time when the Ukrainian military was very weak) to ease their military-civilian transition. By the current definition, at least, militarization forestalls critical thinking and drives people toward destructive activities (Cohn 1987; Enloe 2000; Cockburn 2010; Sjoberg and Via 2010; Dowler 2012; Gavriely-Nuri 2013; Cohn 2013). This is far from the whole story, however, because it leaves out the conscious and deliberate practices nonstate actors use to mold others' thoughts and feelings about war.

My Place in the Café

The argument that follows is based on several visits to Café Patriot that took place while I was carrying out ethnographic fieldwork in Ukraine between 2015 and 2017. I was introduced to Yuri and Eduard (Ostap was out) by a friend who had been displaced to the city and was close to one of the owners. On the first visit, I carried out a formal interview. Except where noted, all of the statements quoted below are from the taped and transcribed interview that took place on July 21, 2017. The conversation took place in Russian, the first language of the café owners. On subsequent visits, I had meals at the café and observed its normal operations more informally. Upon returning to the United States, I followed the café in the Ukrainian news media. When the café closed, a Ukrainian assistant located the owners and spoke with them about what had happened since my time there.

In the midst of ongoing bloodshed, rapport is notoriously difficult to estab-lish, but Yuri and Eduard welcomed me as they would a journalist, food critic, or tourist. The café was their pedagogical project, so they were used to educat-ing visitors. As an American, I represented an unusual opportunity for interna-tional exposure: would they receive notoriety in the United States as a result of the interview? I was also less threatening than a local, who might have had a concealed role in the conflict. However, an unaccompanied woman visiting their country was outside established norms, and I understood I must have seemed unusual when they asked me more than once what my purpose was in visiting their café. Still, my status as a foreign female conferred a certain advantage and helped me to establish a rapport with the owners that would have been unlikely had I been male, and especially had I been Russian.

In what follows, I first put the café in context and explain how it challenges prevailing theories of militarization. Then I discuss my findings, starting with the affective "architecture" of the café and its antidepressant focus. This is followed by an exploration of the owners' reflections on masculinity and its hybrid forms. The café's affective architecture can shape responses to the café but does not control them. I therefore turn next to patrons' reactions. The final section considers the local authorities' attitudes toward the café and its eventual closure.

The Café's Place in Ukraine

The café's place in the territorial conflict can only be understood after recalling that, as noted in chapter 1, the Ukrainian military had been significantly downsized (Wezeman and Kuimova 2018). Under the Budapest Memorandum on Security Assurances, signed in 1994, Ukraine agreed to give up all of its nuclear weapons and signed a nonproliferation treaty in exchange for assurances that its territorial integrity and political independence would not be threatened (Synovitz 2014). There were comprehensive plans to reform the Ukrainian military to meet NATO requirements, but those plans did not come to fruition at the time, and Ukraine's military hardware became outdated. Conscription was phased out to make room for a future professional army. At the time the war began in 2014, military ranks had been drastically reduced (Sanders 2017), and untrained volunteer fighters like Yuri, Ostap, and Eduard were sucked into the resulting vacuum. These are the international and intra-Ukrainian dimensions of the territorial conflict in which Café Patriot is situated.

Members of Ukraine's volunteer battalions included police and military veterans, entrepreneurs, students, Maidan activists, and even individuals with criminal records (Puglisi 2015). They had various explanations for their role in their country's military, including the desire to stand up for Ukraine's territorial integrity and defend freedom and democracy. In fact, some commentators have alleged that the battalions represented the most patriotic people in the country (Puglisi 2015, 18). But the various battalions had disparate views on what that freedom should look like, and they often disagreed over which means were justified. Although the volunteer battalions are credited with significant territorial gains (Käihkö 2018), their untrained and unofficial nature made them difficult to control and suscepti-ble to engaging in misconduct (Amnesty International 2014). Official forces alleg-edly also engaged in human rights abuses, but it was the volunteer battalions that took the brunt of the criticism resulting from some high-profile cases (Sanders 2017, 43–44). Put simply, a primary issue was that volunteer battalions often acted without coordinating with Kyiv or one another. Financed by wealthy oligarchs, they threatened to become private armies (Klein 2015). As Ukraine launched a formal army, the volunteers were replaced with professional forces. Some battal-ions were shut down, and others, like the "Donbas" battalion the café owners be-longed to, were incorporated into official ranks.

The United States' involvement in the war in Vietnam provides a useful sign-post for this chapter. American society was divided over the country's role in the Vietnam War. In both wars, the media have been faulted for inadequate and, in some cases, inaccurate coverage. Another reason the Vietnam War is a useful benchmark is that the cold and sometimes hostile reception soldiers received upon returning from the conflict also applied in the case of the war in Ukraine. Al-though the war in Vietnam claimed the lives of at least 58,000 Americans and in-jured 150,000 others, it took a decade for a memorial to be erected.[1] Like Americans over the course of the Vietnam War, Ukrainians during the time of my research were ambivalent about the ongoing military conflict, which remained an unde-clared war at the time. When I was in Ukraine, the farther one moved from the line of contact, the more people seemed to want to avoid the topic. While the offi-cial death toll was 13,000 at the time of my research, that figure was believed by members of the medical community that I interviewed to be an undercount by a factor of approximately seven.[2]

Militarization

The conflict between Ukraine and Russia over Donbas led both countries to strengthen their respective militaries. A central concern regarding the civilians in a situation like this one has to do with the possibility that society itself may be-come militarized. A risk is that the individual may be "disciplined into perform-ing as an agent of violence" (Torres and Gurevich 2018). It is important to make a distinction here between maintaining a strong military capacity, sometimes called *militarism,* and *militarization,* which refers to widespread social and psychological preparedness for organized violence (Higate and Henry 2011, 134). Militarism and militarization are linked because a society that has undergone militarization is more likely to condone expansive military goals. For both social-psychological and geopolitical reasons, then, militarization warrants attention.

Scholarship on militarization and militarized masculinity sees these processes as malignant because they entail the metastasizing of military values and mindsets (Peterson and Runyan 1999, 258). Feminist theorists have therefore argued that militarization collapses what are believed to be healthy boundaries between military and civilian spaces (Enloe 2000; Lutz 2002; Dowler 2012). Militarization was also a significant concern among certain publics in Ukraine at the time Café Patriot was open. We may recall that the conflict had largely stabilized, and the line of contact ran down the middle of the Luhansk and Donetsk republics. People in western Ukraine knew that living conditions in the east were often deplorable and that conflict-related deaths were ongoing, but the self-proclaimed DNR and LNR seemed for the most part to be minding their own affairs. Arguing that the people in the occupied territories had chosen a path of Russian-backed rule, many people were eager to distance themselves from the conflict.

Theories of militarization caution us that allowing the osmosis of militarization is a way for authorities to garner acceptance for expanding the military. What theories of militarization fail to appreciate, however, are multiple vectors of influence. In the café, it was demobilized veterans breaking down the (only fantasied) boundaries between the conflict zone in the east and a place of peace in the western part of the country. In reality, it was only a question of time before all of Ukraine was drawn into conflict, making theories of militarization seem painfully naïve and shortsighted in light of what Russia had in store for the country. Clearly, Ukraine could have benefitted from a swifter and more aggressive response to the 2014 occupation of Crimea and the initial Russian military incursions in Donbas.

The (In)visible Hand

So did Café Patriot represent the spread of militarization? It certainly brought military paraphernalia and reminders of the conflict in the east to the western part of the country. In writings on the topic, militarization is described as working much like an "invisible hand" that ushers in military values and "creeps" into a culture to "insinuate itself" (Enloe 2000, 3; Hedstrom 2018) in ways that are "often subtle, hidden, concealed, or unidentified" (Woodward 2018, 719). The effectiveness of the process can be determined by the extent to which it goes unnoticed (Hunt and Rygiel 2006, 5). The worry is that civilians, without ever putting on a helmet or using a rifle, may become militarized in their thoughts and in the goals and values they pass on to their children (Enloe 2000, 2) in locations where there is no need to expend resources on armaments or use violence to resolve disputes.

Café Patriot provides a useful lens for interrogating the feminist line of thinking on militarization (Uehling 2020). Granted, the interactive elements of the Café aimed to make war rather tasty and fun. But it acted more like a *visible* hand because of the owners' conscious and strategic efforts to prompt critical thinking among civilians and aid soldiers with their military-to-civilian transitions. While the concept of militarization supposes the inscription of military values is an unconscious and uncontested process, the owners operated from the assumption that people are conscious, choice-making agents, much shrewder than theories of militarization allow.

The idea of militarization as a form of indoctrination was most famously encapsulated by Enloe's often cited example of the satellite-shaped pasta in Heinz soup, which ostensibly normalized military activity for mothers and their children (2000, 2). In her view, the pasta's shape had a subtle, unconscious effect on the people designing, producing, and consuming it. Subsequent scholars have provided similar examples of only seemingly benign cultural products that worked in analogous ways such as the khaki-colored icing on a cake in a shop window. The offending cake was decorated with toy soldiers and miniature military hardware, leading one author to surmise that "militarization is as commonplace to a society as baking a cake!" (Dowler 2012, 497; emphasis in the original). The examples they use to illustrate their points about unconscious indoctrination are unfortunate because there is no empirical evidence that the shape of one's pasta or cake decorations can alter one's thinking in a deep or sustainable way. Indeed, the empirical and analytic weaknesses of this line of thinking were obvious to the owners of the Cafe. Rather than rely solely on visual optics, they used the café's décor as a starting point for engaging very directly with the thoughts and feelings of patrons and veterans of war.

Café Patriot and Everyday War

Ultimately, the owners commoditized war in the theme café not to normalize war, as militarization supposes, but to question it. Consistent with everyday war, their objectives were to enhance communication between the military and nonmilitary sectors of their society, and to strengthen human connections, especially with regard to caring for underserved veterans. The concept of everyday war, which encompasses the conscious and strategic ways people engage war, is thus a more robust way to think about what was happening inside the Café. In contrast to settings where militarization is found to exploit intimacies (Fattal 2019, S57) or result in a failure to recognized emotional investments (Åhäll 2018, 5) the café owners' everyday war was filled with attending to volunteer soldiers' social standing, employment status, and emotional wellbeing. In short, the restaurant was not intended to glorify the use of violence but to advance the dialogue around it, something that in hindsight was needed.

The Café

The café's aesthetics were designed to support this questioning. The main room contained about nine tables, each with a military-style lamp hanging low over its surface. The lamps threw soft yellow light out from under their hard metal rims, and I felt as though I had stepped into a museum's diorama of the World War II partisan underground. The tables and chairs were constructed out of planks to resemble a military field kitchen. They were painted in a camouflage pattern to mimic the atmosphere of a base camp, but varnished to make them smooth to the touch. In short, it used light, sound, texture, and color to elicit feelings. Studies of airport layouts and restaurant color schemes attest to the strong link between architectural design and affect (Kidd-Nakai 2015). In this respect, the café was a study in opposites. The seating was upholstered in an army green, but the fabric was velvet. There were lethal weapons hanging from the ceiling, but they were painted with flowers. The waiter was a grizzled veteran in camouflage, but his demeanor was consistently gentle. There were bullet casings amassed in compartments in the floor under plexiglass at my feet, but smooth jazz floated above my head. These jarring contrasts put me somewhat on edge, but as I realized, this reaction, an uncomfortable mixture of anxiety and entertainment, was part of the objective.

When the tour and the interview were complete and the audio recorder shut off, Yuri and Eduard suggested I try the cuisine. In the appetizer section, one could find "Ukrainian happiness," consisting of thick slices of *salo* (fatback) on black bread with a garnish of horseradish—a staple comfort food across Ukraine. Likewise, the first course included borsch—iconic of Ukrainian national identity but at the same time claimed by Russians *as* Russian. As such, the soup itself is an apt metaphor for the conflict: like the soup, Donbas is claimed by two countries. Another specialty at the café was pizza. From this category, one could choose "Partisan" (a reference to World War II), with white mushrooms and fresh herbs, or "Patriot," with both bacon and salami. Both pizza names have militaristic meanings in keeping with the café theme. Café Patriot displayed a European orientation by eschewing standard Russian beet and potato salads. The menu provided the owners with a communicative vocabulary that complemented their more explicit verbal efforts to create a pedagogical environment through conversation. While feminist discussions of pasta and frosting imply food items advance militarization, I suggest it is not that simple. Menu items are inherently limited in their power to persuade patrons of the rightness of Ukrainian patriotism. The menu may flag Ukrainian-ness, but in contrast with Enloe (2007), Dowler (2012) and other feminist theorists, I suggest people are fully capable of ignoring obvious symbolism and forming their own independent interpretations.

When it came time for me to order, I noticed the watermark on the paper menu depicted an androgynous-looking fighter. This seemed to align with the owner's willingness to question the meaning of masculinity. While the items on the menu are likely to appeal to both men and women, the implements were very masculine. For example, my chicken wings arrived on an enormous wooden "plate" the size of a cutting board, accompanied by an enormous knife. The sheer physicality of the experience was a bit impressive. Later, my friends would ask how I could enter the contentious space in the first place: Could I be sure the landmine holding down the napkins was effectively deactivated? I had, like many people trying to live through war, learned to take risks like these in stride. Did I think it was safe? Yes, relatively speaking because hazards far greater were part of my daily life.

"An Alternative to Depression"

Yuri arrived at the concept for the café after he demobilized and applied for a number of jobs but was rejected despite his qualifications. He suspects he was turned down because many people consider veterans "unbalanced" and prone to "losing it." Yuri envisioned the café as a way to work against this, stating, "When they come, they will understand we are normal people." This approach aims to build a small world inside the café, or, to use Rosenwein's term, form an "emotional community" (2006, 19), using authentic objects and their corresponding "energies" to heal from painful experiences. The manager and cook, Eduard, phrased it this way: "We try to make sure that all the military objects here are not from the store. They are brought from the ATO zone. With them, we moved forward, and everything carries some value in itself, and is filled with the energy of trenches and battles." The way they have curated civilian and military emotions by means of carefully selected objects and images illustrates more concretely my point about the deliberate, conscious, and relational dynamics at play within processes of militarization, as well as, somewhat paradoxically, its contestation.

Opening the café felt especially pressing because when Yuri returned from the front, he encountered indifference—as well as thinly veiled hostility—in interactions with nonmilitary Ukrainians. The differing perspectives of the military and civilian inhabitants of the country were especially pronounced. The café aims to address the dissonance surrounding what was often deemed at the time a "bullshit" war. Scholars of everyday peace look for ground-up efforts directed toward calming animosity (Vaittinen et al. 2019). The animosity most at issue in the café was public sentiment toward ex-fighters. As Yuri summarized: "It's difficult for people who left the war to return to society, to adapt. We all have the problem of feeling a little uncomfortable. So we think that there should be a place where people with the same views and thoughts can gather together. Well, when we were starting this restaurant, we didn't see it as a place only for military men because if they communicate only with each other, that too is a problem. They need to communicate more with the outside world." Yuri very quickly realized he was not the only one who felt depressed and isolated. The café was a way to make his own emotions, and those of other veterans, more manageable. In our first conversation over coffee, Yuri explained that the café offers "[an] ability to start anew and an alternative to depression after the war." Taken together, then, the cuisine, the décor, and the jobs it provides make the café an "alternative to depression," in more senses than one.

Demilitarizing Masculinity

Militarization is believed to reinforce an exaggerated gender binary in which men are taught to disavow signs of weakness and disengage from any emotions that would undermine their ability to fight (Peterson 2010), because to be "authentically" male in conflict entails the ability to control incapacitating emotions. Until relatively recently, little attention was paid to the ways in which militaries rely on far more diverse, plural, and contradictory forms of masculinity (Belkin 2012; Sylvester 2011; Duncanson 2015; Wilkinson 2018). As Bulmer and Eichler argue, veterans' transitions to civilian life challenge the coherence of the idea of militarized masculinity (2017, 162). The doxa that the hypermasculine politics of war should be linked solely to men is worthwhile to question (Sylvester 2011, 120). These efforts can be augmented by considering how veterans' interstitial position between military and civilian realities created space for a hybrid form of militarized masculinity. After all, masculinity is hardly an undifferentiated or stable category. Overemphasizing the prevalence of militarized masculinity risks making men themselves less understandable (Schaeuble 2014, 205). Indeed, my venture into Café Patriot shows that the ex-combatants were engaged in an ongoing process of self-reflection with respect to their gender identities. Veterans' new insights were being actively translated into the affective architecture of the café in the form of care for patrons and one another. This was a café where plush toys were often pinned to the wall next to firearms. The empathy the men found for one another became an ethic of care and means for shifting norms surrounding masculinity. This provides a corrective to those lines of thinking that postulate men themselves, more than the systems of which they are a part, as the problem (cf. Cockburn 2010, 144). The café owners' calibrated efforts to nurture veterans, educate patrons, and valorize their own military service therefore exemplify everyday war.

Yuri's explication of veterans' emotional lives is a perfect example of a more nuanced understanding (cf. Hunt and Rygiel 2006; Peterson 2010; Sjoberg and Via 2010) in that raising the issue of depression exposes veterans' vulnerability. In acknowledging the troubled emotional lives of soldiers returning from the war, the owners have modeled an alternative way of being men that includes being honest about their complicated emotional lives and providing emotional support to one another. Research on militarized masculinity that takes men as the locus of the problem risks overlooking men as reflective and choice-making agents. While there is a rich literature on veterans spanning medicine and the social science fields of psychology, sociology, anthropology, and geography, feminist theorizing on militarization has yet to be cross-fertilized by these advances.

The café reinforces the point that there can be multiple masculinities at work. The video rolling on the flat screen TV in the corner of the café depicts men in nurturing roles. There are also images of men with their rifles at the ready, defending Ukraine. The majority of the images in the video slideshow, however, show men cooking, bandaging, and embracing other men. Yuri explains that they intentionally selected these scenes for the restaurant. In so doing, the owners of the café produced a variegated image of what it meant to be men at war.

The café would not have been opened without military friendships. Yuri uses emotional terms to frame his process of becoming a more compassionate person and adjusting to his demilitarized identity. As he describes it, his life was transformed in a positive way as a result of the territorial conflict: "Before the war I had no friends, only comrades. . . . I am a very difficult person to communicate with. Also, I have an authoritarian side, I love to command. I love to make decisions myself. And I had no friends at work, I had acquaintances only in my football team. But I had no best friend. I really did not like to get along with people. The war changed everything. It's true. And my attitude toward people has changed." Yuri explained that he was pursuing a career in business in Moscow when the conflict began. He felt ashamed that he had not done more for his country of birth. He saw the conflict as an opportunity to prove he could be useful. With acumen acquired in the business world, he quickly rose to the equivalent of a commander in his volunteer battalion. A divorced man with grown children, he reports starting to feel emotions on the front lines that he had not felt before. He emotionally connected with, and became invested in, other fighters' welfare. A specific moment of awakening he described was rushing a comrade with potentially fatal wounds to a hospital and understanding the personal loss he would feel if his comrade died.

This feeling of allegiance is in itself unremarkable. Soldiers all over the world have attested that in battle, they fought more for their comrades than for their nation (Belkin 2012). But Yuri brought his feelings of empathy for others with him into demobilization. His daughter offered the observation that he came home a "different man." As we drank our coffee, Yuri and Eduard told me that they often talk about how having a "soft" side does not make a person weak. Yuri frankly regretted that he "woke up" to the significance of friendship late in life. His description of this process demonstrates how military masculinity may be reshaped through self-reflection. I suspect Yuri's attitude had a lot to do with his perception that in his mid-fifties he was "near the end" of his life. This created a sense of urgency around making his social world right. Consideration of these veterans reveals something of the "mechanisms" (Duriesmith and Ismail 2019, 3) for demilitarizing masculinity.

And Yet, Aspects of Militarized Masculinity Remained

To say that the café constituted a coherent project of demilitarized masculinity would of course be an exaggeration, and along with displays of caring and humor, aspects of standard sexist and misogynist military culture were also to be found coexisting in the same space. On the way out of the restaurant, I noticed two small metal plaques hanging opposite the crate with bullet casings. Both depicted young women wearing bright red lipstick smiles. One of the women had a phallic-shaped armament pointing upward between her feet. The other was depicted with a firearm blazing near each breast. The images evidenced the complexity of the café where the macabre atmosphere was tempered by things like the plush toys pinned to the walls next to rifle displays. The copresence of objectification and empathy as well as kitsch and authenticity prevented a single interpretation, and potentially fostered critical thinking.

Patrons Feel War

The patrons of Café Patriot were diverse. At any given time, one could see hip young women there sporting the latest styles, and young, middle-class families with a bit of time, spending money entertaining their school-aged children with the café's war paraphernalia. The owners estimated that civilians comprised a little less than half of the clientele. People with a past or present connection to the conflict were slightly in the majority. Tables with both men and women talking quietly over beers were common. During the day and the early evening when I made subsequent visits, the café appeared to appeal to men and women about equally. Guests spoke Ukrainian, Russian, and sometimes a combination. The owners were adamant that language not be "policed" in the café, noting that many Ukrainian army battalions communicate solely in Russian. Thus, speakers of Russian and Ukrainian were equally welcome. Political allegiances were far more salient than family heritage and language preference.

Patrons' reviews of the restaurant often praised the café's use of authentic military objects. Taken together, the militarized paraphernalia, veteran staff, and overall aesthetic created a unique brand of everyday war that many found moving. As one visitor stated: "The peculiarity of Patriot is that it is possible not only to see the latest history of Ukraine, but also to feel it" (Pavluchkovich 2017). The patron's choice of words reminds us that a visit to the café is an embodied experience that for each patron had its own emotional choreography. Patrons often described how the café had left them with an uneasy or uncanny feeling. Pavluchkovich reports the following remarks made by another patron: "It is precisely when ordinary civilians wear armor and take up a machine gun that they come to understand what war is for the first time. After all, this ammunition does not just look beautiful in photos or lie here for exoticism. It saves lives. And when you feel for yourself—it all comes to matter so much! And our guys are wearing this constantly, not just five minutes before the photo. People literally for the first time really think about what is hiding behind the word 'war'" (Pavluchkovich 2017). This patron suggests that the materiality of the objects initiates a tangible awareness about the war that potentially deflates romanticized depictions of conflict. At least for him, the tension he felt between the "beautiful" weaponry and the potential for death triggered a process of critical reflection.

During my fieldwork, the Ukrainian government was actively recruiting for the new professional army with billboards on streets and placards in metro stations. In the café, however, the idea of enlisting is presented not only as less abstract, but also as less heroic. The café translated flashy posters about recruitment into a sense of what it might be like to serve, and a relatively unglorified version of the war emerges. For example, enlistees should expect to receive inadequate rations that will leave them relying on friends to bring them jars of soup. They should also expect to have only primitive medical care and to have to bring their own pistols and running shoes because the military is short on weapons and standard military-issue boots are outdated and uncomfortable. In short, the images circulating across the flat screen showed the frayed edges of the Ukrainian military.

Was the owners' critique, paradoxically, another form of militarization? I would argue that it is not because the café primarily supported those who were seeking a way of staying *away* from the war, not returning to it. The beer consumed in this space was a means of coping with civilian life and resisting the attraction of going back to a soldier's reliable paycheck. Granted, patrons like the little boy I described may have left hoping to become a soldier. However, whether or not he retains a memory of his visit and becomes one is dependent on a host of variables. In fact, these variables get at the crux of my argument about militarization. Incentives to go to war are complex, and conjecturing about direct connections between militarization through branding and successful indoctrination, as Enloe (2007, 7) and others have done, is unlikely to yield new insights. To understand militarization, it makes more sense to attend to the specific and intersubjective relational processes at work in different contexts. As the specific context of Café Patriot reveals, processes of militarization, like those of demilitarization, are in reality complex and ambivalent. Actors "work through" the meanings of military signs in civilian spaces in multiple ways.

A Contested Process

What people experienced in this space is not wholly determined by the owners' emotional cuing, of course. In a country fighting an undeclared war, the café could only provide the emotional scaffolding (Griffiths and Sarantino 2009) for a wide range of individual responses. Reflecting on the way some patrons were attuned and became enmeshed in the atmosphere, while others did not, Eduard stated, "There are different people who speak different languages. Some come with the words "mazafaka" [by which he meant "mother fuckers"—G. U.], others say we have a heightened sense of justice, and others are hiding their eyes." Eduard's observation suggests that regardless of the empathy and critical thinking they hoped to generate in the café's space, what people actually felt in that space was not necessarily, as has been argued by other authors, up to the objects themselves (cf. Navaro-Yashin). Nor was it necessarily what the curators had in mind. For example, as one can gather from the Englishman's expletive (cited above) and another patron's comparison of ATO fighters like Yuri and Eduard to dogs, the owners' status as former volunteers complicated the impact of their project.

Reactions to the screening of a film about the war in Donbas demonstrate that responses to the café varied a great deal. When *Home* was shown in the café, some patrons complained the film impaired their ability to relax. A reviewer of the event described the negative reactions of some patrons this way: "The guys sat for fifteen minutes, thanked them [the owners] politely, then apologized and left. I'm calling this tortured conscience (Mirovich 2017)." The men's departure underscores that however much Yuri and Eduard wanted the café to wake people up to the war, some people did not want to think seriously about the military conflict on the opposite side of the country. In his interview with me, Eduard voiced skepticism about the ability of the café to change attitudes across the board: "Fifty percent of the people in Ukraine do not want to know about the war. They have a happy life and they are no longer interested in anything [else]. Others are afraid of the news, afraid to look into our eyes. The people who come here are basically patriots, volunteers, and people who know that a war is going on." Eduard's comment illustrates that the café's owners are acutely aware of the limitations of what the café can accomplish. After all, people gravitate to and help to create moods that make them feel comfortable. This is equally applicable to satellite shaped pasta (cf. Enloe 2007, 1) and khaki-colored frosting (cf. Dowler 2012, 497). Eduard's observation about the differences among patrons and people in Ukraine remind us to be cautious of exaggerated claims about the power of militaristic symbolism.

How is the café situated in relation to the conflict? One patron ruminated on whether it would be safe for people from Russia to visit the café and concluded: "The veterans of the ATO know very well the difference between ordinary citizens of Russia and the 'volunteers' [to the separatist forces], and no conflicts are likely to arise" (Mirovich 2017). This implies that the owners appeared to be judicious enough not to extend fighting itself into the café. What they hoped for was the opposite: an end to the conflict.

While some people—especially these demobilized fighters—wanted to bridge the civilian-military disconnect and foster dialogue about the conflict, others wanted to deny these tensions exist. The literature on everyday peace processes applauds education efforts such as the café and has amplified the significance of relationships to achieve a peace that is sustainable (Dutta et al. 2016, 81). The café was a paragon of everyday peacemaking, with its movie nights, invitations to dialogue, and emphasis on tolerance and understanding. Ultimately, however, the tensions that the café tried to address are only partially about the military conflict between Russia and Ukraine. They had also to do, more specifically, with who goes to war, on what conditions, and with what benefits within Ukraine.

The Café Closes

In March 2018, Café Patriot was closed after being open for approximately nine months. The primary reason for the closing was resistance to it on the part of local government officials who openly opposed maintaining the café's license on the (interestingly feminist) grounds that it collapsed the distinction between war and peace. According to Eduard, the officials told them outright that Lviv is a place of peace and no evidence of the war should be visible. If they wanted a war-themed café, they were told, they should go back to the warzone and open it there.

The authorities' discomfort with the café's messaging came to a head when the owners announced they would place a portrait of Vasilyi Skripak on the façade of the café. Skripak was a world-renowned Ukrainian opera singer who had worked as a soloist with the Paris opera for two decades before returning to join one of Ukraine's extreme right-wing nationalist battalions, "Pravi Sektor" (Right Sector). Skripak perished from a sniper's bullet in 2016. To fighters, he became a symbol of volunteer heroism. For the authorities, however, he symbolized one of the distasteful aspects of Ukrainian politics. Right Sector formed during the 2013 revolution and was instrumental in overthrowing the government at the time. The authorities were concerned because the battalions had threatened the state's monopoly on the legitimate use of force (Sanders 2017). In addition to openly threatening journalists with whom they disagreed, Right Sector got into an armed standoff with official government forces in 2015. They threatened to send fighters to Kyiv and demanded the resignation of the country's interior minister (Sanders 2017, 43). It warrants emphasis that the café owners did not themselves belong to Right Sector: the café positioned itself as agnostic on these matters and allowed any battalion to leave its insignia among others on the wall. The nod to Right Sector through the portrait, however, raised the specter of a threat to government authority.

Yuri and Eduard readily admitted the volunteer battalions had made mistakes. However, Yuri hypothesized that the real issue was a more basic fear of veterans: "From the outset, they were afraid of us [veterans] on a psychological level. Unfortunately, we feel it sometimes. Very often they try to discredit us. . . . I mean, they think that if one man does something wrong, we are all like that. Unfortunately, the government is interested in discrediting all [the volunteer battalions]." They suggested that the volunteer battalions' contribution, staving off a total Ukrainian defeat in the beginning of the military conflict, was eclipsed by the mistakes of a few. To authorities in Lviv, it was plainer: the Skripak portrait glorified the threat that the battalions represented. Considering authorities' willingness to tolerate a different, World War II–themed café for years on end, Yuri's interpretation carries weight. Café Kryjivka, or "Bunker," openly celebrated Lviv's former Nazi affiliations. That café offers a classic example of militarization: it is designed not to foster dialogue as Café Patriot does, but instead to allow patrons to act on their anti-Russian sentiments through simulations of physical violence. Kryjivka provides an onsite shooting range where patrons can fire blanks at Stalin and Lenin from authentic period weaponry and hit a punching bag with an image of President Vladimir Putin. Concerns about preserving peace, then, cannot be the sole reason for closing Café Patriot.

There are also interpersonal reasons for the café's closing. As Eduard suggested, "It turns out it is easier to fight together than to run a business together." Each owner had his own point of view about how the restaurant should operate. Yuri had shared with me that he prefers to be the one in charge, and this must have worked better for him on the battlefield than in the kitchen. After the café's closure, the owners shared with my assistant that they were reflecting on and learning from their mistakes and that they anticipated trying again with a similar business venture in the future.

We can think about the "failure" of the café as evidence of its success. The café posed a threat to the state's narrative about the war at the time, and local authorities were sufficiently troubled that they wanted it to close. The veterans' descriptions of how they tried to curate two different sets of emotions and the local authorities' actions to shut down the café demonstrate in concrete terms how working through militarization is a process that entails acknowledging, feeling, and negotiating one's relationship to war in the context of civilian life.

Thinking geographically for a moment, the founders of the café succeeded in "shrinking" the perceived distance between the eastern and western parts of the country, folding the mental map so that the eastern region besieged by fighting was allowed to touch the western area attempting to remain sheltered. Still, however, the intervention was incomplete because what people experienced in this space depended on both the owners' selection of objects and the patrons' (including authorities') thoughts, feelings, and politics.

This exploration of the café stands to sharpen our thinking along three principal lines. First, the literature on militarization describes a process in which the boundaries between civilian and military are effaced in problematic ways. In the case of the café, strategically bringing the civilian and military together (against the will of the local authorities) served as a foundation for dialogue. Second, the literature on militarization explores the process as insidious. The café owners, in contrast, used military paraphernalia deliberately to incite everyday war and thereby arouse civilians' critical awareness. Third, while most scholars remain committed to the idea that militarized masculinity—and war itself—is organized around devaluing emotions, I have shown how the demobilized fighters curating Café Patriot found latitude to thematize the war while also demonstrating a form of masculinity that includes emotional vulnerability.

If everyday war refers to the conscious and deliberate practices people used to participate in the conflict, the veterans engaged through counseling veterans and educating patrons. Everyday war is distinguished from everyday peace (and war itself) by its objective of achieving a greater sense of connection, and the veterans launched the cafe not to mobilize against Russia, but to nourish their friendships and national belonging. The complex dynamics surrounding Café Patriot show how the concept of everyday war, with its emphasis on conscious and strategic efforts, is more applicable in this setting.

The policy implication in my finding is that militarization is more open to negotiation than has previously been recognized. In this case, the owners sought to critique Ukrainian military policy and gain the acceptance of a society in which they felt underappreciated. The owners were primarily critiquing the military leadership, which had left them inadequately supported and their contribution under recognized. The people who become objects of social scientific analyses are rarely the dupes they are so often made out to be, requiring us to recognize militarization as complex negotiations about the reality of military conflict in nonmilitary spaces.

When I left the café, the check was not provided in a little box or tucked in a little book, as is customary in other Ukrainian cafés. The check was placed on my table in an empty ammunitions casing painted with decorative flowers. I had the privilege of leaving the underground restaurant simply by stepping back into the bright sunshine outside. For veterans, of course, it will never be that simple.

INTERPERSONAL PEACE
The Micropolitics of Friendship

The previous chapter was concerned with the process of militarization and Café Patriot's aim to bring civilians, volunteer fighters, and the official military into greater awareness of the costs of the war as well as one another's challenges. Despite their geographical distance from the conflict itself, patrons of the café reported being able to sense the conflict through the café. Even though authorities in Lviv, where the café was located, wanted to "invisibilize" the conflict, then, it was palpable for those who frequented Café Patriot. In this chapter, we consider a realm of sociality closely related to the café: friendship. Imagine yourself following some of the patrons of the café home and sitting down with them to see what transpires in living rooms and at kitchen tables during a time of war.

One of the most troubling features of the conflict in Donbas for those who experienced the intersecting forces of military conflict and national rhetoric was that it reconfigured relationships among people who knew—or at least thought they knew—one another. The literature on war's implications for civilians has traditionally focused on trauma, and the medical and psychiatric literatures on this topic are especially rich. Efforts to understand the specifically social sequelae of war are in their infancy. This is unfortunate because, as Halpern and Weinstein pointed out, "it is the interpersonal ruins, rather than the ruined buildings and institutions that pose the greatest challenge for rebuilding society" (2004, 264). Even though friendship is known to contribute to the ability of a society to reconcile (Licklider 1995, 681), the diplomatic "track" system that classifies and organizes different kinds of peace-making activities is primarily focused on outcomes rather than the private and informal interactions discussed here. Additionally, the works that do address relationships tend to be concerned with unexpected violence among neighbors, colleagues, or former friends, as books with titles like *Killing Your Neighbors* (Holtzman 2016) attest.

But another outcome also warrants scrutiny: situations in which the descent into violence does not occur. As I learned in the course of my research, even though some interpersonal relationships were among the unrecognized "dead" in the war in Donbas, friendship was a site that continued to matter for mending a country divided by armed conflict. Efforts to rebuild relational worlds— the topic of this chapter—were continually underway, even as the microcosmic worlds of warmth and intimacy were undermined by the conflict.

Svetlana's Kitchen Table

In spite of the bombing taking place on the outskirts of her city, Svetlana sought to create a sanctuary from violence in her home. After all, she had male friends fighting on both sides of the conflict. Svetlana suggested to me over a heaping basket of French fries that the picture most people have of Donetsk is distorted. In spite of the ongoing violence, and regardless of the unscrupulous separatists who became de facto authorities, she argued, daily life continues. Even though the region is marked by ongoing fighting, people still go to school, graduate, get married, celebrate birthdays, and mark anniversaries. To make her point, she told me that while she still lived in the city of Donetsk, men who were enlisted in opposing military forces sat across from each other at her kitchen table. As she explained: "I have two friends in the military, one of them is on one side and the other one is on the other side. But nevertheless, we sit at the same table."

"Do they talk to each other?" I asked.

"Yes. One gets a salary there in the DNR [the self-proclaimed Donetsk People's Republic], the other one gets a salary here [in government-controlled Ukraine]. One friend is DNR, and the other one is Ukrainian, he is in the National Guard in the ATO [Antiterrorist Operation] zone. They talk to each other as we do, you and me."

"And what do they talk about?"

"Well, about everything that is not related to the violent situation. I want to tell you that in my everyday life, even at work I don't talk about war. I don't want to, everyone has his own truth, you know."

In other words, people who drank tea with one another in the evening could be put in a position to kill one another someday. It was, in effect, an *interpersonal* politics to set aside *geopolitics*. Considering the conflict's lethality, this is an enormous feat that goes beyond the cliché of agreeing to disagree.

The scene she describes is especially remarkable given the time period and her physical proximity to the conflict—close enough to feel the sonic blasts through the plaster. Svetlana lived in the city of Donetsk through the siege of the Donetsk airport, the most prolonged fight between pro-Russian separatists and the Ukrainian National Guard before the 2022 Russian invasion of Ukraine. A skirmish over the airport early in the war left Ukrainians in control, even though the city of Donetsk had already become the capital of the breakaway DNR. A second and decisive battle took place between September 2014 and January 2015. The fight became so legendary that the soldiers striving to retain control of the airport came to be known as "cyborgs" for their apparent "half-man, half-machine" ability to survive inside the besieged airport. They continued to fight with little sleep or nourishment. These soldiers were vastly outgunned by Russian and Russian-backed DNR soldiers, however, and the DNR was able to take control of the by-then charred remains of the airport with heavy artillery fire.[1]

This chapter asks how the scene at Svetlana's table was possible. I endeavor to answer the question using the concept of "everyday peace." In this chapter readers delve more deeply into how everyday peace entails practices on the part of individuals or groups that help to avoid and minimize conflict in divided societies (Mac Ginty 2014, 553). Studies of everyday peace suggest that it is through mundane, so-called everyday practices that civilians resist being drawn into the conflicts that surround them. Considering the practices of nonelite and nonmilitary actors in their efforts to negotiate their own, interpersonal peace outside the trenches and battle fields supports an increasing body of research that shows how peace can be enacted at multiple levels.

Expanding the field of inquiry in this way requires recognizing even the most politically marginalized people as "competent commentators" (Berents 2015, 186) capable of engaging with, and making practical sense of, their conflict-riddled world. In tracking multiple nonelite actors in their everyday efforts, scholars like Williams (2015) emphasize that peace is less a state to be arrived at than an ongoing process of negotiation. That process is evident in Café Patriot, across kitchen tables, in public transport, and in social situations transpiring in both literal and figurative minefields. Once civilians living their daily lives are taken seriously as peace-building actors, it becomes clear that war and peace are less a binary than a continuum.

But capturing the latent possibilities for peace entails further extending Berents's (2015) observation that people are capable of interpreting their political landscapes. The activities they carry out to maintain relationships and their own equanimity in the midst of a brutal conflict must also be considered. Svetlana's kitchen table is an example of a site where friendship is nurtured through avoiding sensitive conversational territory. The efforts, which are continual, keep her social world stitched together. We can therefore use Svetlana's kitchen table to talk about what have been called the micromechanisms (Williams 2015) that maintain an everyday kind of peace.

While famously difficult to define, friendship is understood for the purposes of this chapter as the mutual affinity one shares with another human being in relations of trust and support. Of course, any understanding of friendship must be situated within a particular historical context. There is no a priori criterion for a relationship to qualify as friendship: it varies from one individual and time period to the next (Licklider 1995). The support it offers may be emotional, intellectual, material, or some combination of these, but as Desai and Killick (2010) have put it, with friendship, the feeling *is* the relationship. Although there are numerous sociological and psychological scales to measure friendship, in a qualitative study such as this one that takes a phenomenological and hermeneutic approach to experiences in war, scales do not generate the kinds of insight needed here. I am more interested in the ways the people I spoke with made sense of their changing relational worlds. I therefore operationalize friendship for the purposes of this chapter by taking the perspective of my interlocutors: a person's friends are who they say they are.

I come to the topic of friendship in Ukraine as a beneficiary. In my fieldwork over the course of more than twenty years, I have benefited—and my research has been advanced—as a result of the warmth, care, and support extended to me by people from all over the former Soviet Union. It was during the fieldwork I did in the 1990s, when I lived in Crimea and Uzbekistan for an extended period that I began to appreciate the incredible richness of friend relationships in this part of the world. My friendships in America seemed to operate according to a very different logic based on enjoyment of free time and convenience. By contrast, the friendships I experienced during my fieldwork were more "in sickness and in health" types of relationships. My friends assured me that when these ties proliferate over a lifetime, it can also encumber one. But this also supports my point: whereas the ideology surrounding friendship in the United States— or my experience of it, at least—was characterized more by voluntarism and informality, friendship as I experienced it in Ukraine was characterized by more durable bonding that was consistently taken very seriously. In addition to the data I collected, this experience of friendship informs the chapter.

Friendship occupied a special place in the value system of people who lived in the Soviet era, when people rated their friendships as more integral to their well-being than home, education, or jobs (Shlapentokh 1984, 61). This is perhaps because friendship acted as a buffer from an authoritarian state (1984, 58). Friends provided one another not only with camaraderie but with valuable and scarce material goods from vodka to dog food, and crucial information suppressed by the authorities. The legacy of this system is felt in the sharp distinction still drawn between *znakomyy* which refers to an acquaintance, a buddy or a "mate" (*priyatel'*), and a friend (*drug*). Under contemporary conditions of capitalism and democratization, what friendship means is evolving and quite variable. Regardless of this variability, friendship was an important site for building everyday peace in the midst of violence. This everyday peace, however, is inherently limited.

Thinking about Everyday and International Peace

The concept of everyday peace emerges from growing recognition within the field of international relations that key insights have been missed as a result of the focus on the state as the primary mover of politics. This new awareness accounts for the increased interest in quotidian practices, the everyday, and human emotions (Shim 2016; Solomon and Steele 2017). Thinking on "everyday peace" has sought to "decenter" the state. Put simply, decentering the state means treating state authorities and international organizations as only one set of actors that create and sustain peace. Considering a wider set of peacemakers requires a corresponding shift from "top-down" to "bottom-up" perspectives (Mac Ginty 2010; Mitchell 2011; Richmond 2015). The research on everyday peace tries to demonstrate that the state is not the only significant peacemaking actor and that studying the activities of civilians yields crucial insights about military conflict more broadly.

What these approaches often betray, however, is the value of "bottom-bottom" or *lateral* peace-building activities. The risk inherent in bottom-up approaches (and indeed in the ways in which the concept of everyday peace has been deployed) is that the language reasserts a hierarchical value system—the very hierarchy it was intended to question. Many otherwise valuable studies of everyday peace end in vague allusions to the value of everyday peace for advancing large-scale peace efforts (cf. Berents 2018: 175; Williams 2015: 182 Mac Ginty 2014: 548), failing to emphasize the lived reality, as I try to do here. As Guillaume and Husyman (2019) argued, simply adding previously ignored actors is not sufficient.

Everyday peace has a way of becoming romanticized. This is especially unfortunate because everyday peace is so unlikely to contribute to international peace-making (Mac Ginty 2014, 551). Practices of everyday peace tend to operate independently of diplomats and international peace-building actors like the United Nations. Often times, the small-scale efforts to create peace have different goals from the ones promoted by national leaders or intergovernmental organizations. LeFranc discusses this limitation by questioning the ontology in which politics work through a "chain of interpersonal relations" (2011, 14). Her critique underscores that peaceful individuals do not necessarily or automatically constitute peaceful societies as a collective. Varying practices and goals result in a mix that van Leeuwen et al. (2012) refer to as a peace-building "heterotopia."

Exploring localized practices makes the contrasts between how peace is conceptualized by people in positions of authority and how "ordinary," nonelite people think about peace more vivid. In Svetlana's case, providing refreshment was the platform for fostering camaraderie between rank-and-file soldiers of opposing military sides *at the same time* that the Minsk peace accords had broken down and fighting had reached its worst levels to date. Everyday peace is constituted by an ongoing set of choices about one's words and behavior (Mac Ginty 2014, 550). Along with that agency comes the obvious fact that peace is not always possible, or necessarily the highest priority.

The Minsk Accords were the center of the international peace process in Ukraine. As soon as Minsk I was signed in September 2014, however, breaches occurred almost immediately and escalated to a full-scale conflict within three months. After then Chancellor Merkel and then President Hollande worked out a second cease-fire in an all-night negotiation, the new plan resulted in another failed cease-fire. The Minsk agreements appeared to be a farce to people who could see and hear the fighting continue, and suspected that leaders in the Russian Federation and Ukraine had an interest in continuing the conflict (Grossman 2018).

The Minsk agreements are a good example of what has been called a "liberal peace," attained through the efforts of international actors to negotiate peace for warring parties. While preferable to all-out war, a liberal peace such as the Minsk Accords fails to address core concerns and local interests (van Leeuwen et al. 2012).

The peace at Svetlana's kitchen table provides a contrast to the ongoing failure of peace at the international level. Her apartment was a place where soldiers on opposite sides of the military conflict could share food and companionship, establishing civility in the midst of military violence and belying conventional ideas of wars as fundamentally oppositional affairs. Peace experts underline that the experience of people living in areas of conflict are vital to the success of peace efforts (Mitchell 2011; Randazzo 2016). Along these lines, Lederach explains that without taking into account the complexities of the local situation, peace-building efforts are likely to fail (2005). The idea that an attitude of tolerance for social or political difference embedded in some, but of course not all, practices of friendship constitutes an untapped resource for larger efforts misses the essential point that the true value of everyday peace may not lie in what it can contribute to international efforts, but in what it offers its protagonists: a way to reinhabit a fractured world.

The introduction provided a skeletal definition of what is called the everyday. We may recall that the everyday is what is routine, habitual, and oriented toward meeting basic needs. But everyday life takes effort to maintain. There is real work behind constructing life in a way that has a mundane flow to it and maintaining that everyday rhythm in spite of inevitable disruptions. The sociologist Erving Goffman brought this home when comparing social interaction to theater and demonstrating how individuals maintain their social relations not only by constructing identities but also by engaging in continual impression management (1959, 208). This kind of management was especially difficult when the political rug was pulled out from under people's feet. People heard their friends and family members, from one day to the next, reidentifying as a different ethnicity or pledging allegiance to a different political party than in the past.

In what follows, we first consider cases in which political enemies, like soldiers fighting on opposite sides, could be personal friends. We then examine the patterns of everyday peace in which people tended to either depoliticize friendship as a way to maintain their social circles or politicize friendship and see their circles tighten as a result. Another pattern was placing blame on the media for using its power to "zombify" and persuade the population. Notions of zombies and zombification provided a spongier vocabulary for discussing otherwise tragically nonsensical events in which decades-long friendships fell apart over the conflict.

Political Enemies Become Personal Friends

During my fieldwork I witnessed everyday peace being created not only among military personnel but also among political rivals. Oleg, a former pro-Ukrainian political prisoner of the DNR, illustrates how everyday forms of peace were actively cultivated. We met in an IDP-serving organization's cool, cave-like basement after he came in one day to get advice on his résumé. The first thing I noticed about Oleg was his ready smile. His habit of spreading his giant arms when speaking seemed to suggest a willingness to embrace the world. He had light blue eyes and white hair, cut short and trained into pointy spikes. In accordance with his personal philosophy of full disclosure, Oleg introduced himself as a member of an extreme right-wing political party. He began his story at the point when Russian-backed separatists gained control over his city of Makeyevka. The group that came to power targeted him because he was part of the campaign staff of an opposing political party. Perceived as a threat, he was placed on a list of people to be removed from political activity.

One morning, he opened his door to four men, all masked in black balaclavas and dressed in civilian clothes with St. George's ribbons, symbols of the Russian Federation, pinned on. They were armed. To avoid jeopardizing his wife's safety, he readily consented to go with them. Once in his yard, however, he tried to avoid arrest by making a dash for it. One of the masked men brought him down with a shot to his back. He was handcuffed and thrown in jail in the nearby city of Gorlovka, where he underwent interrogation and received some medical attention while staying in the basement for about thirty days. The injury, fortunately a surface wound, wasn't life-threatening, and he suspected it even caused his captors to treat him with more leniency than other detainees. While he was imprisoned, members of his political party attempted to purchase his release. They were flatly rebuffed. After a month of being kept out of politics, however, he was released unconditionally. He suspects his captors may have reassessed the risk he posed or lacked the resources to sustain him.

When they let him go, they gave him back his cell phone and, at his request, some spare change for bus fare. While on the bus, he called his wife, who had been trying to secure his freedom. A human rights group she had been in contact with swooped in and put him and his wife on the next train to Ukrainian government-controlled territory. This could be where the story ends, but Oleg maintained a surprising amount of contact with the former captors: "I am only glad to keep in touch with those people, actually. But not all of them are glad to keep in touch with me. There is nothing about their behavior that would irritate me enough that I wouldn't be willing to speak with them."

"Even those who had opposite political opinions?" I asked.

"Yes, exactly."

"Did you talk to them?"

"Yes, I did. I did talk. I even talked to some rebels, on the telephone and Skype."

"Regarding what?" I wanted to know.

"Well, everyday things."

I was surprised that in spite of what he had been through—after all, he had been shot in the back—Oleg did not appear to harbor any resentment toward these individuals. This attitude enabled him to continue relating with them on the level of the everyday. Oleg explained that after he was evacuated, his neighbors called to tell him that his house had been broken into. He contacted his former captors: as the people responsible for maintaining law and order, the former rebels and now de facto authorities resecured the house. After the incident with the house, one of the separatists called him to discuss the car sitting in his garage. When the man—and Oleg refers to all of these individuals as "separatists," although many of them obtained official titles in the DNR—asked about the car, Oleg simply gave it to him, having left the keys with the neighbors. Oleg told me this with a nonchalant shrug of his shoulders. I was perplexed by what seemed like capitulation to this vigilante justice and asked for the reason. Oleg replied that it gave him hope that his house in Donetsk would be safe and that at some point in the future, he might be able to call in the debt in a moment of need. In fact, Oleg's "separatist" offered as much, saying that if Oleg's life "got bad," he would be there for him. Oleg's story highlights the practical value of everyday peace, which in this case supports Oleg's pursuit of other goals. The connection he cultivated over the phone and through videoconferencing was a vehicle for resolving mundane issues and ensuring cooperative coexistence in the future.

An important piece of the puzzle is that Oleg is keen to return to Donetsk. The vignette about his car shows everyday peace is enacted not just because it represents an ideal, but because it is pragmatic. Put bluntly, his jailers might have been violent separatists, but they are also future neighbors. In addition to pragmatism, faith also played a role in Oleg's ability to reach across political lines. Oleg was confident justice would be meted out by his Christian God. He was therefore not inclined to seek legal justice for the harm that had been done to him, even though it was suggested to him by the international human rights organization that helped him evacuate. Above all, he saw his captors as human. In a political atmosphere in which tolerance, respect, and peaceful coexistence were unlikely, Oleg's ethics supported everyday peace. Thus both pragmatism and religion can inform everyday peace.

Months later, Oleg shared with me that the man to whom he gave his car had disassociated himself from the political party responsible for Oleg's capture and imprisonment. Interestingly enough, from his perspective, this was beside the point because he never had an expectation that their political views needed to be brought into any kind of rapprochement. This is typical of reactions to the chronic uncertainty characterizing contemporary conflicts, in which a primary objective is personal survival (Duffield 2007) and the state demonstrates an inability to protect.

These examples show that everyday peace is clearly possible between military opponents (as in Svetlana's case) and political rivals (as in Oleg's case). Svetlana and Oleg crafted everyday peace where one might least expect it. What happened between people who were less directly involved in the conflict? Turning our attention to so-called ordinary people takes us deeper into the ways in which people practiced peace in the midst of violence.

The Micropolitics of Peace

Disruptions to interpersonal relationships as a result of the war were one of the biggest concerns that people raised during my fieldwork between 2015 and 2017.

When friendships faltered, everything, it seemed, was thrown into question. Oleksandra, who we encounter again in chapter 5, provides a good example. I met her at the screening of a documentary film about female IDPs. Having appeared in the documentary, Oleksandra was invited to take part in a panel discussion following the showing. I thought what she had to say was very important and invited her for coffee to learn more. Oleksandra projected confidence even though she was quite young at the time. Short in stature, she wore her brown hair long, and it flowed down over her shoulders and arms to almost reach her elbows. She was dressed very modestly in a slightly frayed maroon skirt and weathered print blouse, but her caramel-colored cowboy boots showed style. Over coffee in a café around the corner from where the documentary had been shown, Oleksandra explained: "Basically, you understand when this conflict takes place that many friends . . . we simply realized they are not our friends; they are ready to put a knife in our backs because we support the pro-Ukrainian position." This was one of the greatest tragedies of the war: the disruption and dissolution of relationships that had previously been sources of support. Her experience suggests that while it has heuristic value for social scientific analyses, separating the personal from the political, or relationality from nationality, is not so simple in experiential worlds. Just as during the American Civil War, the crises of relationality and nationality were interrelated.

My conversations with people revealed two main strategies for managing interpersonal tensions and reestablishing order in a disordered world. The strategy adopted by Svetlana—avoidance of contentious topics like war—was only one way of maintaining peace. A second strategy was avoiding friends who acted as triggers because they held opposing political views. This was the strategy adopted by Oleksandra. In other words, whereas Svetlana and people like her made peace by separating their personal relationships from political views, others created interpersonal peace by comingling them, effectively "nationalizing" friendship. Nationalization resulted in the loss—or war-imposed hiatus—of friendships. In other words, Svetlana and Oleksandra adhered to two different ethics of care. The first extended amiable relations to all, irrespective of political position, and the second restricted friendliness to a circle of people defined by national loyalty. National allegiance was therefore pivotal to intersubjective worlds: each person had to find a way to organize—in some cases repeatedly reorganize—personal and ideological commitments.

The dynamics surrounding friendship in Ukraine raise a question continental philosopher Hans Georg Gadamer asked in *Friendship and Solidarity*: what happens to friendship in a time of war? He was concerned with what was left of friendship and solidarity in an age of "anonymous responsibility." By anonymous responsibility, he meant a world in which there are shared institutions but also a great diversity of views. With regard to his sense of anomie, he wrote, "We live in a world of interrelated foreignness" (Gadamer 1999, 4). Gadamer's question is relevant to managing friendships under Ukrainian conditions that pit neighbors and friends against one another. Gadamer suggests clarity can be achieved by making a distinction between simple friendship, which he suggests is rather ineffable, and solidarity, a kind of avowed friendship. When Gadamer wrote about avowed friendship, he was thinking about war and the way that the bombings of his city "awoke" strangers to unprecedented acts of solidarity. Similarly, the war in Ukraine required people to become more conscious of their personal relationships. Life in a war zone fostered avowed solidarity, characterized by interdependence and ethical ties (Nielsen 2017, 244). Friendship had to be rethought in terms of both who was considered a friend and how that friendship was practiced.

Svetlana and Oleksandra were not alone in reevaluating relationships. According to the thematic coding of the material I gathered, the majority (65 percent) of those interviewed reported a loss of friends. People in younger age brackets were noticeably more concerned about the loss of friends than those in older demographic categories. Those in the eighteen-to-twenty-nine age bracket, for example, spent about twice as much time discussing how this affected them than those in their forties. Only eight out of forty-five IDP interviewees stated that they had also gained friends. Five of them were careful to clarify that they had new acquaintances, not full-fledged friends. Conversations about friends relied more heavily on the vocabulary of nationalism than discussions of changes to family life, the topic of the next chapter.

Perhaps counterintuitively, concern about the loss of friendship suggests that friendship itself has remained quite alive. Notably missing was the kind of malice that typically characterizes ethnolinguistic conflict. The story I seek to tell about friendship is as remarkable for what it is—a vivid demonstration of the "reach" of political conflict—as what it is not—an expression of deep existential hatreds. In Donbas, loss of friendship was rarely treated as having to do with betrayal or hatred. More often than not, people in Donbas saw their political opponents as the victims of disinformation campaigns.

In what follows, we examine the specific strategies for making and unmaking everyday peace, beginning with a deeper inquiry into Svetlana's strategy of depoliticizing friendship. Then, we visit a shelter for IDPs. The strategies could vary over time. Bohdan, for example adopted the depoliticizing approach only after the painful, if temporary, loss of his best friends. This brings us to the second strategy, politicizing friendship. In the section on this topic, we explore the use of national symbols and the "world collapsing" stakes involved when "people are like bombs."

Depoliticizing Friendships for Everyday Peace

Among the strategies of those impacted by the conflict in Donbas, the best way to keep one's friends appeared to be adopting an apolitical stance. But avoiding the topic of war in a country experiencing a conflict was a delicate balancing act. As Kira put it, "We can talk about hardships that they face (those who stayed in my native city of Donetsk). We've got some hardships here as well, so we can discuss these hardships, but without touching upon political matters. That's how we have managed to preserve our relationships." In other words, challenges like not being able to sleep because of shelling in the night could only be spoken of cryptically as the "inability" to sleep. Not being able to purchase food as a result of shooting in one's street would be spoken of in terms of hunger. People would assure one another that everything was okay, as they ignored the sounds of shelling that could be heard in the background of the phone call. Scholars of everyday peace argue that interactions that place boundaries around conflict subvert the (violent) political status quo (Ring 2006; Mac Ginty 2014). But this approach to understanding the implications of apolitical social relationships ignores their significance for the actors involved, focusing instead on how individual choices might impact the state.

Avoiding political topics came at a cost because it created figurative minefields within interpersonal relationships and required a kind of self-imposed separation from the burning political issues associated with the war. For example, a humanitarian and pastor who ran a shelter for IDPs in Sloviansk, whom I will call "Pastor Sergei," had established firm rules: "We do not watch TV because they [the residents] are coming from the DNR and the LNR, some pro-Russian and some pro-Ukrainian, and if they watched the TV they would start to fight. This is wrong because it is in this way that you ruin your life, disrupt your fate. So it is forbidden to discuss politics."

Pastor Sergei elaborated that the tolerance level for any kind of political difference was so low that even stating one's place of origin could trigger a heated argument close to the line of contact. The highly selective use of the television in the family room pictured here, largely for religious purposes, had a significant impact on daily life because it was literally the only form of entertainment in a rural area where the impoverished residents typically had a phone but not

FIGURE 8. Shelter common area

an internet connection or computer. The everyday peace established in the shelter by decree enabled it to function as a shelter, but it was a negative peace. There were also less austere arrangements in the IDP "hubs" throughout the country.

Learning How to Depoliticize

After our initial conversation in the dining room of the shelter, Pastor Sergei invited me back. He picked me up after church on a Sunday afternoon. On our way to the shelter for the IDPs, Pastor Sergei noted where tires had previously formed a barricade, where a bridge had been strategically bombed and destroyed, where the first civilian casualty in the war had fallen. When we pulled into the driveway, he explained that all of the residents lived in the large, two-story, white stucco building at the center of the property. Before it became a shelter, it was used as a sanitorium—a hybrid between a spa and a health clinic. The building had been badly damaged during the siege of Sloviansk, however, and was only recently restored. The main building was accessed from a circular driveway that connected various gardens and outbuildings. In the center of the drive was a large grassy area with a fire pit. When we arrived, the residents were sitting around a fire, perched on stumps and dilapidated lawn chairs. I was encouraged to sit down on one of the rickety chairs. All of the residents seemed guarded and I felt a little bit like I was crashing a party.

As we stoked the fire, we chewed on sunflower seeds, a favorite if *nikulturiy* "uncultured" local habit. Pastor Sergei busied himself with the garden, trimming hedges and weeding the flower beds. Eventually, his wife emerged with two enormous racks of chicken kebabs and placed them over the fire. One of the residents brought out a large speaker which seemed to lift the mood immediately. The music was upbeat, a hybrid between smooth jazz and Christian pop. When Pastor Sergei put down his hedge clippers and joined our group, he explained that I was interested in understanding what it was like to have been forcibly displaced. He suggested I stroll with residents one by one. Speaking with them individually while wandering around in the yard brought their guards down, and they began to tell me about their lives.

The metaphorical tightrope they walked to avoid political topics was, however, ever present, and each resident in some way expressed a desire to avoid being overheard by the other residents. For example, although quite elderly, Luidmila wanted to sit on the swings to talk with me. We both faced forward, swung, and chatted like schoolgirls. With the afternoon sun warming my face, I could begin to imagine what it would be like to live in the shelter long term, as Luidmila had. Then I spoke with Olga. She wanted to stand behind a large tree, where we were concealed by its fat trunk. As we spoke, she would periodically peek at the group sitting around the fire. Her furtive body language made it feel as if we were in a game of hide-and-seek. After I spoke with Olga, Maya led me to a picnic table where she pulled me toward her, cupped her hands around her mouth, and whispered into my ear, also casting cautious glances to the group around the fire. From the perspective of psychology, all of these comportments might be viewed as trauma-related, perhaps "regressive" behaviors, revealing that the political tensions had become an embodied reality and a subtle, intersubjective, everyday war in the shelter.

By the time I had spoken with several residents, I was quite famished. Thankfully, the chicken was ready. We went inside to eat. Shoes were kicked off by the entryway, and slippers were slid on. A breeze was blowing gently through the open windows of the house, and the residents seemed happy, perhaps in anticipation of the special meal to come. Standing in the doorway to the dining room that had seemed like a sanctuary when I first sat there with Pastor Sergei just a few days before, I felt the vectors of tension intensifying into emotional force fields. The Formica-topped tables, it seemed, had come to stand for entire oblasts that had become de facto republics. Although it remained unspoken, the country's political problems hardened and materialized in this communal space. Still, experiencing mere tension rather than arguments or worse, it seemed, was an accomplishment. People with very different political beliefs not only tolerated one another, but lived together.

Maya came up behind me, and perhaps sensing my uncertainty, gently ushered me to her table. Then Luidmila walked up with a heaping plate of food just seconds later. Soon, more women joined our table. Having been coached by Pastor Sergei, I assiduously avoided any topic that could be construed as remotely political, which was difficult considering the physical and emotional proximity of the war. I was becoming a little bit more like a person who actively depoliticizes relationships, and it was difficult: I began to second guess everything I said. The conversation turned to food, and one of the women asked me what is available at an American deli. I suspected the question was born from shortages and cravings. Given their isolation and limited resources, I worried that a full accounting would be insensitive to their situation. I spoke instead about the foods available in their local markets but not at an American deli: authentic buckwheat kasha, certain cheeses, eggplant caviar, and creamery butter, among other things, are much harder to find.

But Olga's food in her pickle jar is the image that stays with me from the shelter. I watched as Olga took the meal that was being served in the shelter and, instead of eating it, stuffed it bit by bit into a pickle jar she had recycled. First she scraped the grilled chicken off its skewer into the jar, and then pushed in her cucumber and tomato salad before spooning in the rice porridge. Next, she poured in the soup of the day, a clear fish broth with a single dumpling, into the jar. The dumpling sat there, bereft of company, until she emptied her fruit cocktail into the mix. No one at our table so much as blinked. They must have seen her do this dozens of times before. It was hard for me to look at the meal mixed, like a dog's breakfast, through the greasy glass. It was poignant to think about how Olga's choice to save the food for later reflected uncertainty. In serving as a defense against hunger, the jar condenses something of the meaning of forced displacement. An attempt to meet both physical and emotional needs, it seemed, was packed in the pint-sized vessel. The food in the jar was also a microcosm of life after forced displacement which people described as mixed up. And finally, given that her roommate of the opposite political persuasion in the bunk above must have stomached the sounds and smells of midnight consumption, the jar is iconic of interpersonal peace.

Not everyone had a Pastor Sergei to provide rules, and I witnessed numerous cases in which strategies of everyday peace were adopted only after discord had emerged. Many people I spoke with initially lost, and then painstakingly worked to repair, friendships across national lines. A good example is Bohdan, who evacuated his wife and child to Kramatorsk, then returned to Donetsk to care for his elderly parents. I met him at the Kramatorsk NGO that had provided him and his family with support. We sat on a decrepit old couch, with the late after-

FIGURE 9.   IDP hub common area

noon sunshine slanting into the basement office through the deep window wells. Marcus was an energetic figure who moved and spoke quickly. He had turned to the NGO for assistance in starting a small business, and with his firm handshake and straightforward demeanor, I could imagine him succeeding. Having just finished talking to one of the case workers, he sported a brown plaid shirt, nicely tailored pants, and impressively polished leather shoes.

With the tape recorder rolling, he told me how back in Donetsk, he had the Sisyphean task of repairing telecommunications infrastructure. Every day, he drove around his town repairing servers, modems, and connections that had been destroyed in the fighting the previous night. The next day, he would get up and do this all over again. He used the funds he earned to support both his parents' household in besieged Donetsk and the household of his wife and child in government-controlled Ukraine. Bohdan's life was literally divided between Ukrainian government-controlled and separatist-controlled territories. Now in his late thirties, Bohdan spoke of the profound toll this had taken on friendships he had built since his school days: "This is a nightmare! All of us . . . I had a group of friends. I am 37, I have known my friends for more than 25 years. We have been together since eleventh . . . since sixth form, I mean, I've got a tight-knit group, we were very, very close. And when all these events started, we quarreled.

"Moreover, I quarreled seriously with my best friend, he was for this 'indepen-dence,' for reunion with Russia, and I categorically opposed all that. The issue with friends is especially unpleasant because they all started to treat me ... Our feelings toward each other are not so kind anymore, not so friendly, resentment appeared, well, in general, it has had a big influence." Bohdan went without com-municating with his friends for the first two years of the conflict. Eventually, he began to use the other strategy: a tacit rule was established to limit the conversa-tion to topics like weather, health, and local sports. While this is a good work-around that enables them to remain in contact, the nature of the friendship has changed in fundamental ways because it is impossible to speak about crucial con-cerns. Everyday peace required being nimble enough to dodge emotional pot-holes in their path, and this flexibility came at a cost. What happened with his friendships shows how the national crisis created relational crises. As Bohdan's situation vividly reveals, the relational and the national are connected on meta-phoric and literal levels.

Politicizing Friendship: People Were Like Bombs

A different way of renegotiating relationships was to avoid certain friends. Yuliya, a middle-aged professional I met in Kherson, reflected on how she disconnected from her best friends. We sat in deep armchairs in the corner of a hotel lobby with my tape recorder running on the coffee table between us. We talked late into the night in the cavernous room, only barely lit to conserve electricity. Her friends, Yuliya explained, were people she had known for over a decade, since graduate school. Having studied, lived, and subsequently worked alongside one another, they had developed multifaceted relationships. Nevertheless, she told me: "I don't talk to them much because I'm so vulnerable, any phrase can harm me. And people are like bombs, so a phrase can easily explode into conflict." Her statement that "people are like bombs" is a powerful metaphor for how previ-ously stable relationships can be disrupted. Further complicating these matters was the prevalence of PTSD, which can complicate the ability to sustain estab-lished relationships. Her journey through PTSD land was characterized by emo-tional lability. She described crying when she felt happy and hearing other peoples' statements as something akin to psychological "bombs." When I met with her over coffee in subsequent years she was continuing to work on over-coming these symptoms. Yuliya was not alone in recalling the breakdown of friendships tearfully. As Victoria phrased it: "Well, mostly I can't talk to them, I have severed all communication with my friends, and they seem to realize that, so they don't call me, because at first we had such debates and quarrels that I understood, well . . . It's just hard that, as I've said, we had normal relationships before and were close to each other, [crying] but now we can't understand each other at the most basic level. That's why I can't talk to them. My husband is more loyal, he talks to them. But still, every call is painful for him, he realizes that people are absolutely . . . they think differently than the way we think." The notion that they ceased to understand one another "at the most basic level" highlights how the macropolitical conflict was reflected in micropolitical dynamics. Some of the "explosions" had to do with national epithets like *ykrop* ("dill") and *khokhol* (a Cossack hairstyle in the past) for Ukrainians and *moscali* (for Musovites). These (only seemingly minor) insults communicate fears and prejudices with regard to difference.

Yuliya mentioned that her husband dealt with his losses differently than she did. My interview transcripts showed that of the people I interviewed who were displaced, women were more likely to describe friend loss than men. The men whose circles of friends contracted were generally extremely careful to argue that the reason for this was not quarrelling but the geographic distance that the conflict had imposed on them. By contrast, women spoke at considerably more length about feelings of depression, emptiness, and loss. To a certain extent, this confirms the prevailing gender stereotypes in that men are expected to be more "rational" and less organized around relationships than women. It is also possible that the women I interviewed were more comfortable than their male counterparts with talking to another woman and therefore more likely to open up to me about something so personal.

Nationalizing one's circle of friends represented a way of eliminating conflict by avoiding those with different political views. In the context of Ukraine, this meant cutting off ties with those who had different feelings about the 2013–2014 revolution that ousted Yanukovych and his Party of Regions, bringing in a new government in Kyiv. There were a lot of complaints about the Party of Regions as a malignant force for the country. There were also extensive discussions around disappointment with the unrealized potential of the 2013–2014 revolution. These were the main positions people in government-controlled parts of the country felt comfortable staking out. This leaves a great deal unsaid. Discourse on political topics was heavily policed through self-censorship and the sheer political incorrectness of saying anything in favor of the authorities of the "republics" controlled by authorities loyal to Moscow. Here is another tragedy of the war. From the perspective of the people internally displaced within Ukraine, their friends and relatives who supported a Russian course of developments were addle-brained, misguided, or just plain wrong. They had well-crafted arguments against their loved ones' assertions that Ukraine had become anti-Semitic, was in bed with the United States, or had a "fascist" intolerance for Russian language and culture. For the people in their midst who fled to Ukraine when they would have preferred Russia, or who had been willing to support the change in government in the DNR or LNR but had to move as a result of the destruction of their homes and villages, avoidance of political topics was the rule.

National symbols became potent condensation points. Sofia's story elucidates how friendships were sorted by flags, national anthems, children's fairy tales, and language-specific lullabies. I interviewed her, a single mother in her mid-twenties, very close to the line of contact. She wept when she reflected on how difficult the past few years had been. She had moved seven times since the war began. Sofia had fled but returned when encouraged by the first Minsk agreement, only to be displaced all over again by the renewed fighting. She described how national symbols exerted a formidable influence on her ability to sustain friendships. In short, these symbols were tools for constructing and deconstructing not just state-citizen but personal relationships. While still in the zone of conflict, she ended all ties with a close female friend: "My friend heard me sing a lullaby for my child in Ukrainian—well, I still sing it. She said: 'What! What are you doing? We are against Ukraine!!' I said enough! Enough of THAT. Yes, I lost my friends, and I really lost friends, and you understand that it is not you who is different, and it is not they who are different, but something in our heads has really turned over that we can't be together or communicate anymore." In this statement, Sofia softens the blow of losing the friendship by locating the problem in the situation rather than the friend: something "turned over." This works to depersonalize the difficulty, placing blame on the macropolitical pressure surrounding them. This strategy requires emotional common sense (Sylvester 2013) to spare oneself emotional pain and turmoil. At a deeper level, however, the experience she relates of having one's mind altered by the conflict vividly conveys how subjectivity and selfhood were vulnerable to war. The world changed, and so did they. Symbols like lullabies, anthems, colors, and flags were powerful precisely because they condensed national identities. They became a way to reenact—or avoid—the conflict at a smaller scale.

The interpersonal lives of those who "nationalized" friendship expressed the salient political divisions microcosmically in mundane and quotidian war. The extent to which this explicitly served any particular political factions is difficult to map. What is clear is that friendship offered little shelter from the political conflict and instead became another site for working out the conflict's tensions, with varying levels of success. Political conflict does more than traumatize the individual psyche or upset the geopolitical balance: it reverberates through interpersonal relationships and expresses itself in different kinds of everyday war.

"It was the world that collapsed"

The stakes in all of this were high. For some, the loss of friendships meant losing the feeling of being a person who is seen and matters in the world. In some cases, material support was also at stake. Vera is a young woman who fled Donetsk with her husband and two children. Although the transcript of my conversation with her contains occasional bursts of laughter over her pithy remarks, she expressed ennui and suggested there was a way in which her social world had been drained of vitality. Although she came with her small family, she found herself in a social world that seemed to have been impoverished: "My ancestors' graves are there. My friends are there. I mean, [here] I can walk in the center of town and I know that I will not meet anybody who knows me during the entire day! [Repeats the sentence for emphasis.] Well, it was the world that collapsed when we heard the first explosions." Although the "world" that collapsed around her was social, she understood that it also had implications for her material well-being. She described a new financial vulnerability: "Now everything depends on my working capacity. If it drops a little, I just cannot pay the rent or anything and raise my children. These rueful feelings are always there. Because of these anxious feelings I lost 10 kilos." Social worlds, then, had to be reconfigured around the conflict, and people brought a variety of strategies and amounts of effort to this process. Vera lost both the feeling of mattering as a social being and her financial safety net.

Losing friends could be a matter of life or death: friends were a source of unofficial information that could be lifesaving. Politically active people told me that their friends were the ones who alerted them that they were on blacklists and helped them to escape. Friendship was also literally lifesaving when public transportation was too slow or too damaged and it was necessary to rely on friends to escape.

Everyday Peace through Zombification

Many whom I interviewed attributed estrangements to the influence of news media. Holding media propaganda responsible became an additional tactic for maintaining what might be called "everyday peace" but is more aptly categorized as everyday war. That the media was perceived as a powerful actor should come as no surprise considering how information is a perennial "weapon" used by news platforms to push particular political agendas with increasing sophistication (Jaitner 2015; Polyakova 2018). In Ukraine, Russian information sources were often described as *maskirovka*—disinformation campaigns that can spread conspiracy theories, vitriol, and libelous stories in a bid to magnify social divides (Polyakova 2018).

Media disinformation was felt to exacerbate tensions throughout the region. A woman I met at a barbecue held by a nongovernmental organization, Xristina, reflected on the friend loss that both she and her husband had experienced: "And I have a decent number of people I know who simply refuse to talk to me. They are people who, as I was leaving, actually yelled at me, 'You're a fascist!' 'Nazi!' and everything under the sun. Psychologically, that's hard, to be perfectly honest. Now it sounds pretty funny, but in the moment, when you live in that political dirt, and the media dirt is the same, you get lied to from every side. It's very difficult because many people believe in things that don't exist." The idea of people believing in things that do not exist brings home the power of the media to shape perceptions of reality. The "dirt" and "lies" she speaks of were an integral part of the everyday kind of war. Xristina attended the barbecue without her husband because he was too embarrassed to be seen in public. His teeth had been knocked out by a blow to the face back in separatist-controlled Luhansk when he made a pro-Ukrainian comment within earshot of some others.

Xristina was not alone in communicating the idea that people believe in things that do not exist. To a certain extent seeing someone else as confused was a conflict-calming mechanism. Their harsh words or other personal lapses could be attributed to an "altered reality," "cotton-consciousness," or "zombification." Some suggested that those exposed to Russian propaganda, in particular, walked around as if zombified. If apparently hate-filled or delusional political views could be seen as a form of contagion, it was possible that people under their influence might recover. Deleuze and Guattari write that "It is in war, famine, and epidemics that werewolves and vampires proliferate" (1987, 243). It could equally be said that for a country like Ukraine, with three uncontrolled provinces, zombification is the perfect rhetoric to assert people are not acting out of the integrity of their own political beliefs, but have in fact lost their political subjectivity. If people are not themselves but instead embody and speak for the political forces acting through the news media, then they occupy an ambiguous—and less contentious—zone between east and west, Russia and Ukraine, family and politics, life and death. As I elaborate more fully in chapter 7, however, speaking of zombification was still a rhetorical form of everyday war, by which I mean a modality for treating the people with different political opinions as lesser humans.

Maintaining relationships in spite of the political conflict was especially valued by people who saw the conflict as a real-world *Game of Thrones*. The American fantasy television series depicting violent struggles for power was widely followed in Ukraine during my fieldwork. While the series (from 2011 to 2019) has many plot lines, a primary thread is the web of alliances and conflicts among noble dynasties who are competing for the power of the throne or seeking to free themselves from it. As such, the show bears a resemblance to the battles for wealth and power among Ukrainian and Russian oligarchs. Allowing a friendship to end was senseless to those who viewed the conflict as a contest orchestrated by these elites for their own gain. From this perspective, the conflict had little to do with whether Ukraine should pursue a European path or a Russian one. Rather, the war was a game of thrones carried out in real life, obscuring the oligarchic theft of resources that should have been public goods. The apparent complicity of some Ukrainian authorities made things worse. As Mykola summarized it: "the territory wasn't so much captured, as it was surrendered. I mean, all cities surrendered. The trade with the occupied territories continues, so there's no war on the economic level, it exists only on TV, between people, in the moods, the war in the moods." The war in Donbas was a "war in the moods," at a number of levels. We have already seen how the emotional lability resulting from traumatic experiences made many personal relationships impossible to continue. At another level, this young man points to how emotions may become weaponized when propaganda incites strong feelings, and strong feelings led people to enlist in the fight itself. The phrase "war in the moods" captures succinctly how the military conflict buffeted peoples' emotions and relationships.

Everyday War in New Acquaintances

We have explored three main strategies for maintaining everyday peace: avoiding the topic of politics, avoiding the people with whom one disagreed, and ascribing discord to the zombifying powers of the media. Avoiding people with whom one disagreed and associating only with like-minded pro-Ukrainians (what I am calling the nationalization of friendship) could open new avenues for friendship. As humanitarian worker Raina stated: "My circle of friends widened because I moved to Kyiv and I can say that I've got new friends here, such patriotic people from Maidan with whom I live in perfect harmony, who love me and whom I love. I value each of them, I would feel badly if a lost any of them." Raina was quite effusive in her enthusiasm for newly found friends. She made these new friends in the process of volunteering to help with humanitarian relief. Sitting on the bed in her tiny room in an IDP shelter, I could see the awards for service plastering her walls. She was well-known for her tireless work as a triage person: she greeted trains with evacuees. Many of the women arriving from the conflict in the east, she recounted, were in advanced stages of pregnancy. Her task was to direct them to hospitals and available bed space based on information that was continually being updated through extensive networks of volunteers. When we spoke, she served as a manager or kind of "resident assistant" in a shelter for IDPs outside the capital. Raina was providing public goods as a private citizen, a situation that I saw repeated in myriad ways both close to and far from the line of contact. Raina's example shows how the nationalization of friendship could, on occasion, form the basis of service to the nation. It also became the basis for the logic underpinning everyday war: its useless to reason with "those" people.

To return to Svetlana's kitchen table, the peace that reigned over cups of tea was possible because Svetlana had implemented a practice of peace-building: avoiding contentious topics. The strategy had the psychic cost of creating a state of cognitive dissonance in which individuals were simultaneously at peace and at war with one another. What Svetlana and her interlocutors gained as a result was a respite from the conflict and potentially a basis for amiable postwar relations.

The reflections on friendships explored here demonstrate how the geopolitical conflict erupted and overflowed into the interpersonal realm so that the conflict between the two countries was often expressed in the intersubjective connections between people. For those with strong political positions, the circle of friends typically contracted. For those who wished to be apolitical, friendship had to be practiced differently. While the literature on everyday peace is often ebullient about its potential (cf. Berents 2018, 175; Williams 2015, 182), we can begin to see how this peace is a reflection of war.

Ultimately, the conflict forced people to become more conscious, selective, and self-reflective about whom they allowed in their inner circles. Although relationality was reconfigured in the process, friendship itself was not at stake. Thus, friendship did not lose its value as a result of the conflict, but its qualities changed. Talk of friendship provides a valuable window on the "war of moods" in PTSD land: these relationships provide an important vantage point on the subjective experience of life in country in conflict, and more subtle, everyday forms of war.

HOME FRONTS
Romantic Partnerships and Families during War

"There were many divorces due to quarrels. Men and women, families separated. And it [was] terrible [how] grown-up children lost their elderly parents because of politics, that's a catastrophe!" —Tamara

This chapter explores how people made sense of changes to family life. The quarrels referred to by the IDP quoted above were political ones. Whereas some people were in favor of a European direction for the country, others saw the future of Donbas as lying with the Russian Federation. These opposing political views were profoundly disruptive to families. People I spoke with were troubled by the arguing, the silences, the slamming doors, and the abruptly ended phone calls among family members. It seemed their social world was falling apart. Other kinds of relationships took up the slack when family ties became strained. Above all, the conflict in eastern Ukraine prompted a reorganization of the relationship between relationships.

Lidiya provides a good example. We sat on a magenta sofa in a "hub," a social service agency that helps IDPs from Donbas. Lidiya's toddler played with brightly colored plastic toys in the corner while we talked. I asked her if any of her relationships had changed as a result of the war and she replied: "Yeah, I ran into that. Everyone has run into that. First off, I ran into that when we . . . were still back home, and we got bombed, our relatives all refused [to take us in]. Right then." Part of the reason was political: her immediate family knew she and her husband were pro-Ukrainian, whereas they themselves planned to stick it out in Russian-controlled Donbas no matter what. Another reason was that despite being closely related, they did not want to become responsible for feeding and clothing the young family on an extended basis and the relationship quickly soured: "They said, 'We don't need any freeloaders.' Our relatives said, 'We don't need you.' And that was that. That's how we spoke. After that happened, we went to an unfamiliar city." Lidiya's distant relatives, people she was not even well-acquainted with came through for her family by raising funds for transportation to government-controlled Ukraine. Then Lidiya and her family received a warm welcome from the volunteer community in southern Ukraine: "Turned out they wanted us more here. We got helped out here, at least they gave us the dorm. And they gave us a roof over our heads, we had our own room, we feel cramped in that small room, but we live in it to this day." Family relationships were severely strained by conditions of conflict, but the ethics or ways of caring for strangers created an expansive safety net. In this way, new networks of care and aid replaced some of the former functions of family, salvaging a livable world.

Ultimately, the constellations of problems that war creates cannot be successfully understood in isolation—they are interconnected. Scholars' analytic categories like family and nation are heuristic devices: they facilitate some kinds of analyses while foreclosing others. In everyday experience, family and nation were connected in many ways. What happened in families in response to the Russia-Ukraine conflict has much to tell us about the personal costs of macropolitical conflicts in general.

The Relationship between Relationships

This chapter further extends the concept introduced earlier that "people are like bombs." The metaphor is apt as a way of thinking about how contemporary conflicts erupt at multiple sites, including within interpersonal relationships. Because of changes in the conduct of warfare, contemporary conflicts tend to lack discrete front lines. We can think of friendships and families as additional sites where conflict refracts. I suggest that what happened in Lidiya's family, and families like hers, is best illuminated by thinking in terms of an intersectionality of relationships.

This affords a reconceptualization of the relation between family and nation. Historians like Benedict Anderson (1991) have described the nation as "family writ large" to explain nationalism. The basic idea is that the nation, which is an imagined community, is shaped by the power dynamics between genders. A look at national narratives around the world shows that, indeed, nations are often described through the iconography of the family and domestic space (McClintock 1993). And nations are often anthropomorphized as motherlands and fatherlands. Countries are referred to maternally as "she." Why? McClintock suggests the family offers a useful model, adding that the model makes social inequalities, especially gender inequalities, seem natural (1993, 63). In this way, the patriarchal nuclear family is naturalized as something enduring and male dominance is affirmed. Here, we reverse the idea that nation is family writ large and consider what is to be gained by viewing family as nation writ small. During the conflict over Donbas, the political conflict could shatter families, or make them sites of everyday war.

Intersectionality

This chapter delves into the inequalities between different kinds of relationships, which is also to say different kinds of caring. I take caring behavior as something that can be enacted by men or women. The intersectionality that interests me, then, is between different kinds of relationships. The relationships between romantic couples were strained by partners being pulled in multiple directions. In many cases, couples and their families held together. In some cases, however, prioritizing a parent over a partner or the call to serve one's nation over marital unity led to physical separation and broken marriages. A profound tension between ethics of caring for oneself and one's partner versus fulfilling one's duty to nation and country had a way of pulling some couples apart.

The concept of intersectionality emphasizes the webbed nature of social categorizations. Intersectionality theory asserts that people can be disadvantaged by multiple sources of oppression. Identities based on race, ethnicity, class, age, sexual orientation, gender, disability, or other factors overlap. In other words, forms of discrimination coexist and become interdependent in ways that can be difficult to untangle. The term intersectionality became popular after Kimberlé Crenshaw used it to summarize what black feminists had been observing with regard to the predominantly white and middle-class bias of the mainstream feminist movement (Crenshaw 1989). To view different kinds of relationships as intersectional is my way of drilling down into care ethics, which were far from homogenous. As applied to the conflict in Ukraine, people were not just deeply disappointed but strategically disadvantaged when their relationships became "casualties" of the conflict.

The reorganization of the relationships between relationships is foreshadowed by Soviet history. Shortly after the 1917 October Revolution, the Code on Marriage, the Family and Guardianship was ratified. It mandated women's equality and visualized the withering away, or *otmiranie*, of the family. In the Stalin period, the idea that loyalty to nation ought to come before loyalty to family was promoted though parable, propaganda, and idealized figures. People resisted this privileging of the collective over the individual in complex and often covert ways—for example, by repurposing Soviet military holidays to honor previous traditions and family interests. Eventually, changes were made that allowed people more privacy. Still, socialist ideology gave considerably more latitude for state intervention in private affairs than was the case in many other countries, and people were conditioned to accept that in some situations, the collective comes before family.

In the remainder of the chapter, we explore how this played out in various types of relationships. We start with marriages and romantic partnerships, then move on to what people had to say about rifts between siblings and between parents and children. The disruptions reveal the significance of everyday war, and help us appreciate, in the last section of the chapter, the importance of repair.

Romantic Partnerships

The challenges couples faced were partly ideological (when members of the pair had different stances on the war), partly related to gender aporia (with new sources of stress—old roles no longer worked and new ones had yet to be configured), and partly the result of physical and psychological trauma. Thus, dyadic relationships became crucibles where much larger forces intersected. Couples had to balance the competing demands placed on them by political convictions, loyalty to parents, and the bond they shared with each another.

What people had to say about romantic partnerships was in part a reflection of gender norms in Ukraine. According to a 2018 study that drew on a sample of 1,500 men across the country, gender attitudes have remained staunchly traditional. The Deputy Minister of Education and Science is quoted as stating that "even though the age of wooly mammoths is in the past, aggression and power are still considered to be essential for men" (United Nations Population Fund 2018). According to statistical surveys like those conducted by the United Nations Population Fund, gender norms in Ukraine revolve around male dominance in the family. While this is admittedly a snapshot and the picture may vary across age and class, the majority of men support the idea that women should maintain their traditional position in society by taking responsibility for tasks like cooking, cleaning, and caring for children. For men, showing signs of "weakness" in public or private was considered shameful.[1] But the conflict in Donbas created havoc around these norms.

Hierarchies of Care: "Where is my borscht?"

Daily routines around who carries out such tasks as making the coffee, going to work, shopping for groceries, or cooking often take shape without discussion. When the conflict over Donbas erupted, these routines were crosscut by national passions and political ambitions. The resulting strains illustrate the importance of multiple and competing ethics of caring. As a humanitarian who was also an IDP, Alina put it: "When a wife who is totally into volunteering comes home, her head feels twice its normal size, she's carrying issues of life and death. And her husband says: 'Where's my borscht?' She looks at him and asks: 'What borscht, what do you mean?'" Her statement about her head evokes how volunteering gave people like herself a new sense of meaning and purpose in their lives as well as new forms of stress.

Like the women who found new roles for themselves in factories and ship-yards during World War II, some women and men developed a sense of direction and purpose in fighting, or aiding those adversely affected by war. "But what happens next when that wife no longer prioritizes her role as her husband's nurturer, and the borscht is not made?" asked Alina, rhetorically. "Unfortunately, there was a wave of couples divorcing, volunteers divorcing, families of volunteers divorcing. They were so immersed into that, well, so to say, [they] went crazy. We know that the divorce rate has grown." In describing the humanitarian volunteers as going "crazy," she underlines just how strong the desire to help became. She felt fortunate because her husband, a pastor, shared her passion. After they themselves were displaced, they formed something of a humanitarian "tag team." She wrote grant proposals, secured funding, found supplies, and traveled all over Europe to recruit assistance from international humanitarian organizations. He ministered to the displaced and provided leadership in a large shelter—which I subsequently visited—that was running a number of different psychosocial programs. Her observation suggests that in addition to hierarchies between genders, then, there are balancing acts to be managed between kinds of care. People who were intensely engaged in assisting others understandably struggled to balance this with care for self and intimate partners. This couple, according to the wife, has maintained a harmonious relationship in spite of their volunteering efforts. One of the costs of their volunteering, however, has been that they are rarely home with their children, who are now parented primarily by their grandparents.[2]

A Broken Mirror

A humanitarian social worker I will call Ksenia helped me understand more specifically how these conflicts unfolded. One day over Americanos at an outdoor café, she described a recent conversation with one of the strongest, best organized, and most resourceful military commanders she knew. Ksenia was part of a group of humanitarian volunteers who delivered medical supplies, blankets, and groceries to the front for the first three years of the war. She came to know this commander—let's call him Petro—on these supply runs. Based on interacting with him over a three-year period, she viewed him as a guy who always seemed to, as she put it, "have it together." But one day he sent her two pictures of his bruised, blood stained, and cut-up hand. She was baffled. The comment said only that all he had left was to destroy himself. Ksenia continued relating the story by glancing between me and the cell phone where her conversation with Petro had taken place. She wove his understanding of the situation with her own. Ksenia prefaced her remarks by stating Petro had just returned home one evening. She described how Petro opened the door, and his wife shut the door. He pushed open the door again, but his wife shut it again. When he cracked it open a third time, the wife began to throw every object within reach through the opening at him. Ksenia looked up to say: "You can't do that!" As a result of her humanitarian work, Ksenia was very aware that people with combat-related trauma can respond violently to touch, especially when that touch is not expected. Nonetheless, when he enterred the apartment, the wife began hitting her husband. Petro was able to check himself, however. Ksenia looked down to read how he recounted his experience: "Something happened to me, I was out of control, I just pushed her aside because I knew I could kill her. I knew something was happening to me, but I couldn't control myself." (As written in the text exchange on the humanitarian's cell phone).

The couple had a large mirror in their foyer that Petro himself had hung. Once inside, he said, he just whaled on the mirror as a way to avoid hitting his wife. His punches broke the glass, gashing his hand. The intensity of this moment is clear in Petro's admission that the wave of emotion was so strong he could no longer contain his rage, and that he could have murdered his wife. The mirror that took the punches provides a powerful illustration of the self-destructive forces resulting from his experiences at the front. His wife's blows were only one trigger for his outburst, though. The words exchanged at the time also set him off. At the crux of the conflict between many romantic couples in Ukraine were their respective stances on the war. Petro related the last thing his wife said to him before he exploded: "What were you doing there? Why is there a war, who the hell needs it? It's bullshit, not a war!" (As written in the text exchange on the humanitarian's cell phone). For a man who had not only risked his own life but had lost close friends to the fighting, the statement was like a gut punch. So he "exploded" like a bomb. Not only was it risky to touch the traumatized ex-combatant's body, it could be risky to touch the topic of war with words.

Petro's resort to hurting himself instead of his wife is significant because of what it is—a poignant reminder of the self-destructive impulses engendered by military conflict—and what it is not: a story of intimate partner violence.[3] Physical violence could be resisted or not, and romantic partnerships were potential casualties of war.

"Blood and Water"

In addition to balancing volunteering or military service with intimate relationships, couples often had to balance their consanguineal (blood) and marital (affinal) relations. A young woman named Mirabelle who divorced explained her decision to prioritize her parents: "I wanted to get my family out of there, and he didn't, I mean, he didn't want to leave his parents. So in that situation he stayed with his parents, and I left with mine. I valued my parents more at that moment, I mean, I guess [I valued] their safety." It was the territorial conflict that precipitated this decision. Under regular circumstances, her care for her parents and her new husband would not have been in conflict. With tanks encroaching on their city, however, they were forced to make a decision, and they chose their respective parents over their marriage. The loss of her husband was compounded by the loss of her career. She had left a lucrative job in the mining industry, where she had just received a promotion. Since the employment profiles are so different from east to west, a position in the mining industry was simply not going to materialize outside of Donbas. Upon settling in the government-controlled part of the country, Mirabelle returned to school to begin new vocational training. She also met a young man whom she plans to marry.

Like literal fault lines, the intersectionalities between different kinds of relationships could weaken some bonds in relation to others. Geographical separation was a crucial variable in all this. For example, one woman reported that the physical separation proved too difficult to manage. Pregnant, she had evacuated with two children and delivered a third baby in a shelter a few hours' drive from the front. Her husband stayed in the conflict zone to look after their house and his mother. Two weeks before the birth, she reported, he called to say, "I can't stand it anymore" and they broke up. She subsequently heard rumors that he had "hooked up" with a "loose" woman and left for the Russian Federation, stating he wanted a "normal" life. The combined pressures of the conflict, unemployment, physical separation, and the responsibility of supporting three children had become too great.

"Hello from Versailles!"

I had special empathy for couples who experienced difficulties as a result of physical separation or the conflict itself because fieldwork in a country at war had such a profound effect on my own romantic life. My partner, who traveled to western Europe for work, planned to come with me to the field but changed his mind a couple of weeks into my work. Ultimately, he decided it was too dangerous for him to fly from Paris to Kyiv, even for a visit. It was difficult for me to understand his concern. The growing cognitive dissonance prompted me to become more aware of the ways that I was changing as a result of my work. Risks that appear stratospheric in hindsight appeared to be minimal at the time. Like couples that were separated between the zone and government-controlled Ukraine, we began to use very different metrics to measure safety and well-being. I realized the depth of the emotional disconnect one day when I returned from an especially painful interview in a rural area and received the text, "Hello from Versailles!" upon being reconnected to Wi-Fi.

In sharp contrast, I had just learned of beatings in basement prisons; limbs severed by land mines; roofs blown off of homes; a billboard bluntly declaring "We will not forgive and we will not forget"; phone calls telling people that if they did not leave their home in the next ten minutes, they would be executed; missiles landing in front yards; and stories of people burned alive in their homes. Moreover, the material hardships of the family that had been displaced and was living in poverty was about as far from the Palace of Versailles as one could have been. With the words "Hello from Versailles!" two incompatible worlds collided.

The emotional gulf opening up between myself and people at home was unmistakable. For example, a friend I will call "Jack" called me one day and mentioned that he had taken his dogs to the cardiologist. The cardiologist ran a stress test and changed the dogs' medications, which Jack would be administering several times a day. This was hard to fathom from where I sat. The dogs were receiving sophisticated medications designed for humans when my human friends in Ukraine lacked the most basic medical care—like prostheses to replace limbs lost in the war. Intellectually, I knew the reasons his dogs had better medical care than many Ukrainian soldiers was complicated. My point is that the distance between field and home, regardless of the social media available to reconnect, was immense.

Another friend I will call "Steve" asked me how my weekend had gone. Like cardiac medications for dogs, "weekend" was a concept that felt foreign. Sure, there was some kind of a routine once I was settled someplace. But kicking back for a day or two seemed like a waste. I could only march from one challenge to the next. The interviewing I was carrying out produced affective "through lines" coloring my experience, and descriptions of violence I encountered shadowed me over half-lives. Obviously, the stresses I experienced were pretty trivial compared to those of the people more directly affected by the conflict. Still, my experiences in the field highlight my point about hierarchies of care: I too found the relationship between my relationships was reconfigured.

Fixing the Tap

When people (typically, but not always, men) enlisted, their partners had to assume both the traditional male and female roles. As one soldier put it: "Yeah, we've changed, but our wives have changed too. I came back and she could change the light bulb, fix the tap, she's learned to live without me. She's learned to go to work, handle the kids, cook, press the clothes and do all the work that I used to do. It would have been easier if she hadn't changed, if she had stayed the same, but she didn't, she couldn't." These changes can be multifaceted because once male support is removed from a household, a great deal shifts. And when soldiers relinquish their fighting roles and demobilize, the changes are equally significant. As Father Nikolai maintained: "It is not just a man that returns from the war, it is a father and a husband that returns. This is a terrifying thing because everything has changed. He wonders if he will manage with the new reality. We therefore have to work with everyone, not just the immediate family." Father Nikolai headed a church-based group that provided a wide range of services and case management to veterans and their families. In addition to church groups, governmental and nongovernmental organizations came to the aid of struggling couples.

One way to think about these service providers is as what Foucault called "entrepreneurs of the self" (1979) and Nicholas Rose developed further as "engineers of the soul" (1988, 157) to refer to those professionals and institutions whose purpose it is to motivate and guide people to change or "work" on themselves (Rose 2003, 9). The professionals staffing these organizations were especially keen observers of how war destabilized families (Rose 1998, 153). They were also at the front line of reconfiguring them. These engineers of the soul promoted specific practices for thinking, feeling, behaving, and improving. Nongovernmental organizations became engineers of gendered souls when they worked with the gender identities of soldiers, veterans, and families.

Gender norms have long been a central component of state policy in this region. In 1917, the Soviet Union was founded upon ideals of equality. The Constitution of the USSR enshrined the idea of women's equality in Article 122.

Granted, women's roles were complex. At the same time that they gained freedom to assume economically productive roles and pursue their interests, they
were still expected to shoulder the "double burden" of responsibility for the home
from prerevolutionary times. There was an ambivalent attitude to the mascu-
linization of women who were taking up previously male productive roles like
welding and machine operating. With the disintegration of the Soviet Union,
men and women reacted against official policies of gender equality with a reassertion of traditional and some would say hyperfeminine roles. A gender binary
in which women were to be sheltered from economically productive roles in favor
of being protected and admired as women was then reasserted (Turbine 2012).

Gender roles were explicitly manipulated for a third time (Gal and Kligman
2000; Reeves 2014) in the post-Soviet period. This reconfiguring departed from
the Soviet models of gender equality without going so far as to embrace Western feminism (Turbine 2012). None of these approaches fully emancipated
women. What tended to come to the fore was an emphasis on what were called
"natural differences" between men and women. Comfort with the notion that
males are naturally "breadwinners" and females are meant to fulfill nurturing
roles has tended to gain credence (Turbine 2012, 1854). A forty-five-year-old male
I spoke with put it succinctly when he argued, "Society works better when men
are men and women are women."

"We Teach Them How to Be Feminine"

I review these shifting norms because the codes for behaving as a man or a woman
were scrambled by the conflict. Women learned to fix the tap, men learned to cook
and sew. Organizations seeking to ease the military-to-civilian transitions latched
onto encouraging men and women to return to traditional roles. When overem-
phasized, the guidance suggested caricatured gender identities. That state funding
went to these efforts further underscores my point that the family is the nation
writ small. The state made it their business to attend to gender norms, connecting
the world of war and the life of family. With funding from the Ukrainian government and her municipality, a social worker with a humanitarian focus I will call
Daria framed her work as teaching women how to be feminine again. She described an event she was planning: "So we're getting them together at this restaurant, [and] there are booths outside, and in the booths there are power outlets, and
there'll be a hairdresser, a makeup artist, a manicure artist, and two photographers.
And we'll make it a relaxing evening for them. And the theme that our psychologists are going to work with is 'femininity,' how to stay feminine. And it's not just
makeup, it's going to be a workshop on how to, well, put on makeup. And every

stylist will tell every woman what is good for her, not just in abstract terms, but individually, like, 'you need eyeliner like this, eyebrows like that, toner cream like this . . .' Right?" This humanitarian social worker-turned-gender-specialist later reported that the women were happy with this event. It remains unclear whether clients liked these activities because the event was a reprieve from daily routines; because it was offered free of charge; or because they sincerely wanted to reconnect with "femininity," construed as greater attention to hair and makeup, and a less assertive role in the family. It could also be that participating in this type of activity was more innocuous than focus groups and other forms of group therapy carried out with veterans and their families. As played out in the western city of Lviv, at least, gender identities were an explicit target of change for social service providers seeking to help couples and families recover from the ripple effects of military service. Going back to the status quo was viewed as progressive from the perspective of social workers tasked with reestablishing family harmony. Teaching women to be more feminine in the traditional sense of the word was a way of chipping away at the forms of micro-agency embodied in changing a light bulb or fixing the tap. It seemed they were acting on the assumption that as long as women remained dependent on men, the family as a social unit could be preserved, and preserving the family could ward off more comprehensive social disintegration.

Brother against Brother

Like marriages, relationships within nuclear families were also crosscut by loyalties to the nation and emotional investments in other relationships. Changes to family life, whether in terms of configuration or communication, were less prevalent than the loss of friendship,[4] but this didn't make family discord any less troubling.

Talk of actual brothers estranged as a result of the territorial conflict provided a ready cipher for talking about the conflict itself. After all, an enduring metaphor for the relationship between the Russian and Ukrainian peoples has been "brotherhood," with the mixture of affection and rivalry that entails. As one woman, Lola, stated: "And we can call this war a 'civil war' because it is brother against brother, cousin against cousin. And it cannot be forgiven. I mean, the First World War, Second World War were conflicts between nations. Russians, Germans. And here relatives are against each other. I mean, blood. Blood is at war with blood. That is the most dreadful . . . I can confidently say that it doesn't unite us, vice versa, it worsens us because in eastern Ukraine mothers cry, and in western Ukraine mothers cry. And taken all in all, these mothers will hate each other because lots of people have died. And when children die, people get very angry. And to forgive—I think, people won't forgive." Lola's statement interweaves family and nation: she uses the vocabulary of nation states to talk about relatives that turn against each other, and the relatives appear to be her primary concern. The fact that they are of the same "blood" means there is no end to the tears or any real possibility of forgiveness. She uses the metaphors of "brothers" and "blood" at battle with each other to express the war's personally and politically destructive power. The war is tragic not only because two countries have gone to war, but because families are destroyed. From Lola's perspective, it is now difficult to foresee an end to the war because the feelings resulting from brother killing brother are so much more difficult to manage than killing a foreign enemy. Lola reveals a crucial connection between family and nation, which are more than metaphorically connected because their crises have become intertwined. Her statement further supports the contention that not only is the nation the family writ large, but in times of conflict, family becomes the nation writ small.

A specific example of "brother against brother" demonstrates war's fallout within families. A family I learned about while in Sloviansk had two sons. One was pro-Russian, the other a volunteer for a Ukrainian battalion. When the pro-Ukrainian brother returned home from a tour of duty, sharply opposing political views prevented the two bothers from even speaking to each other. Then the pro-Russian son was diagnosed with late-stage cancer and died soon after. As the story was told by one of their parents, the brothers were simply unable to resolve their political disagreements and remained estranged while living in the same house. The brother who survived lived with deep remorse. While family might be viewed as a protective shield against the "outside" world, this family's experience shows this is not always the case.

Sisters: "Politicians have banged our heads together"

Conversations often had a way of sliding from the topic of patriotism to that of family, as Danilo's comment illustrates: "We are not part of some Commonwealth of Independent States, we are not dependent on the politics of Russia. Let them allow us to develop independently. On the basis of what? Values? Language? Blood? I don't think you can definitively say on what basis. It is everything together, values, language, blood. I have relatives that live there and others that live here. Do they become enemies? No, they stay relatives!" The metonymic slide here from the state (the Commonwealth of Independent States) and nation (parsed as values, language, and blood) to his relatives was swift. He traversed this linguistic territory without any words to mark the transitions. A single tonality, it turns out, could encompass relations to the state, the nation, and kin. His comment about the country's political status was also a comment about family, telescoping the nation onto the family as the site where national allegiances are worked out.

What inspired him to glissade between nation and family, it turns out, were his observations of his wife's yelling matches in which sisters accused one another of being fascists, *banderovtsi*,[5] and zombified. They argued for hours. People asserted that not only their own families, but thousands of families had experiences like this in which "politicians have banged our heads together." The metaphor of authorities "banging" siblings' heads together shows just how imbricated were nation and family. Siblings' conflicting opinions serve as a concrete example of how the nation was writ small in the family. At the same time, however, the idea that it was the authorities that had "banged" their heads together suggests that the source of the conflict was outside the family. The problem had less to do with family itself than with the way the conflict was being carried out. Ultimately the territorial conflict set off a multitude of emotional "sparks."

The Generational Front: "All Soaked with Hatred"

So far, marriage and sibling relationships have been discussed. Similar dynamics unfurled between what is reputed to be one of the strongest of bonds, the bond between parents and children. Olena, a volunteer humanitarian recalled: "When the conflict began, not only our opinions went their separate ways, but I was actively helping the Ukrainian side: we brought aid to soldiers and to civilians . . . we arranged evacuation to Ukraine's territory. But [my mother] was all soaked with hatred toward Ukraine, she couldn't understand me." This humanitarian was involved with a group of volunteers who were filling in gaps left by a weakened military. She had been helping the Ukrainian side by delivering first aid supplies to the front line. It took about twenty-four hours to get there, driving through the night with a tag team. Once there, the volunteers made their way up the line of demarcation between the warring parties, as supplies allowed. The mother-daughter rift demonstrates just how close to home the political divide could cut.

Ideological divisions created conversational landmines that could easily erupt. As Tamara, a woman whose family chose to stay in Russian-controlled territory described it: "At first it was very hot. Not only hot but . . . [we were] smashing the phone down, tears, there was, um, anger, aggression toward me because I help Ukraine." The word "hot" conveys the emotional intensity of these exchanges. The redrawing of "interior frontiers" (Balibar 2001) weakened but did not appear to alter the geomorphology of families: most people seemed to think navigating the conversational landmines was vastly preferable to severing communication. As Liuba observed: "Well, I'm here in Ukraine, [and] they're there. I mean, we call each other, [but] we only talk about, like, 'how are you,' 'Everything is fine, it's all good,' 'How's your health?' 'It's okay.' We try not to [discuss politics], because, well, there are many cases when families just . . . they talk, right? And at some point, they have different points of view about some political [issue] . . . And, like, well, that leads to fights, and that's bad." Whether the mayhem was in one's own family or others, discussions of what had gone poorly seemed to amplify concern and contribute to a widespread belief that the social world had stopped turning.

Reconfiguration and adaptation was more prevalent than complete destruction. Limiting family conversations to questions like "How's your health?" (when the sound of grenades could be heard in the background) maintained a curious but durable bond holding families together. The families that were separated by the line of demarcation, in particular, lived in "selective deafness" in which the risks of the military conflict could not be discussed, even when the conflict was audible all around them. Moreover, people in both government-controlled and nongovernment-controlled territories told me that they suspected that their calls were monitored by authorities. Their worst fear was that as a result of "political" conversations, the separatist authorities would accuse them of treason. Only some families risked conversation about substantive topics. Phone calls between geographically separated kin were less about exchanging information than verifying that the channels of communication were intact. Multiple times in a given day, these calls wove emotional connective tissue for relationships imperiled by the war.

Nation Writ Small

Although the territorial dispute penetrated home fronts and ricocheted into intimate relationships of all kinds, efforts toward repair were ubiquitous. Vladimir did not avoid the topic of politics with his mother and father, who were living in the conflict zone. He reported trying to deescalate topics as they naturally arose to avoid reprioritizing the intersecting loyalties to family, profession, and country. This was an ongoing process because he went to visit regularly. His dad "stuck to his guns" about politics because there was really only one political perspective available to him where he was living. When I asked him if they discussed politics, he replied that what his father heard on television negatively predisposed him toward then Ukrainian government-controlled Kherson. He tried to reassure his father: "[When] I went there—I said 'dad, calm down, they treat us fine, fine, why do you say that?' I told him 'Calm down, come to your senses, and don't watch that TV.'" Established relationships were maintained through a continual process of reflection and repair. Since 2014, a variety of stories have painted Ukrainians in a negative light using allegations of everything from cannibalism to rape and torture. In the chapter on friendship, we explored how hewing to the surface in conversation, simply not talking about the war, was a strategy of everyday peacemaking that camouflaged the selective deafness of everyday war. Likewise, many families tried to avoid contentious discussions.

If the people I interacted with described a crumbling social universe, what they were enacting was continual reflection and repair.[6] This is perhaps most evident in communication patterns. Families maintained dense webs of communication, even if they had to avoid topics that could be construed as political. The vast majority of my interviewees stayed in touch with family in the conflict zone from whom they were physically separated either daily or several times a day. They described checking in on one another as they went to work or came home, inquiring about health and children's schooling and in general reassuring one another they were "okay." Only two of the people I interviewed maintained contact with their families as little as twice a month, and only one person got in touch with family in the contact zone no more than a few times a year.

Kira, an internally displaced person living in Lviv who had experienced sharp disagreement with her sister in Donbas, found an opportunity for rapprochement when her nephew arranged to visit her with his mother. He wanted to look at universities, and the visit provided a chance for the two sisters to break a long silence and talk again. But considering all she had heard about "fascism" in western Ukraine, the sister from the east was nervous about speaking Russian in the west. The ethnonational framing of the conflict that was felt sharply at the beginning of the conflict had been firmly imprinted. From the western, pro-Ukrainian sister's perspective, her pro-Russian sister living in the east appeared "drunk" on language politics. The Ukrainian central authorities' goal of "Ukrainianization" mixed with Russian propaganda and provided a volatile national cocktail in minds that were already primed to be sensitive to ethnonational difference. When they rode the bus together during the visit, Kira's sister who lived in eastern Ukraine, where Russian predominated, scolded Kira for speaking Russian in a place that was rumored to be intolerant of Russian speaking. But she had to acknowledge that Kira was comfortable speaking Russian in government-controlled Ukraine for a good reason. The rumors had been exaggerated. Still, the propensity to look for an enemy remained. As Kira described the visit, "When she was leaving by train, she told me: 'Well, I saw that there's no fascists in Lviv, of course, but I think they are somewhere else, I think they're in Ternopol.' But [overall] her attitude had changed significantly." With some of the misconceptions about the language politics dispelled, the sister began to shift her blame from ethnonational prejudices to state policy: "For all these three days, she didn't say a bad word . . . I mean, all that rhetoric has changed. Now she says: both governments are to blame, Putin, Poroshenko they're to blame, well, those on top, they're to blame." I spent time with this woman each consecutive year of my fieldwork and learned that her family relationships gradually improved over time.

Home Fronts and Family Preservation

The extensive discourse about the prevalence of family dissolution indexes contemporary concerns but also highlights many activities devoted to family preservation. Galya's family provides a good example. She moved with her husband and two children to the southern city of Kherson. She described going through difficult economic times, but on balance she felt the family had become closer. With tears in her eyes, she recalled her son's desire to direct his birthday money to food for the family as an example of the way that the four of them formed a united front. Another woman, Marna, stated that as her circle of friends contracted, the value of her relationship with her husband and children was enhanced. She referred to her husband as her "best friend."

People were troubled by the implications of leaving aging parents in Donbas. For example, Mykola, in the middle of a conversation on a completely different topic, spontaneously launched into a kind of requiem for a grandmother whose death was only discovered by the stench of her rotting body: "I'll tell you a gruesome incident: sometimes, err, the only way to realize that someone has died is by the smell. Well, [it was] when a grandma died in her flat, lonely, like that— and there's a lot of elderly people who are lonely. Well, it's an uncomfortable topic." It's impossible to know if this grandmother died in a state of loneliness or simply alone. What is knowable and worth underscoring is the concern the young man raises. Fears and concerns about dying alone index, among other things, the ethical obligations he felt toward her. Whether one's death will "matter" and be mourned or be accompanied by indifference motivated people to visit the elderly and try to persuade them to leave the DNR and LNR. Those I spoke with were often torn between staying to help aging parents and leaving to protect the next generation. This young man's image of a grandmother dying alone is especially poignant because she could be anyone's grandma.

A central through line of this book is that the war attuned people to human vulnerability and elicited caring for others. That thread runs through this chapter in the form of an extensive conversation on divorce and family upsets that ran alongside evidence of families holding together. As a result of the war in Donbas, family and nation experienced not only interrelated but also mutually entangled crises. Family and nation are traditionally analyzed separately. For the people living through the conflict over the Donbas and Luhansk provinces, these categories were superimposed, the complexities magnified by the issues of life and death. In thinking about the forms of intimacy forged in and around the territorial conflict in Donbas, concerns about family and marital dissolution elicited efforts toward repair. This powerful tension shows how intimacy was shaped through war, conflict, and displacement.

As suggested above, one way to think about the war's effects on intimate relationships is in terms of intersectionality. The war upset the relationship between relationships: volunteering to help with humanitarian efforts could take precedence over long-established rituals of sharing daily meals; brothers could become political adversaries; and strangers or distant relatives could suddenly become close allies. While the nation has long been figured as a family, the family can be viewed as a mirror of the nation, or a crucible of working out its tensions. Families who disagreed about politics adopted the same strategies that were found among friends. They avoided contentious topics while remaining otherwise close, took breaks from one another and distanced themselves, and often blamed the media for the "zombification" of relatives through unbalanced news reporting.

Evidence that family is nation writ small was especially present in the work that organizations were doing to counsel romantic partners and families. In cases I found, counseling entailed encouraging people to hew closely to traditional gender norms. The family, too, is an imagined community. Taken together, all of this affirms the extent to which relationships are not self-contained in their operations or energies. Romantic and family relationships became crucibles for larger political, economic, and military forces. In the next chapter, we explore this more deeply through cases in which family relationships inspired investment in the fighting.

BOOTS, GLOVES, AND TACTICAL KINSHIP

Everyday War

Oleksandra described the discomfort of the large heavy boots as if she were the one wearing them. Her care for her father, a man three decades her senior, is motherly, daughterly, and in a way chilling, all at the same time. Oleksandra's father volunteered to fight against the pro-Russian insurgents that declared a separatist republic in Luhansk. As a patriot, Oleksandra explained, he saw fighting as part of his moral duty to protect Ukraine's territorial integrity. Although past an age when he could be recruited into the military, he saw joining a volunteer battalion as part of being a man. The trouble was he did not have appropriate footwear or any of the other essentials for his position as a sniper. The Ukrainian military had issued him rigid leather boots that were at least a size too big. Oleksandra worked hard to purchase lighter ones in his size. Then, she secured him a bulletproof vest, camouflage, a knife, and special night vision goggles. In short, Oleksandra's daily life was organized around supplying her father for the military engagement. This chapter considers what happens in families like hers when they become a part of the conflict itself. If earlier chapters have considered how everyday peace can be cultivated even between combatants fighting on opposite sides, this chapter exposes the seepage of war into the places one might not expect to find it.

When kinship became tactical like this, it amounted to everyday war. Given the diffuse nature of contemporary warfare that is waged without discreet frontlines and involves different kinds of nonstate actors, it is worthwhile to consider the quotidian, perhaps mundane, practices that advance conflict from the sidelines. This chapter explores the meaning of these practices through two cases. In the first case, Oleksandra's loyalty and sense of connection to her father led her to normalize the killing he was doing as a sniper and enabled her to throw herself wholeheartedly into gathering supplies for him. Unwavering in her commitment, she made an emotional investment in her father's fighting capacity that exemplifies what Lauren Berlant called "cruel optimism." Cruel optimism describes situations in which something a person desires and works toward actually thwarts that person from thriving (Berlant 2011, 1). The second case is concerned with a mother-son relationship. Larysa lost her nineteen-year-old son to the conflict. Although the pain she was experiencing as a result was beyond words, she claimed that if she had another three sons, she would encourage them to enlist as well. Given the extent to which the country did not respect her son's sacrifice, this, too, was a form of cruel optimism. Larysa was very cognizant that there was not a lot for her to gain in return. Still, what both Larysa and Oleksandra wanted was not to kill but to belong.

Cruel optimism and tactical kinship provide more granular detail to this exploration of the logic behind people's willingness to participate in war. Anderson (1991) suggested that to understand how it is that people come to willingly kill and die for their nation, it is necessary to consider the nation as an imagined community. An imagined community is not to be confused with an imaginary community. Saying that a community is "imagined" captures how even though members may never meet, they very powerfully conceive of themselves as a collectivity. Considering intimacy between mother and son, father and daughter, or husband and wife provides an additional way to see into this process. Their emotional connections are what "hinges" the personal and the political (Ahmed 2004; Wetherell 2012; Burkitt 2014). The ostensibly "private" world of relationships and the public world of military maneuvers, as we will see, are intricately connected.

This chapter picks up an important thread from chapter 2, where I tried to show that the feminist conceptualization of militarization as an insidious and largely unconscious process misses the highly conscious efforts of people like the Patriot Café's owners. The concept of militarization has a way of divesting people of agency and failing to register their strategic efforts. Unlike militarization, thinking in terms of everyday war and tactical kinship reveals the conscious choices people made to support friends and kin who were fighting. This is far from an insidious or unconscious process: Oleksandra and Larysa share their conscious reflections and deliberate choices to act out their love for family members *through* the undeclared war. This, then, is everyday war. Unlike Galtung's idea of negative peace, it takes place when there is still ongoing fighting. Unlike everyday peace, it rejects the naïve optimism that interpersonal peace can be scaled up to a regional or national level. And unlike militarization, it highlights the conscious continuation of conflict at an interpersonal and intersubjective level.

Boots and Gloves

Oleksandra and her father were displaced from Luhansk, Ukraine. The first time I met Oleksandra, I was impressed by how poised she was in her crisp flowered sundress and how calmly she spoke despite the destruction she had witnessed. She had left when Russian-backed forces had just reached her city, but not before the heavy artillery arrived and the first bombing campaign began. When we spoke, Oleksandra was being sheltered by a church that had spaces for a small number of IDPs behind the chapel. She was unemployed and without a permanent home. What she saw as most vital, however, was her role as a provider for her father. As we spoke about her life, it became clear that every week was marked by visits to businesses and NGOs to drum up cash to purchase more equipment. This was the center of her new routine, the structure of her new normal in displacement. Last week, she sent him camouflage. Next week, she planned to send him tactical gloves. Tactical gloves, I asked? "Yes. They are the ones without fingers, totally leather and specially designed so that your fingers don't slip. For example, if he picks up a weapon, right? And if it is really hot, he is going to be all wet and sweaty but in the gloves the weapon will not slip out of his hands. There is also a special rubber area so that he would not be blistering his hands from firing, you see. They are considered tactical." This description of gloves reveals just how readily she could imagine her father sweating in the summer sun. She is intimately aware that a tactical glove over the palm of the same hand that used to hold hers would prevent his gun from slipping. Even as we sat chatting in a blissfully air-conditioned café, with enormous glasses of iced tea beading up on paper doilies in front of us, Oleksandra remained empathically connected to her father, who at that moment, she told me, would be suffering through the heat and insect bites that came with life on the frontline. Judging from her description of his hands and a visit to the front I will describe, the emotional connection between them is a strong one. But the purpose of the gloves must not be overlooked. She knew that her father needed the gloves to kill Russian and Russian-backed opponents without blowing his own foot off, or worse. Oleksandra fully understood that her father was a sniper, and that the gloves would help him kill adversaries, some of whom were her former neighbors. Her role as a provider was necessitated by the Ukrainian military's lack of resources—as noted in chapter 2 with reference to Café Patriot—for volunteer fighters and official soldiers at the beginning of the war.

Oleksandra began fundraising for her father early on in the conflict when, as she put it, soldiers were being sent "bare-assed" into war. At the time we spoke, a massive volunteer effort supplemented the Ukrainian military's efforts to equip soldiers headed into the conflict zone in eastern Ukraine. Volunteer fighters became less significant as the Ukrainian military regained its strength, but in several key battles their contributions were decisive. Oleksandra was working independently, but a variety of individuals and groups (many of which formed on the revolutionary square), were also contributing their time, care, and attention to official and unofficial fighters. Organizing on social media platforms like Facebook generated funds and supplies that filled gaps in military supply chains.

For a young woman who was homeless and unemployed to focus her energies on purchasing her father tactical gloves upsets the comfortable illusion that we can separate family and war, public and private. Oleksandra was both a loving daughter and what I call "tactical kin" because her care for her father contributed quite literally and directly to the fighting. Her experiences demonstrate concretely that there are two sides to everyday kinds of peace: strategies for minimizing violence were not relevant for Oleksandra, who was focused on her father's survival. At the same time, her actions were not based in animosity toward Ukraine's military opponents.

It was a pragmatic, self-defensive stance that never (at least in my presence) overflowed into animus. In other words, her "everyday war" was strangely tethered to everyday peace. Everyday war could be seen as the diabolical twin of everyday peace. A rough definition can be hammered out by inverting Mac Ginty's definition of everyday peace (2014, 553). Everyday war describes practices on the part of individuals or groups that aid and abet conflict in divided societies. Everyday war is also constituted by an ongoing set of choices about daily activities. Oleksandra's story dramatizes how civilians can be drawn into the conflicts that surround them, especially when the state is weak or nationalist sentiment is high. The practices of nonelite and nonmilitary actors that advance the conflict, unseen and miles from the trenches, show how war is enacted at multiple sites and on multiple levels.

How did Oleksandra's efforts matter? Helping her father meant enabling the military conflict and affecting the outcome of the war. As Puglisi has argued, "under-equipped and lightly armed, they held the front, thus giving the Ukrainian authorities the time to regroup and organize a defense" (2015, 9). Even Anton Gerashchenko, a member of parliament and an adviser to the Ministry of Interior, conceded that had it not been for the volunteers, the line of demarcation with the separatists would have run along the Dnipro (Puglisi 2015, 9). In

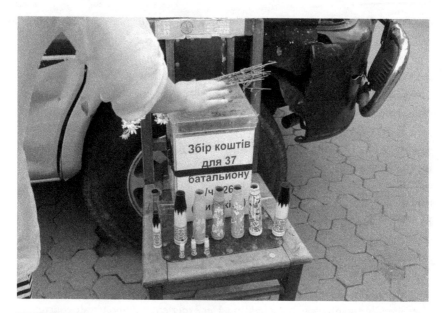

FIGURE 10.   Donation box for the war effort

other words, Ukraine could have been faced with trying to win back half its territory instead of portions of two eastern provinces.[1] Oleksandra's contribution was tiny in the larger scope of the war. But she also was not alone. The image above shows a donation box where people otherwise enjoying a Sunday afternoon stroll in a city square deposited their spare change. During the early years of the war, this sort of collection was ubiquitous. The box shows one of the more quotidian ways people participated in everyday war.

Oleksandra told me the hardest part of being internally displaced was not losing her home, her friends, or even her enrollment at an institute in Luhansk. The most difficult thing was having her father leave to fight in the conflict zone as a volunteer: "It is very hard to go through my father leaving for the war. I am in general a nonsmoker but when my papa, well, I just started to smoke, and smoke, and smoke." And smoke and smoke she did. When we had finished our tea and the recorded part of our conversation, she chain-smoked as we strolled down to the river, where we talked about everything but the war: our pets, our furniture, favorite breakfast foods. But the incessant smoking indexes just how stressful her father's volunteering efforts were. This tactical kinship was not cold blooded. Rather, it was emotionally charged by all that a father-daughter relationship can signify in the life of a young woman: he had been her provider, protector, and role model.

She persevered in part because of what Berlant calls cruel optimism. Berlant used this idea to illuminate how people in the United States and Europe have remained attached to unobtainable fantasies of having a good life with upward mobility, job security, and social equality, all of which have become more elusive when economies are organized around the neoliberal principles that prioritize corporate profit over state supports of the most vulnerable workers (Berlant 2011). The notion also illuminates aspects of Oleksandra's fantasy surrounding involvement in the war. Oleksandra imagined Ukraine regaining lost territory and being able to celebrate: "We once had a dream with my pro-Ukrainian friends that we would have a march in *vishivalka* (embroidery) *all over* Luhansk. We would go through on foot and sing the hymn of Ukraine, and I promised everyone pizza at my place! I promised the guys pizza and I hope I get to fulfill that promise." The pizza-and-embroidery event is indicative of what Anderson (1991) called an "imagined community," by which he meant a collective construction through language and practices. Oleksandra and her friends relished a collective image of parading through the streets wearing national embroidery (*vishivalka*) and capping the event off with a theme party (albeit one that is culturally hybrid). But the fantasied "after party" is unlikely to come to fruition, and Oleksandra knows this. She admits that as the war drags on, it becomes increasingly unlikely she will ever be able to return to her former home. Her pro-Ukrainian political views would prevent her from living with any sense of security in the pro-Russian Luhansk People's Republic. What her everyday war secures is inclusion in a wider national collectivity.

This collectivity is likely to disappoint. I mean this quite literally: her father spent days in dugouts and blinds in the trees, watching for action, but the military could not provide something as basic as a bulletproof vest. From this perspective, emotional investment in the nation takes on a self-destructive quality.

Thinking more economically, Oleksandra and her family had lost their home, their car, and their jobs. Every hour she spent provisioning her father was also an hour spent postponing her own local integration within a state that had forsaken both of them. Oleksandra was not eligible for IDP incentive payments because she was not working. The payments were so small she had not thought them worth pursuing. What is "cruel" about some attachments, Berlant teaches us, is that when an attachment becomes integral to one's coherence as a person, one's reason for being, it can occlude other ways of seeing and being in the world. Oleksandra's optimism wedged her into the workings of war.

Oleksandra's attachments to family and nation were thoroughly entangled. She described an ideologically frictionless home environment in which loyalty to her father mapped seamlessly onto loyalty to nation. Even though one parent was ethnic Russian and the other ethnic Ukrainian, their political-ideological allegiance lay firmly with Ukraine. This was part of her early political socialization: "I memorized the [national] hymn at [the age of] five. Yeah, at five years old I sang it at my father's place of work for the first time. So I knew the hymn of Ukraine from childhood. There are things that are passed from one generation to the next in our family." Oleksandra beamed with pride when she told me she knew the anthem from the time she was five years old. And we can imagine her father's pride when the high-pitched, little girl voice projected his own nationalism. With family members in agreement, their bond was readily retooled into the service of the war. This family "inheritance" of patriotism further elaborates the dynamics at work in cases of cruel optimism, which congeals at an affective level before it is accounted for in intellectual ways. Thinking in terms of cruel optimism peels back the emotions to expose the costs associated with habitually national ways of thinking and the impulse to invest in political life. With attention to things like education and employment occluded, thinking in terms of family and nation was paramount.

In addition to demonstrating the imbrication of family and nation, Oleksandra's story demonstrates how conflict upsets generational roles. Anthropologists (Carston 2007) have argued that role reversals demonstrate the instability of kinship. The slippage of generational boundaries might enable a family to cope, the thinking goes, but it also places a weight on children who must take on the functions of adults. To my way of thinking, however, if the family remains a unit regardless of the roles that are taken, and against the backdrop of the family conflicts considered in the previous chapter, generational role reversal suggests durability. Oleksandra's tactical approach to kinship serves both family continuity and nation-building.

Oleksandra's description of her experience provides us with a way to think about military conflict in the same frame as that of family. A connecting link is emotion: conflicts become emotional investments even for distal actors like Oleksandra, who lived a good four-hour drive from where her father was stationed. The conflict had been unthinkable in Oleksandra's childhood, when Russia and Ukraine were close allies. For a young woman to work to purchase her father gloves to be a safer sniper demonstrates the intimacy of war and conflict. Nation is scaled down to be writ small. Just as war affects family, families affect war.

From her descriptions, it seems Oleksandra's father was as attached to her as she was to him. When there was a lull in the fighting in his region, the men with whom her "papa" served decided to take her and her sister back with them from a supply run. She had not seen him for approximately six months. The fighters decided to make it a surprise. Oleksandra and her sister were hidden in the back seat with a blanket. When he opened the door to investigate what had been referred to as "equipment," she and her sister jumped out. As he wept, they wrapped themselves around his neck.

The whole ruse shows how military and civilian family life had permeated one another. The "guy's" cover story that his daughters had sent supplies, and the willingness of these guys to transport his daughters to the front, underscore the military-civilian osmosis that was taking place in small, capillary ways.

This case is most striking, however, for what it was not: filled with enmity. Oleksandra never expressed any malice or hatred for the people her father was killing. She suspected some of them were classmates and neighbors. Oleksandra was keenly aware that her filial piety—her family politics of loyalty—was intricately linked to, and supportive of, the war. What her investment in the war cost her was a fuller engagement in the life of a young woman. The militarization of her life may have been insidious but, harkening back to the second chapter concerned with Café Patriot, it was far from unconscious. Her militarization was deliberate, strategic, and tactical in the literal sense.

"Family Matters are Secondary"

The second case features a family involved with the official military. Larysa lost her only son to the conflict in eastern Ukraine. He died fighting in an elite Ukrainian airborne division that was attempting to regain territory lost to separatists. That would have been a terrible loss in and of itself, but it was made more painful by the fact that Larysa's mother and sister financed and supported the separatists. I was encouraged to call Larysa by a program director at a municipal veteran's association who knew Larysa well and thought she would be eager to speak with me. I was reluctant to call her, however, because I did not want to cause her further trauma by probing her painful story.

With the reassurance of the program director, I made the call, and Larysa readily agreed to meet with me. She suggested we meet at the IDP-owned and operated café called Two Rabbits, in Lviv. I arrived early and ordered an enormous pot of tea—the largest they had. I was going to need it, I felt, and perhaps I could share it with Larysa. I fidgeted with the position of my pens and notebook, pulling them out of my bag and then putting them away again, for what seemed like an eternity as I pondered what to say. Larysa entered in a black cotton T-shirt and black skirt, with her peroxide-blond hair gently pulled back by combs.

Larysa positively boomed an enthusiastic "hello" to the owner behind the counter. From my perspective, she had a powerful presence that seemed to fill the entire room because she spoke loudly, moved her arms expansively, and laughed easily. We spent the first minutes ordering cake to go with the tea. I explained the purpose of my work: to understand the firsthand experience of people affected by the conflict. I also gave Larysa multiple provisos: she could end the conversation or take a break from it at any time; she could choose not to answer any question for any reason at any time; I would phone her the day after our conversation to find out how she is feeling; and the social worker at the municipal veterans' center who introduced us would be available by appointment if she needed to talk.

Larysa seemed larger than life in comparison with the portrayals of military mothers that so often lack character development: we have only to think of the popular 1998 film directed by Steven Spielberg, *Saving Private Ryan*. The epic war film shows the brutality of war through realistic battle scenes and the emotional struggles of the soldiers as they try to make sense of the war. It has been called one of the greatest war films ever made, as well as one of the greatest films of all time (Rubin 2018). There are two women in the story, the mother whose sons would be sacrificed for their country, and Ryan's wife, who offers reassurance that he led a good life. But these women remain two-dimensional characters: we do not learn of their struggles or motivations. And yet, the mission to save Private Ryan was launched because General George Marshall learns that three of the four sons in the Ryan family had already been killed. To prevent the mother from losing all four sons, Marshall orders Private Ryan to be brought home. In spite of this guiding ethos, viewers have to rely on their imaginations. All that viewers see of her are her hands washing dishes and a brief glimpse of her face before she stands on the porch to receive the news of her three sons' deaths. Otherwise, the scene is filmed entirely from behind her back. The camera focuses on the men bearing the news while Ryan's mother slowly lowers herself to the ground to brace herself for the emotional blow. This chapter fills in some of what films like this one leave out to provide a clearer vantage on how love for one's child and love for nation are connected.

Tea, Bread, and Salt

I decided to open the conversation by asking Larysa to tell me a little bit about herself. She explained that she was born and raised in Luhansk and recently began identifying as Ukrainian even though Russian was her primary language. She pulled a picture from her purse, and showed me her son Adam. A skinny young man with wide eyes and an angular jaw grinned at me. She described him as a happy-go-lucky kid, a "goofy" guy who was a great joker and a terrible student.

Larysa explained her sister worked in the administration of the breakaway Luhansk People's Republic. As Larysa saw it, her sister was partly responsible for

Adam's death because she supported the Russian-backed separatists through her job. Larysa also stressed that her mother contributed funds to the separatist cause. Put bluntly, they welcomed the separatists who ended his life. This, too, was tactical kinship. Larysa aligned with her son on the pro-Ukrainian side against her sister and mother, the young man grandmother on the Russian side: "He died, for you to understand, twelve minutes away, if running, from my mom's place. He died where he was born. I don't talk to my mom. It's very painful. Because I think that she indirectly caused the death of her grandson. Indirectly—she greeted Putin's soldiers with bread and salt. Putin is *her* president." With this simple phrase, Larysa conveyed that her mother was far too welcoming to Putin's forces. Bread and salt are presented as a traditional welcome in Slavic cultures. A ceremonial greeting with bread and salt is offered to formal and respected guests. This is embedded in a broader tradition that values giving the best one has to guests. One explanation for the tradition is that salt was not always easily obtained. In the Russian empire, for example, a high salt tax made it prohibitively expensive for many. There are other layers of meaning built into this: bread, a staple of the diet in both Russia and Ukraine, is probably the most valued food. Larysa, a professional psychologist, told me she is a person with a rich vocabulary of emotion words. But that vocabulary was useless in the face of this loss, which she experienced as a void that was inexpressible. She described herself as "crippled" from the emotional turbulence resulting from his death, which leaves her little emotional strength to devote to other matters. Having identified this void, we spoke around it by touching on related topics like Adam's now adult sister and his schooling, before returning to the topic of Adam's death itself.

As she spoke, a lump formed in my throat and began to cause me searing pain, and my unsuccessful efforts not to cry made my chest ache. I was so emotionally overloaded that I began to feel dizzy and light-headed. My visible distress seemed to bring us closer, however, by making me a person who was present with her in her grief, rather than trying to assume an objective, scientific stance. The conversation spiraled into this pain until we were both deep into it, with tears running down both our faces.

"Ukraine Above All Else"

Upon later reading the transcript of the interview, I could see that chronologically, the narrative was a jumble. Larysa jumped forward and backward in time, moved more by her feelings than the sequence of events. Whatever the trajectory, each vignette bent back to a single idea: Adam died for his people, not his government. The meaning Larysa made of her son's death, and her current estrangement from her mother and sister, was that "the people" come before family. Larysa explained that when the war broke out, her son arrived at a state of national consciousness he had not experienced before: "Nationalism awoke in him. When we were oppressed by aggressors, it awoke . . . he said: [he was going to fight] 'to prevent Putin from coming here, for you to sleep peacefully.'" That a territorial dispute would incite nationalism in a young man is unremarkable. But what also requires attention here is the combined reference to territory and a mother's peace of mind. In Larysa's retrospective imagining, we can see how the young man's desire to protect and defend his country so that his mother could sleep at night conflated mother and nation. Pioneering work on the part of writers like Yuval-Davis (1989, 1997) has illuminated just how tight the woman-nation-state conjunction has tended to be. Women literally reproduce nations, and they also come, symbolically, to stand for it. Their bodies become the territory over which men must fight in order to ensure the continuation of national identities and ideologies (Sjoberg and Via 2010).

Larysa makes sense of her loss, retrospectively at least, by making it part of defending the nation. Speaking in Ukrainian, she says, "Ukraine above all else . . . God, it's not translatable into Russian. First of all, uppermost, the most important thing. Yes, Ukraine. First is Ukraine. The rest is family matters, that's secondary. And the time came when only this remains in my heart. To say that it hurts is an understatement. I live with pain." The attachment Larysa feels to her country stands out in bold relief in the statement "Ukraine above all else." Her approach alchemizes grief into purpose. Larysa felt she had fulfilled the duty of a mother and citizen of her country by producing such a patriotic son.

The Pain of National Optimism

Considering what happened after Adam's death opens up more facets of Larysa's loss. In the parking lot of the morgue, Larysa was approached by a social worker who needed to complete some documents. Larysa described her voice as offensively jolly when she asked if Adam had any scars or tattoos for identification purposes. The conversation alarmed Larysa because it suggested his physical condition might prevent her from recognizing him. Shocked, she asked, "What's left of him?" But the social worker did not know and could only state: "I don't know, I'm just a social worker, I was sent to ask." As Larysa explained, "I don't know about other mothers . . . but [at that moment] there's a picture in my mind that he is lying there in pieces, that I put on gloves, and that I look at each piece, looking for something. And I say, I say: 'Oh! The teeth . . . Are there teeth left? I'll recognize the teeth.'" As a result of this exchange, Larysa flashed through nightmarish scenes in her mind. The stage for this hellish drama had been set by authorities whose emotions pertaining to the war seemed always to be wildly out of key. Although the woman who approached Larysa was ostensibly "just" a social worker, it was arguably her job to deal more sensitively with clients.

Lieutenant P. is Rude

Larysa knew that her life would never be the same. Her distress was compounded by the cavalier treatment her son's corpse received from Lieutenant P., who, while Larysa was still standing in the parking lot, emerged from the morgue and proclaimed in a loud voice, shrugging in dismay, "It's a total mess!" In fact, the corpses were such a "mess" that they would require a thorough *ekspertiza* or investigation. Larysa recalled him shouting these comments within earshot of at least fifteen other grieving family members, also awaiting a chance to view the contents of coffins. As Larysa told the story, he continued to sound off with remarks such as "It's impossible to recognize anything!" Lieutenant P.'s behavior clashed so intensely with any notion of respect and consideration for the mourners that it provoked her to wonder whether the military even valued her son's service.

At this moment in our conversation, Larysa inhaled deeply and paused. She told me that at that moment, it seemed that the wind had become still; the birds had stopped singing; and the squirrels stood frozen, listening carefully from the trees. Not even a leaf rustled: silence. It was something metaphysical, as if the wind, the birds, and the squirrels participated in the human grief, aligning themselves with the mourners for a moment. It was precisely this kind of alignment that was missing in the conduct of the professionals she encountered.

After more waiting, the father of another deceased soldier who had seen Adam lying in the morgue told her, "He's handsome!" That gave her the courage to go in. Her hopes for an open casket funeral were quickly dashed, however, because he was badly disfigured by lividity, the swelling and dark purple coloration that result when the heart stops pumping blood and the red blood cells settle according to gravity. This provoked a veritable war of moods. Her goofy, gregarious Adam and death itself seemed so incongruous that his dead body, from Larysa's perspective, "didn't make sense." Her story continued with a lurid account full of reproach directed not only at the state but also at herself: "It was so unpleasant . . . Well, I understand, it was summer, the heat. But the stench was unbearable. The morgue . . . I don't know . . . whether it's like that everywhere, I don't know, but it shouldn't have been like that. It was wrong. Wrong. My final glance at him. That image will remain . . . till the end of my life. And it shouldn't be like that. And those feelings, I hate myself for that stench, for the fact that I could not bear it. No Adam anymore. . . . it's my only . . . the body of my only . . . (Crying)." Describing the seven-day-old remains, Larysa was forthcoming about the most unglamorous part of war: the sweet and sickening stench of decomposing human flesh.

The comportment of the social worker and Lieutenant P. was inappropriate and upsetting the citizens they ostensibly served.

Motherland Protector Day

All of this emotional (mis)management reached a crescendo at the Motherland Day observance Larysa attended. Hypothetically, the holiday solemnly honors those who are or were serving in the armed forces. Informally, it also became a day when women honored the men in their lives, just as men honor women on International Women's Day. Considering the holiday was created in the Soviet Union, President Poroshenko changed the date of the holiday to underscore Ukraine's independence from Russia. Larysa left her home for the event expecting somber words and perhaps some coffee and sandwiches. She arrived to find a concert. In describing the scene, Larysa provided snapshots of other attendees, whom she knew as members of her local community. Each was grieving a loss. Some had lost a limb, others a loved one. Larysa could only tolerate a few minutes of the festive atmosphere before she felt she had to leave. She had begun to divest herself of any optimism that her sacrifice would be acknowledged.

"The People"

People for whom her son had given his life were at times insensitive and disrespectful. She described the types of conversations she began having: "The first question was always 'Why did you let him go?' Once I was asked this on TV. I told them: 'It's painful, but the most painful thing is this question.' I said: 'I'd prefer you to hit me and go on your way rather than ask something like that.'" Repeatedly pressed with this question, Larysa told me, she had also been known to respond that her son had died so that other people's sons could study and work. At the time her son enlisted, it was entirely possible to bribe the military not to draft one's son. But Larysa was too patriotic and respectful of her son's desire to serve to pursue this option. So she learned to warn people not to blame her with this question.

From Larysa's perspective, the social worker, the lieutenant, the military command that organized the Motherland Day observation, and the other mothers all had a distinct tendency to disregard her sacrifice. And the condition in which her son's remains arrived was a further indication that the nation she had prioritized did not reciprocate with respect.

As part of a strategy to make sense of the situation, Larysa assigned her son larger-than-life significance: "My son is not only my son, he's Ukraine's son, he's buried at the cemetery where Krushelnytska is buried, where Ivan Franko is buried, you see? Ivan Franko! I never thought that my son, my son . . . I've finally understood the phrase "heroes never die." Ivan Franko (1856–1916), was a famous poet, writer, and political radical who founded a national movement in western Ukraine. In a way, Franko is to Ukraine what Thomas Jefferson is to the United States, wielding an enormous influence on Ukrainian political thought.

Heroes never die, she explained, because they "live," figuratively speaking, in the hearts of those who remember them. "*My* grave will be forgotten, [placing hands on chest] trampled away, [making an expansive move of her right arm] but tours will visit his grave. The name and the surname, his face, his smile will be printed . . . he'll never leave. They'll always be . . . Even if Ukraine will collapse, you see, he'll stay in hearts, he'll stay . . . in hearts of patriots. There have always been patriots, there are patriots and there will be patriots who carry the national idea. I've finally understood that. What do they mean? They never die!" In this passage, Larysa has the fantasy that her son's grave will become a tourist destination. Cemetery tourism is common in eastern Europe. What will be said in front of his "goofy" face, however, will depend in part on the outcome of the conflict and may not be as favorable as she imagines. The vision of her son living on in the hearts of patriots of Ukraine, and being visited by schoolchildren in the years to come, however, provides an emotional salve. The way the war was going at the time it appeared to be more likely that Adam would be criticized, like those who returned from the Vietnam War, as an accomplice in an oligarchic turf battle. Like Oleksandra's fantasy about the pizza party, cruel optimism makes itself known through her fantasy about how he will be revered. In reality, the love Larysa showed for her nation was not returned. Larysa's description of the way public servants handled her son's death suggests she was quite conscious about the cruelty of her national optimism.

Nevertheless, coming to ideological consciousness as a Ukrainian led Larysa to subordinate her family to the interests of the people. The statements of so-called ordinary Ukrainians like Larysa reflecting on their experience explicitly tie together the inside (the inner, emotional world of a person) and the outside (a polity). What happened to subjectivities like Oleksandra's and Larysa's as a result of the conflict matters because tactical kinship is part of the war and an additional way to see into it.

Love, A Common Horizon, Remains

Tracking these processes reveals a more distal vantage point beyond the various disappointments associated with national belonging. Larysa maintains her bond with her mother, stating: "I'll give her a chance to sober up and come to her senses, right?" She added "I don't renounce her, God forbid, she's an amazing woman, I love her very much. I just don't call her so as not to hurt myself." Not even her mother's contribution to her son's death can kill the love she feels for her mother and sister. Again the enmity, vitriol, and hatred one might expect in a situation like this one are not part of her description.

Larysa and I hugged goodbye, and I gathered my things and left. Larysa stayed behind to chat with the owner of the café some more. I cycled through feelings of grief, loss, and anger for several days before I found the energy to continue my project. A local friend suggested my work would be easier if I were more detached. She may have been right, but in keeping with the discussion of anthropological fieldwork in the introduction, I suggest an ethnographer's embodied presence and receptivity is still a valuable tool for gaining insight. Plus, being a receptive and empathic listener seemed to create a more capacious conversational space for Larysa to share her story.

Oleksandra and Larysa show us in fine grained detail how emotional attachments to the nation take shape. The question as to how people become willing to die for national collectivities has traditionally been answered with the concept that nations are imagined communities (Anderson 1991). To stop there stands to overlook the intimate and indeed cruel ways nation and family coconstitute one another. Oleksandra's and Larysa's experiences make the connection between kin and nation more tangible. Nationality works through, and is configured by, relationality.

While in some ways Oleksandra's and Larysa's self-identification as specifically national subjects is satisfying, it is also problematic. They are enabled to support the nation, but this is also their disabling. One of the benefits of thinking about how "cruel" and "optimism" conjoin, then, is that it prompts thinking carefully about how hope gets attached, in uncomfortable and maybe even maladaptive ways, to the collectivity.

The cases of Oleksandra and Larysa provide a contrast to those in the chapter on friendship, in which everyday peace was forged across political sides. In both Oleksandra's and Larysa's cases, family members provisioned the fighting in conscious and strategic ways. Put bluntly, family was emotionally enlisted. At the same time, both cases are instructive because of what they leave out: the racially, ethnically, or religiously based enmity common in war. Ultimately, everyday peace has a shadow in everyday war—the quotidian investments that facilitate the conflict. Everyday war is most of all distinguished by its purpose. What Oleksandra and Larysa sought to accomplish as a result of their contributions was not more death or destruction but a greater sense of belonging to their family and nation.

INTERTEXT

"I Need a Peaceful Sky"

The statements that follow evoke something of what IDPs from the conflict zone in Ukraine experienced. The lines are selected from the sixty-five interviews with people concerned with the war in Donetsk and Luhansk. The reasons they left—and the conditions they faced—are expressed in the lines below.

People with machine guns came.

A friend of mine said "I saw your name on the list of those who are to be shot."

You know, the soundwave from a missile is very large.

By the side of the road lay a boot with a piece of leg.

Groups of bandits were going through the city, sacking everything.

I was in stupor, I was . . . I was like a child.

We took mainly summer clothes because we thought we'd return.

From the very beginning I couldn't accept those gangs.

It happened with the full support of the local authorities.

They started bombing from Yakira street and my windows were shaking.

I was home alone, and it was terrifying.

There were innumerable tanks . . . cannons, tanks, everything was so scary.

My son was 6 at the time. He took his toy gun and started shooting.

The threats were of a very serious nature, along the lines of "your children aren't going to come home alive from school."

Well, there was no . . . there was no government at all.

There was no police, I mean, there were masked people.

I didn't want to lose my apartment, but when a guy got his legs blown off in my stairwell, I . . . I decided to leave.

Words just fail me: you walk, and something explodes right over your head with a huge "boom." Windows are rattling, and you recall school lessons: "duck and cover."

They were shooting from the school where our children studied. From the school.

There are suburbs, so they go into the suburbs and shoot from there.

They go into the villages, and shoot from there.

When our bus was leaving . . . they started firing. . . . I took cover, and I wondered whether I'd stay alive or not.

Well, I saw everybody seizing their phones, all faces are twisted.

It was scary to travel because there were lots of crushed tanks.

There were lots of burnt corpses lying on the road.

When we entered the territory under control, I still remember that feeling that I'm, as if I'm somewhere . . . I don't know . . . I'm in some heaven.

I need a peaceful sky.

These statements communicate some of the pain associated with becoming aware that life cannot go on as expected. The chapters that follow flesh out what these sentences telegraph.

PRAYING TO BE KILLED AT ONCE
Ways of Coping with Military Violence

"Did my girlfriend tell you about Dzerzhinsk? Well they bombed the
mining college, the central streets were plowed up by tanks, the White
House was ruined. I mean, even the central department store, everything was blown up.

Bombing went on for a day. Then: ruins.

And the following morning, the children were running around, gathering the shells, [and] taking selfies in front of burned cars."—Mykola

This anecdote was told by Mykola with a grim smile that acknowledged the human
capacity to adjust to anything and carry on. This chapter asks how it was that life
on the front lines came to be treated as normal, and how subjectivity, or the individual's felt interior experience, was managed in relation to military violence. I
argue that in addition to being divided by a political line of demarcation, Ukraine
was characterized by two significantly different ways of coping with the military
violence emotionally. Mykola was troubled by the way the destructive power of
the military confrontation was quickly minimized and made to seem ordinary
through the play and the selfies. He was not alone in making observations like this
one. The tendency to treat the violent conflict as normal was a major preoccupa-
tion among the people I spoke with between 2015 and 2017.

What they observed with astonishment was the sheer nonchalance with which
residents of the conflict zone engaged in the tasks of daily living in spite of ongoing violence. They told me how pensioners lined the streets to sell jars of milk and
homemade cheese. Those with gardens laid out for sale their bunches of delicate

herbs, tied neatly like bouquets of flowers, while there was active shooting audible on the next street. People became adept at gauging the amount of time it would take for Russian-backed forces to reload their missile launchers (about fifteen minutes, I was told) and used the time to scurry out for milk or bread—a practice that sometimes ended in death. Children could pop out of school to enjoy a slide during recess, but the playground was likely be located close to the trenches used by the Ukrainian military and schools themselves were military targets.

What requires explanation, then, was why these individuals chose to stay in the conflict zone when their lives were imperiled by it, and how they viewed their imperiled lives. As Paul Willis argued in his famous study of British working-class youth who end up in low paid jobs, "it is much too facile simply to say that they have no choice" (1977, 1). He argued that the situation could be understood as a form of class culture shaped by experiences. Challenging the thesis that lower-class men were trapped and subjected to rules not of their own making, he argued convincingly that far from being simply manipulated, they had created their own ways to resist. This too is part of everyday war.

Researchers interested in the displaced and the dispossessed often turn to Agamben's notion of bare life in a state of exception to analyze how these situations come to be, and their larger import (Ramadan 2013; Puggioni 2014; Marr 2019). A significant line of thinking within this tradition is concerned with the extent to which people living in abjectivity have agency (Owens 2009; Ross 2017). Too often, these discussions are calibrated against exogenous standards of agency, occluding how people frame their own situation. In observing the minimization of violence, we may say, as Paul Willis did in reference to the "lads" who rebelled against school only to spend the rest of their lives laboring in unskilled and low wage jobs that there was an element of self-damnation (Willis 1977, 3). What is crucial to remember, however, is that the self-damnation entailed in carrying out one's activities in areas of active conflict was, paradoxically, experienced as exercising choice and having freedom.

In the Donetsk and Luhansk provinces, material considerations were undoubtedly central to why they lived as they did. Many of the people who lived there had initially fled for their lives but had been unable to make ends meet in government-controlled parts of Ukraine and therefore returned. The population in the conflict zone was also disproportionately elderly. The combination of small (or unpaid) pensions and the inability to compete in the contemporary job market led many a pensioner to stay in his or her home, come what may. It must also be acknowledged that a significant portion of those who lived surrounded by conflict supported the de facto authorities. What interests me here is less the structural violence of living in a war zone, although that is certainly important, than the thoughts and feelings they articulated with regard to their choices and experiences.[1] There were, in effect, two different emotional comportments or styles with regard to the suffering imposed by military violence.

This chapter further develops the theme of care by attending to the people who were troubled by the normalization of violence. Some of them expressed concern and some made it their work to care for the people who seemed to have stopped caring for themselves. This ethic of care was especially prevalent among psychologists and social workers who traveled in and out of the conflict-affected zone. The other way of being in this world was not at all about "working through" or "healing" from trauma. From this perspective, people "unhitched" themselves from the widespread ethos that places an emphasis on optimism and making continual efforts to better oneself. To them, it did not make sense to worry about "trauma" or think about escaping the historical contingencies of life. They had what Lauren Berlant called "crisis ordinariness" when she argued against relying on trauma to anchor discourse on a crisis-filled present (2011, 9–10).

In what follows, let us first explore how the people who were troubled by the normalization of violence described what they saw as contrasting emotional states. One of the stories I heard from a number of people concerned grandparents in the zone assessing risk differently from their adult children outside of it. Metaphors that people within the range of the military violence are like amphibians or like "little soldiers" were also common, and the sounds of the military conflict were compared to those of weather conditions. In the second half of the chapter readers dive more deeply into how the violence was understood inside the conflict zone through the reflections of Aleksey. Too poor to relocate, and having lived as a laborer during the Soviet years, Aleksey's story illuminates how Soviet working-class life prepared him to take the military violence that began in 2014 in stride. As such, the high tolerance for violence is conditioned by history and socioeconomic status.

Dimensions of Care
First Example: "A Person Can Get Used to Anything"

Maria was among those who were profoundly concerned about the high tolerance of violence she saw among the people living in the zone of active conflict. Although trained as a teacher, Maria became a humanitarian and mental health support provider, managing a shelter for internally displaced persons when they began flowing into her town of Kramatorsk. She also routinely traveled to the buffer zone around the line of contact and the NGCAs to provide humanitarian assistance and mental health services. Not far from the current line of demarcation,

FIGURE 11.   Dolls used in therapy with traumatized young people

Kramatorsk had once been under siege and occupied by the pro-Russian separatists. At the time Maria and I spoke, Ukrainian forces had regained control of Kramatorsk. Speaking of the people along the line of contact she states: "They learned to live under gunfire, they learned to live without heat and electricity, they learned to live in basements, they learned to walk through minefields. At some point in the beginning it was frightening, but with time that edge is erased. Of course it's not safe. They don't think that it is. Over these years I came to understand that a person can get used to anything."

What concerned Maria was that events like hearing sniper fire on one's residential street were no longer treated as dangerous. As Maria says in the passage above, "a person can get used to anything." It was as if the capacity to feel fear had been dulled by sustained exposure to the military violence. Maria suggested that the full impact of the conflict over Donbas is yet to be determined because the profound effects on children will unravel in communities for generations to come. She had made it her full-time job to care about and for these children.

Among the many thoughts and feelings they expressed about the war, what stands out as salient in the interview material, then, are two complementary and yet divergent tendencies: minimizing the state of violence in which they lived, and interrogating that very strategy of minimization. Phenomenologically speaking, what was alive for the second group was concern about damage to the minds of the people they knew, loved, or worked with and by extension future

PRAYING TO BE KILLED AT ONCE   115

generations of Ukrainians as a whole. Their ethic of care was wrapped up in ways to foster the well-being of people more adversely affected by the military conflict than themselves.

Second Example: "The Broken Branch"

A story that captures the geography of emotional responses especially well is the story about broken fruit tree branches. It was told in the first person by a number of different individuals, all of whom suggested it happened to them. The story has to do with the common practice of sending children to their grandparents in the country for a summer respite. A man I will call Ivan who fled Donetsk with his wife and daughter, for example, recounted how his mother back in Donetsk began to miss her granddaughter. She called to request that he drop off the child for a summer visit. In his rendering of the request, his mother described the bounty of the garden her grandchild would be able to enjoy. But then, in passing, she informed him that, "by the way," there had been shelling, and it had torn a big branch off the apple tree. He recalled: "And I just can't get my head around it: how can a person tell me about shelling *and* ask me to send her my four-year-old daughter for the summer because fruit has ripened?" In calling attention to his own befuddlement, he lays bare the radically different frames of mind he and his mother occupy with regard to coping with military violence. Excavating deeper, the story is emotionally freighted by Soviet culture, in which summer dachas became iconic of well-being. The quintessential good life in this region includes a summer cottage, even if it is very modest. The story shows a place of comfort, safety, and nurturance becoming the inverse: a place of random and unpredictable perils. Grandmothers typically represent benevolence, but this story describes a grandma who is off the rails, having lost the ability to assess risks to her loved ones' safety.

In relating the story about the fruit tree, Ivan models how to view the conflict bifocally. There is "normal" life, in which the fight or flight instinct is intact, and life in which that instinct appears to be missing. What emerges as a result are two very different ethics of caring. The man who told this story contrasts his ethic of care with that of his mother.

Third Example: "Little Soldiers"

A psychologist I will call Anna who lives near the line of demarcation and drives into the conflict area on a weekly basis made a similar point and also takes a bifocal view. Referring to her patients inside the zone, she states: "I can say these are almost all people for whom an understanding of safety has been destroyed. . . . This is both surprising and horrifying. It's true that people live, for all practical purposes, full lives, and, for different reasons, get trapped into a state of chronic stress in which they do not react to danger signals. They no longer react to sounds of danger. Safety is destroyed. Well, it is a basic instinct that is destroyed." The way she describes it, emotional expression underwent mitosis: some people's chronic stress destroyed their ability to fear danger. Others, like herself, sustained the ability to sense danger. They bear a moral responsibility to help those who have ceased to help themselves. The psychologist further developed the significance of these different emotional frames by explicitly flagging their historical continuity. "For decades we were taught that we had to be, if not like little soldiers, at least withstand everything, it was the system of upbringing in life, education, you see." The reference to "little soldiers" intimates that far from new, this attitude toward hardship actually has a long history. The texture of these lives is more complicated than we might first imagine because it is not solely a matter of the present. They are like "little soldiers" because in the twentieth century alone, Russia underwent two revolutions, and carried out a bloody civil war. The Soviet Union that emerged from that ruble was then devastated by two world wars, and lost millions more lives to forced labor camps, collectively known as the Gulag. It would be a mistake to understand the high tolerance for suffering as engendered solely by the conflict that began in 2014.[2]

Fourth Example: "It's Like the Frog in the Pot"

People who survived and subsequently reassessed their understanding are valuable sources of comparative insight. Sasha survived the siege of Donetsk by grabbing what sleep he could in an empty bathtub, fully clothed, where he knew the absence of windows increased his chances of surviving through the night. People who lived through other sieges in Sloviansk, Debaltsev, or Iliavosk had similar tales. All of them noted that when it happened sequentially, they became numbed. As Sasha described it: "One person is shot, then two, then three, then ten. If it was all at once [making sound of gunfire] bu bu bu bu bu, you would run away. But when it happens little by little . . . You know, this is like the experiment with a frog. If it is put in water, and then the water is gradually heated, the frog will die before it has the sense to jump out. It's like this situation." Likening his response to that of an amphibian is suggestive of a subhuman existence. Drawing a human-frog parallel figures the civilians in the conflict zone as reacting at the level of physical reflexes, reflexes that have been disabled and can no longer save them. It's a poignant irony that this is actually a myth: if a real frog is placed in a pot of water and the temperature is very gradually increased, it will indeed jump out because it can. Conversely, if a real frog is dropped into a pot of boiling water, its muscles are quickly immobilized and it will die. Whether the conditions changed quickly or slowly, people saw their past selves and their compatriots in the conflict zone as emotionally disabled.

Fifth and Last Example: "Rain and Sunshine"

Describing the military conflict using terms for weather was also common. Kyrylo, who runs a humanitarian aid project in the zone, described this most powerfully. I met Kyrylo through a television journalist who had traveled extensively to cover the conflict and thought very highly of him. When I met up with Kyrylo and spent an afternoon with him, he told me that he had been traveling between government- and separatist-controlled areas on a weekly basis for a couple of years. His experiences in the nongovernment-controlled areas caused him to become particularly concerned, like Maria, about the children growing up in terrible conditions. The generation that is coming of age in a protracted and undeclared war, he argued, provide a unique window on war itself. The five- and six-year-olds who listened to shooting on a daily basis, he suggested, heard it as rain. This is to say that it had the effect of "white noise," or a soothing "soundtrack" that can be ignored by the conscious mind. At a symbolic level, the weather analogy suggests children ceased to make a distinction between truly life-giving elements like rain, and those that spell destruction like mortars and bullets. I was haunted by these observations because a developmental milestone for children living in peace is being able to name animals and match them to their sounds. What the children he encountered could match were the sounds and the names of ordnances. Distinguishing millimeters of an ordinance was far more consequential to survival than knowing the barnyard animals of yore. The larger the ordnance the more imperative it was to descend to a basement or root cellar, and children learned to make distinctions like these by themselves.

To recap, the people in relatively safe and government-controlled areas agonized over the normalization of violence and its implications for the country as a whole. The social and psychological service providers among them by and large subscribed to a pedagogy based on helping people in the zone to recover their instinct for self-preservation, their craving for social justice, and their optimism about things like rehabilitation and recovery. This was their ethic of care: food, shelter, counseling, and sensory and play therapy were all extended to the people traumatized by the war. But the people making their lives in the midst of terrible violence, and against less than favorable odds of survival, saw things differently. Next, let us consider their way of being in the world. How did the people whose lives were most precariously situated make sense of their predicament?

Survival Mode: Aleksey Minimizes the Significance of Violence

Aleksey's story takes us more deeply into what it means to experience the military conflict as a poor Ukrainian civilian living in a nongovernment-controlled area (NGCA). I met Aleksey in a homeless shelter outside of Kyiv. What I noticed first about Aleksey was his unflinching gaze. Sitting in his wheelchair in a bright yellow shirt, he stared into my eyes and did not look away. Aleksey was in a wheelchair because his right leg had recently been amputated just above the knee. The end of his right pant leg was folded neatly under the stump. Aleksey perched his elbows on the arm rests and leaned toward me. We started by chatting about the vibrant house plants growing in coffee cans on the windowsill, practically dancing in the sunlight. When I asked him if he would like to tell me a little bit about himself, he didn't waste any time getting straight to the point: he had had a job, a family, and an apartment before the war, but when the conflict spread to his region, he lost them all.

Too poor to relocate, Aleksey endured repeated bombing campaigns in his neighborhood. He recounts: "Well, of course, during the shellfire you have unpleasant feelings. Because you don't know what will happen. I am telling you, I just go out on the balcony, and it starts banging [arms waiving]. Shells fly, and you don't know whether it will hit you or not. But what to do? Everybody lived like this. I placed my trust in God. That's how we lived." Aleksey's description of his "unpleasant feelings" suggests considerable presence of mind. The dispassionate tone he strikes contrasts with the shock and dismay expressed about the fruit tree branch and the frog in the pot.

Even after the glass in his apartment's windows had been shattered by sonic blasts from nearby shelling, Aleksey continued to live in his unheated apartment without running water. Electricity was intermittent. During this time, Aleksey's foot began to hurt. His tone was matter-of-fact as he recounted removing a sock in his chilly room and seeing two toes that had begun to "rot." Without access to medical care, his abscesses worsened. Still, Aleksey inflected his situation with gallows humor: "So I ate raw semolina. I can offer a recipe for weight loss [laughing]. If someone wants to lose weight, there's no need for any diets [waving his right arm through the air]. Two weeks of eating semolina: two spoonfuls of semolina, two teaspoons of sugar in a mug of water. Per twenty-four hours. In three weeks, you will be able to reach in and feel your spine through your stomach." The mock medical tone of the phrase "per twenty-four hours" makes light of this episode. Aleksey did not describe himself as losing his composure. Rather, he recounted with considerable pride that like the people with more resources, he had survived. In a situation in which rage and self-pity would also be under-

standable responses, his ability to joke about the "recipe for weight loss" nor-
malizes a horrific predicament.

Death was his best-case scenario. Aleksey told me that he would hobble out on
his balcony, and pray to die "at once," meaning go quickly, without suffering. He
figured this was preferable to continuing a bare existence that is somewhere between life and death. Aleksey was unable to hide in the basement like others because
the pain in his lower leg prevented him from descending the stairs. While his
neighbors were cooking on small fires outside the apartment block, Aleksey barely
eked out an existence in his third-floor apartment. It might be tempting to understand his story solely in terms of structural violence or bare life, focusing on the
forces and forms of sovereignty responsible for his plight. My approach is more
concerned with understanding the subjective elements of Aleksey's response to his
situation, which amounted to a complex interplay of embodied responses, historical paths, and personal biography. A conscientious engagement with other's emotions avoids taking human experiences of pain or fear as universal, attending to
their historicity (Tolia-Kelly 2006, 213). Along these lines, Aleksey's commentary
certainly invites deeper questioning about how he experienced the "getting used to"
without premature conclusions about the adequacy or inadequacy of his response.

Curious about what motivated him besides stoicism and gallows humor, I
asked Aleksey what it was like to live in the shelter where we were sitting. When he
shrugged off the question with "I'm fine," I prompted him to elaborate. After pausing for moment, he blurted out, "Like in a fairy tale!" before falling silent for a long
time. My heart pounded as I worried I had probed too much. Was this anger and
sarcasm? When he elaborated, it became clear that relative to his previous life
when he did shift work as a welder, he actually considered life in the shelter to be
pretty good. His assessment was tied up with Soviet working-class experience. To
give just one example, he described working on the Baikal-Amur Mainline, where
they were continually undernourished and it was so cold, they changed their
clothes under the blankets. Considering structural violence alone says little about
the intricacies of the subjective experience of conflict. From Aleksey's viewpoint,
he had scored a pretty cozy spot at the shelter. Surveying the potted plants on the
sunny windowsill and detecting the scent of traditional borscht with dill and a
hunk of fatty beef simmering in the kitchen, I could understand what he meant.

Aleksey's attention to the history of his feelings provides valuable dimension
to the geography of emotions surrounding the war. His life as a laborer had
moved him around the Soviet Union quite a bit, and while he said he did not
exactly feel fully at home in the shelter, it was a lot better than most of the places
he had previously been. His socioeconomic background is therefore integral to
his emotional style: Aleksey makes sense of his cold apartment with its shattered
windows not in terms of a traumatic experience but rather on a continuum with

previous hardships he experienced as a welder working for various state enterprises across what was then the Soviet Union. His references to his life in the Soviet Union help us understand that the reaction to violence we see in the present is part of life in PTSD land: it is tethered to experiences as well as norms and expectations in the past. Among the workers on the Baikal-Amur Mainline, it was likely emotional nondisplay that engendered respect from peers. Aleksey therefore demonstrates the veracity of the idea that considering how common crisis is to history, it is important not to limit oneself solely to the medical framework and logic of trauma (Berlant 2011, 10).

Aleksey's approach creates a strong contrast with the way that Oleksandra and Larysa were dealing with the consequences of war (see chapter 5). Unlike Aleksey, they were magnetized by the prospect of patriotism and derived meaning and purpose from embracing Ukrainian national pride while directly contributing to the military conflict. In refusing to make a national or self-improvement project of himself, Aleksey disavowed the cruel optimism of envisioning a future that had no chance of materializing. In fact, when asked about his hopes for the future, Aleksey replied in his characteristically blunt style that he did not have any hopes. He told me he believed that God's will for his life would be fulfilled, stating, "Let it be as it will be." For Aleksey, there was nothing to strive for, no happier future hovering on the horizon if he could only improve himself in this way or that.

Although his confinement in the zone of conflict left him, basically, to rot, Aleksey withstood his hardships with equanimity. His approach to life recalls Hegel's definition of the life of the Spirit, which is a life that accepts and lives with death instead of shunning it (Hegel [1807] 1977). He did not seek self-improvement, only the best life possible under the circumstances. In making this argument, I try to avoid platitudes about human agency and resilience. As Das has pointed out, even when it is impossible to transcend spaces of abjection such as the conflict zone, it is still possible to make them one's own (Das 2012, 208). The experiences related above align with Das' view: people lived through the military conflict in part through adopting the attitudes toward their predicament that served them. They did not talk about rising above so much as embracing what was.

"The Child May Die, but the Child Will Die with Me"

Aleksey was not alone in refusing to strive. Awareness of having been positioned to die was expressed by many others as well. The same social worker we encountered at the beginning of this chapter, Maria, told me a story that illustrates this concretely. She recalled approaching parents in the front line city of Jovenka to evacuate them. But the parents did not want to evacuate their families and they refused the proposition that, at the very least, their children could be temporarily sheltered in safety while they remained to guard their homes. As she described it, the mentality was this: "the child may die but the child will die with me." Her efforts to assist these families did not turn out as she had hoped because not even the prospect of death would persuade them to be separated from their children. This attitude represents a step into what I am calling everyday war because they seemed to be valuing the preservation of family unity over life itself.

I often wondered what these parents were thinking. After all, staying would come with an array of risks, such as the danger of sending children to school across minefields. Parents in the area explained that while it was certainly harrowing to allow their children to leave the house, they were still making mental calculations about the risks they were taking. The school building was the strongest structure for miles, and in the event of a mortar attack, children stood a better chance of surviving at school than at home. They had been to the government-controlled parts of the country and had not found a way to subsist and remain an intact family. They all knew couples who divorced after opting for the mother to take the children to safety while the husband guarded the house or cared for the elderly. Hewing too closely to the logic of trauma misses the "crisis ordinariness" (Berlant 2011, 10) unfolding here, and everyday war.

The internally displaced who were not able to make ends meet in government-controlled Ukraine and returned to the separatist-controlled areas were especially disenfranchised: divested of political relevance by prohibitions on voting and receiving their pensions, they exercised their agency in the limited way available to them—by being able to choose at least the location of their death, if not the timing. Scholarship on agency has produced volumes on how best to define it. Rather than engage these arguments here, I want to acknowledge how the people I encountered spoke about it. The families with school-age children and Aleksey had given up any romance with agency that is directed toward striving and betterment, or acting as an autonomous and "productive" member of society. "Damnation" to use Willis' (1977) term is paradoxically Aleksey's liberty, autonomy, and nonconformity.

The research presented in this chapter reveals that within the war over Donbas, both the territory and the emotions surrounding the military violence were divided. In the areas most affected by fighting in Ukraine, people became habituated to military violence and adapted to living in and around it. At its most intense, this meant risking death to keep one's family intact. In government-controlled Ukraine, by contrast, people had a tendency to express dismay about both the violence and other peoples' willingness to tolerate it. Recognition of the heterogeneity of attitudes toward violence and the symbiosis between those doing the caring like Kyrylo and Maria, and the cared-about like Aleksey further supports the thesis that the war in Donbas elicited caring responses. This in turn has value for studying how contemporary wars in general, which scoop up unprecedented numbers of civilians, are best understood.

Readers may be indignant that Aleksey prayed to go quickly, or that parents allowed their children to cross minefields on their way to school. I suggest the "getting used to" things is neither right nor wrong but worthy of consideration in its own right. Taking either of these modalities as simply normatively right or wrong, good or pathological, I suggest, is not very productive. Resisting the temptation to impose an exogenous normative framework cracks open the raw reality of finding peace in the face of violence. After all, both responses were significant ways of coping through protracted encounters with the toxic concatenation of military conflict and state neglect. The next chapter continues the exploration of coping with conflict by sharing the somatic language that people used to describe their disrupted lives.

EVERYDAY SCI-FI AND PRACTICAL ORIENTALISM

Earlier chapters have explored everyday war and everyday peace: the ways that people affected by war negotiated their differences through quotidian practices of bracketing out disagreement or, alternatively, a wholesale reorganization of their social networks. This chapter links up with that discussion and takes us further, into what I call "everyday sci-fi." I use the term sci-fi to capture what people described as a collective imagining, a shared making-sense of what seemed like life on another planet. In conversation, conflict-affected people I spoke with painted a world so uncannily altered by violence that it felt as they were living in a science fiction drama. This is not to say they spun fictional tales, but that when the military engagement spread to the place they were living, the familiar became very strange.

The process of entering what I am calling a sci-fi awareness was aptly described by Natasha. We got to talking in the shop she owned one day while business was slow. Natasha wore her dark brown hair skillfully coiffed, with helmet-like precision, into a short bob. A seamstress by training, I only ever saw her in well-tailored dresses that contrasted with the cheap imported clothes most people wore. Although initially she did not plan to leave the conflict area, the fighting in Luhansk quickly became too intense for her to reasonably stay. In her city of refuge, she focused on growing her business—a shop where she created custom-made clothing. The shop Natasha created for meetings with clients was homey: imagine a carpeted space with comfy chairs, examples of her clothes hanging in the windows.

The hominess provided a stark contrast to the scenes of departure from Luhansk she described. Prior to that departure, Natasha told me, an otherworldly quality seemed to overtake her city: "We had a period when animals, dogs were silent for a month, not barking at all." She speculated that this was because of the Russian Federation's experimentation with new technologies that alter brain waves. She explained her experience with the dogs as being like an *existing* science fiction movie she had seen about the Soviet Union, in which high technology sonic waves were used to subdue the population. In the film, the intelligent people "with brains" had wild headaches. The rest were brainwashed into docility. Like many, she believed the Russian Federation was using rays and magnetic fields to exercise mind control over their opponents, whether military or civilian.

Natasha's description of a world in which dogs did not bark captures the sense of the uncanny reality that permeated this world. Whether or not dogs truly ceased to bark is less important than appreciating the way the silence of the dogs came to stand for just how much things had changed. Following this month of silence came a month of uninterrupted howling, during which the dogs completely refused to be quiet: "Dogs were howling under our window . . . Owo-o-o-o . . . a dog. They say it's an omen: if a dog howls, death is near." Living there meant a constant adjustment of what was considered normal. As a result of spending time in intimate proximity with war, then, their perceptions were altered in a way that changed how they thought about their surroundings. To Natasha's way of thinking, the dogs were prescient, foreshadowing the tragedy to come. Imitating the sound a dog makes (and people imitated weapon sounds as well) also communicates the eerie weirdness of life off its hinges. Many suggested their hometowns had become odd, unrecognizable. As Kira tried to explain it: "I'll tell you what hit me: fear. Fear because you see a completely different city. Well, for example, when entering the city, you see billboards without any ads, or with ads that are ridiculously out of date. You realize that something's terribly wrong with the city. It's a weird feeling. It's a kind of fear which is strange somehow, I can't explain it." Through descriptions like these, we have an entrée into the somatic registers of political and military conflict.

In this world that overlay the one they knew before, they developed a new language, a somatic one, to describe their experiences. What they described was a process of registering military conflict in the workings of their physical selves: sight, skin, diaphragm, digestive organs. Thus, they found themselves not only inhabiting a landscape that had been altered by conflict, but taking up an alternative way of being in that world. It was sci-fi in the sense that in the process of seeking safety, they passed through a dystopian universe filled with experimental technology and mutants and they came to see themselves as foreign bodies in this strange land.

The embodied sense that the world—including one's pets, former neighbors, school mates, teachers, shop clerks, police, etc.—had become strange was pivotal in the decision to leave and important to the way the situation was retrospectively reconstructed and imagined. Given how the conflict had caused serious rifts between people who were formerly close, as described in chapter 3 and 4, what could be more fitting than the fantastical language of mysterious "waves" and "zombies" that detached responsibility from the offending parent, lover, or friend? This is a "practical orientalism" (Haldrup et al. 2006; Simonsen 2008; Wall 2011). If orientalism (Said 1995) refers to representational practices that exaggerate difference and presume superiority, *practical* orientalism aims to capture how cultural difference is also enacted in more mundane and sensory ways in everyday life. Deeming others to be stupefied by waves grounded the prevailing anti-Russian discourse in everyday sociality, amplifying what I have been calling everyday war. We may recall that everyday war refers to how conflict entered the intersubjective spaces of relationships, not with malice or the intent to kill so much as the desire to protect, care, or belong. Natasha's narrative about the sci-fi world was also a narrative that cast some people as superior to others.

Trauma and Translation

Anthropologists have dealt with the challenges associated with writing about pain, violence, and suffering from various angles. A crucial question pertains to how one can describe violence without one's account serving a prurient purpose. This is the question E. Valentine Daniel asks in his seminal account of violence in Sri Lanka (1996). He points out even the most earnest writer is faced with a difficult conundrum: escaping prurience and sanitizing one's description through recourse to meta-theoretical points is hardly a solution. A related challenge has to do with the epistemological problem of knowing another's pain and suffering in the first place. As V. Daniel wrote: "Pain stops at the skin's limit. It is not shareable" (1996, 139). In stating that pain is incommunicable and not sharable, Daniel and others have sensitized their readers to the ethical problems and limitations inherent in trying to understand the experience of violent conflict.

If pain stops at the skin's limit, it follows we must think very carefully about the silences of survivors. Veena Das (1995, 2000, 2007) and Eileen Scarry (1988) made especially significant contributions to this effort. One of their central contentions is that the silence that results from extreme violence is a response in its own right. Stated more directly, verbal reconstructions of suffering may work to deny the existential reality of the victim of the violence (Das 1995). Anthropology has a rich tradition, then, of theorizing and debating how violence produces silences that cannot be spoken (Das 1995; Jackson 2004; Castillejo 2005; Daniel 1996). Authors have debated how best to translate traumatic experience into forms that can be understood (Feldman 1991; van der Kolk and Fissler 1995; van der Kolk and van der Hart 1995; Nordstrom and Robben 1996, Pupavac 2002, Kidron 2009, Hautzinger and Scandlyn 2013; Hinton and Hinton 2015 Pillen 2016). Along these same lines, this chapter asks if there is a sensitive, and yet still more capacious way to listen to survivors.

Overwhelmingly frightening, painful, and extraordinary experiences disrupt the ability to recount an experience as progressing in a linear way through a beginning, middle, and end. Still, unverbalized experiences "live" on in flashbacks, nightmares, and somatic sensations (Pillen 2016, 98). There is also a strong tendency to dissociate as a result of overwhelming experiences. Dissociation refers to the sense of detachment from reality that occurs when existing meaning-making schemes are inadequate to making sense of what is happening. It is therefore not uncommon for trauma to lead individuals to develop the sense they are living in two very different worlds (Langer 1991; Pillen 2016). For traumatized persons, the realm of ordinary life and the realm of violence appear separate, unbridgeable (van der Kolk and van der Hart 1995, 176–77).

In what follows, rather than artificially imposing a linear narrative with a beginning (leaving home), middle (embarking on the car or train journey), and end (arriving in government-controlled territory), I seek to replicate how the experience was told to me through organ systems and (only seemingly ordinary) objects. First, we explore the somatic registrations of trauma: the "decisions" that people described in terms of specific embodied experiences, organ system by organ system. In these conversations, various objects figured prominently. We therefore turn next to some of the things they described. I show how they offer entry points for accessing more of the emotions associated with departure. In the next section of the chapter, readers explore the social dimension of this: the feeling they themselves had become alien others and were also encountering culturally different strangers. This "practical orientalism" was also described in embodied terms, showing how cultural difference is not only constructed through discourse, but embodied experience (Haldrup et al. 2006, 177).

The somatic registrations of cultural difference amounted to everyday war and have implications for peace. The last section of the chapter considers the reflections of a psychologist and a social worker who doubted the conflict would be resolved anytime soon based on somatosensory work with the conflict's survivors. Everyday war was fed by the sense, often embodied, that people in the east were now very different from themselves. The chapter therefore considers what can be gained by dwelling at the intersection of embodied trauma and embodied difference.

Somatic Registrations
Skin and Bones

The decision to leave was often described as a visceral one. A woman we will call Zhenia, who left Donetsk after the airport was destroyed, told me she and her husband made the decision without exchanging so much as a word. Originally, they had no intention of leaving: her husband had worked his way to the top of a very prosperous company, and she had become a popular nail technician. She and her husband considered themselves apolitical and had hoped, she said, to avoid "voting with their feet" for the pro-Ukrainian side of the conflict. They spent about six weeks of the bombing campaign in their home, doing their best to maintain habitual routines. One night, however, Zhenia noticed a greenish cast had come across her husband's face when he came in from the balcony. Apparently, he saw a mortar land down the street from their high-rise apartment. She heard him retch in the bathroom and then walk to the hall closet, where he pulled out a small suitcase. With only an exchange of glances, the couple packed a few changes of clothes, got in the car, and left. She told me it was the body that "knew" when the time to leave had come: the decision to leave was not cerebral, but kinesthetic. And the timing could be very different from what had been calculated mentally. It was truly an embodied form of knowing.

Another story about somatically registering the need to flee was told by Svetlana, whose kitchen table was described in chapter 3. Svetlana was nonchalant until her husband felt it was time to go, literally in his skin and bones: "You know, the sound wave from a missile is very large. My husband and I were hanging out watching TV. There was a wall behind him, so he leaned against that wall and he felt [an explosion] through the drywall. And he said, 'that's enough.'" This couple had listened to blasts reverberating across the city of Donetsk for almost three months. It was the sensation he felt in his skin and bones, more than rational thought, that triggered their departure.

The Diaphragm and Breathing

The conflict also worked its way into breathing. Yuliya, a woman who left Luhansk, related this: "And on the last day before I left, I was going to work, to my psychologist's office, and somewhere very close a cannon shot: BANG! And BA BA BA BOOOM. I was twisted [twisting a clenched fist against her mid-section] for a whole month, my diaphragm was twisted with such animal fear, my body . . . well, that's an [an example of] instinct." Afterward, she found it difficult to breathe normally for a long time. Her body had taken the conflict in. In speaking of "animal fear," she calls attention to the way in which living in the conflict zone had activated her sense of herself as a (human) animal. The somatosensory interpretations of the forcibly displaced testify to the catastrophic effects of the military conflict in Donbas.

The same response could also be triggered by witnessing portions of large apartment buildings crumbling; seeing the roofs of schools caved in; or witnessing the destruction of infrastructure such as train stations, airports, or hospitals. For Volodya it was smaller but no less influential. He recounted how he was in the practice of walking to his aged father's home around midday. It was a chance to bring his father meals his wife had prepared and check on the eighty-year-old. One day as he was walking, he noticed a boot laying by the side of the road in the distance. When he drew closer, he realized that someone's foot was still in the boot. That was it. Volodya realized that the military conflict had penetrated even his most routine task: the world had changed.

Intestines and Digestion

Above, I mentioned how one of my interlocutor's husbands vomited after witnessing something on the balcony. The decision to leave could be registered by the digestive system in other ways as well. As any soldier who has seen combat knows, it is common for combatants to have a parasympathetic response in which they eliminate the entire contents of their digestive tract. This could happen to civilians as well. Masha had recently graduated from technical college when the fighting began. She described how her intestines were affected by the conflict growing closer and closer to her apartment. Thinking about the day she and her husband decided to leave, Masha said: "I heard him saying [through the bathroom door], 'We're getting the hell out babe, packing our things because,' he says, 'you could croak!' And to be honest, I was on the toilet then, because I had so much fear." For her, the animal fear triggered episodes of diarrhea. And true to the disrupted seriation resulting from trauma, recollecting one episode prompted her to recount a different, later bathroom episode without filling me in on what happened in between. In the second bathroom story, she is in a public toilet and her husband notices a queue forming outside. He urges her to come out and let others have their turn. While the fears of "croaking" are ubiquitous in war stories, and refugees often tell of their fear, the physical dimensions are often bracketed out. In fact, scholars of forced migration have lamented that while the journey a forced migrant takes is likely to retain deep significance throughout his or her life, researchers focus most intently on the reasoning surrounding leaving and the conditions upon arrival (Benezer and Zetter 2014). In between escape and arrival, however, states such as hunger, thirst, diarrhea, or constipation were a central part of the embodied experiences. The putrid odor of sweat coating fearful skin, nausea, dizziness, dry mouth, bad breath, and shaking hands are the undertheorized and unromantic experiential ground of living forced migration.

Perhaps the strong physical reactions stand out in retrospect because there was no way to calculate risk using common sense. A social worker who was working with a group of children told me a story in which several families gathered for an evening meal in one of their homes on a beautiful summer evening. Afterward, the adults went out to the courtyard to smoke and chat among themselves with the children tucked inside. Just then, a missile came down and landed in the center of the courtyard on the adults, mixing their bodies in a bloody pulp. The children came out to find all of their parents dead. Experiences like this one shifted the experiential axis of the world: nothing would ever be the same.

Distress Condensed in Objects
Clothing

One of the things that intensified the sense of life being off its hinges was that people assumed they would be returning shortly. The lack of familiar objects and personal possessions compounded the sense of loss, and people became preoccupied with things that had been left behind. Galya told me that the prospect of the fighting dragging on any longer than a couple of summer months seemed as remote as Santa Claus: "Well, I packed and left with only one suitcase of light clothes, because I was leaving on June 16, 2014. I took only my two kids and summer clothes since actually, when I was leaving, I thought that there would be no DNR [Donetsk People's Republic], LNR [Luhansk People's Republic], these words were like Santa Claus for me: everybody talks about it, but nobody has seen it, I mean, that's impossible." What had previously seemed impossible, however, came to fruition. The mental image of Santa Claus shows how the changes taking place felt fictional, like entering an alternate reality. Fairies, monsters, and folktales were all referenced as my interlocutors searched for words to describe their experiences.

When it came to packing, space was always at a premium. Especially when departure was rushed, there was a risk inherent in pausing long enough to think about the items that would make life more sustainable later. Concurrently, the availability of public transportation tightened, and although private contractors filled many transportation gaps, they were strict about what they were willing to take on board. Many people found themselves in government-controlled territory fabulously unprepared. In a country renowned for long winters, this was a signifi-cant oversight and an indication of the degree to which those fleeing the conflict zone were not in a position to rationally assess the true gravity of their situation.

The Cadillac Eldorado

If bringing only summer clothing represented a maladaptive mix of wishful thinking and willful ignorance, other possessions condensed even more power-ful emotions having to do with loss. Leonid, whom I met at a workshop for IDPs, was a good example. He was eager to speak with me when he learned I had come from Michigan, the birthplace of his favorite car, the Cadillac Eldorado. Leonid was in his mid-thirties and had an angular face that communicated a combina-tion of undernourishment and emotional intensity. His immense cobalt eyes pro-duced an unwavering, penetrating gaze. After the workshop, we sat down at a picnic table, with my tape recorder between us. I was a little surprised when he told me that what he most longed for was his collection of matchbox cars. A pic-ture of the matchbox cars he saved on his phone showed the cars lined up neatly, still in their boxes, on a shelf in his Luhansk study. By contrast, there did not appear to be any nostalgia for his *real* car, which was parked in his garage.

FIGURE 12.   Pen and ink drawing of Cadillac Eldorado car

In fact, he refers to the real car and his apartment mechanically, using the economic term "rapidly depreciating" property. Gently sliding my notebook out of my hands, he picked up a pen and covered a page with a drawing of the Cadillac Eldorado to express his double nostalgia for his personal past and an American past when the auto industry was still in its prime and Detroit could be compared to a thriving European metropolis.

I understood his attachment to the toy cars better when he scrolled through the other pictures on his phone. What he captured on camera as he and his wife were departing were incinerated cars, upside-down cars, smashed cars, cars with flat tires, disemboweled cars, and cars with broken glass. The toy cars were everything the cars in his real world were not: safe, whole, and protected by boxes with cellophane. Leonid told me he was interviewed by a woman from the Organization for Security and Cooperation in Europe who told him to buy himself some new toys. But it is not that simple, he explained. Apparently not: he used so much pressure on the page in my notebook where he drew the Cadillac Eldorado that the pen left brail-like impressions, directly communicating the intensity of his feelings. I suspect that thinking about the toy cars helped him dwell for a while in a neat and safe toy world, providing a momentary escape from the messy, bombed, and precarious world he inhabited.

Household Fixtures and Appliances

Fiona left after she realized the threat of random physical violence had become very high. She told me her story at her home in a village about an hour's bus ride from a major city. She told me how while she still lived in Donetsk, she had marched from her front door down to the nearest checkpoint, which was a few short blocks from her home. She wanted the soldiers to stop partying and shooting into the late hours of the night. They ignored her. Concerned about the safety of her five daughters, she approached them again. This time, however, six men armed with machine guns surrounded her in a tight circle. They were close enough that she could smell the alcohol on their breath. She was misted by beer-scented saliva when one of them told her in a menacing tone that she had better "shut up." Fiona told me she understood in those moments that they answered to no one but themselves and could kill her or one of her daughters without thinking twice. The soldiers who were ostensibly guarding her from Ukrainian forces were drunk. It was an upside-down world where the protectors of the people had turned into menaces, all too ready to shoot and kill. She began the process of selling household items to generate funds for bus tickets. The stepwise nature of this process meant her daughters were sent off one by one.

FIGURE 13.   Rural kitchen of Internally Displaced Person

Fiona's description of these items was quite detailed. At first, I was perplexed as to why she wanted to go over the make, year, and model of items like toasters and washing machines. Then I understood they were icons of the good and cultured life she had lost. First, the expensive and brand-new, state-of-the-art refrigerator was sold. Then, the light fixtures that had been installed as part of a recent "Euro" remodel had to go. Next was the 2012 washing machine, followed by gardening tools, including a pricey shovel that she valued. After the tools were gone, she persuaded a neighbor to give her a bit of cash for their toaster oven. Like the toy cars described earlier, I came to appreciate the objects condensed the life she had to give up: this was not a tangent. The appliances she then had to use represented a socioeconomic step backward to a humble country kitchen in government-controlled Ukraine.

I came to know more about the objects than the offspring whose journeys they financed. The one daughter of hers that I met had gone to Russia but recently sought out her mother in government-controlled Ukraine. On the day I visited, she was tearful and did not seem to want to talk. The descriptions of appliances were a way, different than discussing emotional experiences, for Fiona to communicate about her family and its displacement. Part of the larger significance of the experience of traversing the weird, conflict-filled sci-fi world, whether somaticized or condensed into objects, was that it etched sociocultural and political differences into peoples' awareness. The sharp social divisions evident after the 2022 Russian invasion of Ukraine were preceded by the embodied experience of cultural difference described next.

Practical Orientalism

Embodied recognition of otherness may at first seem perplexing considering that the conflict between Russia and Ukraine was not between peoples who could be visibly distinguished on a phenotypic basis.[1] Looking back on their experience, however, the people who left Donbas complained that everyone was divided into "ours" and "others." They felt that in the newly coined DNR and LNR, they started to be viewed as *chuzhie*, meaning strangers who were foreign, even alien. The dichotomy between *sviy/nash* (ours/us) and others/they has a specific history in Ukraine. In her book about Ukraine's transformation after the disintegration of the Soviet Union, Catherine Wanner suggests *sviy* refers to a common identity built on the shared experience of an oppressive state in the Soviet Union (1998, 9). Alexei Yurchak also explored this internal othering productively, using the word "imaginary" to summarize the discursive practices that go into constituting internal others. He understood this process as based more on local needs and desires than concrete differences (2009). Scholarship also examines how internal othering worked during the conflict in Donbas. Tania Bulakh has traced how the complex internal hierarchy of othering enacted through this "ours-others" dichotomy played out when the internally displaced found their way to government-controlled Ukraine (2017, 53). Bulakh finds the hierarchy of othering to have profoundly affected the way IDPs were perceived and treated in government-controlled parts of the country, although those ways changed over time and depended on where the IDPs had originated.

The distinction between ours and not ours was not only abstract, however. Rather, it was embodied in the form of practical orientalism. Encounters in the social world involve bodies. These bodies constitute social life through relations that involve the senses. And this sociality is not only embodied but also narrated through naming, categorization, and the creation of social distinctions. A saying I heard frequently that expresses this succinctly was that they could no longer stand to "breathe the same air" as "those" people. They were referring to the people who had fomented rebellion against Kyiv or supported the separatist governments of the DNR and LNR. Practical orientalism takes as its starting point the insights of philosophers like Merleau-Ponty (1962; 1968) who were keen to establish the significance of human beings' continual perceiving and reacting to the presence of other human bodies. In this instance, it is about the intimacy of taking air that has been in an enemy's body into one's own. Merleau-Ponty argued it is the flesh that connects self and other because of human vulnerability. He describes how it is the flesh that suffers when it is wounded and it is also a source of healing through human touch (Merleau-Ponty 1968, 137).

Practical orientalism expands on these ideas about embodiment in ways that are especially germane for understanding noncombatants in a war zone. Practical orientalism suggests officials' narratives and rhetoric are translated into practices and become part of embodied experience (Haldrup et al. 2006, 177). As one of my interlocutors phrased it, "suspicious glances drill through you" because "the Russians there hate Ukrainians." Thus, difference is performed and managed in everyday sociality in part through the physical. Classical orientalism as formulated by Edward Said (1995) was by no means deaf or blind to the body. Said takes into close account, for example, how views of others are often sexualized, and how people are separated into types based on physical characteristics. But these observations can be more fully developed in recognizing how people are constructed as other through sensory experience. The notion of practical orientalism (Haldrup et al 2006; Herzfeld 2005) or perhaps *embodied* orientalism uncovers important additional layers of meaning in sci-fi. Sensory-based descriptions of difference contributed to the sense that something was terribly wrong and could prompt displacement.

Describing these sensory experiences required speaking around silences and through a new grammar of "us" and "them." A productive to way to think about the statements about glances that "drill" or the distastefulness of the air itself is that they take place at an intersection between embodied trauma and growing socio-political difference. This proto-othering, if you will, constitutes one of the starting points for a cultural logic that divides Russians and Ukrainians into an "us" and "them."

Olfactory

Above, the putrid smell of sweat on fearful skin was mentioned as a sensory experience of displacement. The olfactory was also part of how people made social distinctions. Pasha, a man who left Luhansk, described the enemy combatants by their smell. To bring home his point that Luhansk had deteriorated into what he called "gangistan," a place run by thugs and gangs, he said: "You know, that smell of three-pack-a-day guys? Well, they were not intelligentsia, obviously! Cigarettes of the lowest quality. As if they gathered some weed, ground it, rolled it in a newspaper, and smoked it." These guys, then, were not the cultured sort. Their smell alone made them lower class. What he deemed to be the more refined population of Donetsk province would never have allowed themselves to chain-smoke Makhorkas, the cheap way to smoke. His description of smelling the enemy exemplifies practical orientalism.

Auditory

As readers may have already surmised, the displaced people I interacted with reacted most strongly to the non-locals involved in the formation of the DNR and LNR: mercenary fighters and Russian transplants who infiltrated local structures of governance. The voices of the separatist insurgents set them apart and established them, in the eyes of the people who left, as imposters who lacked the legitimacy of local actors. Kyrylo, who lives in the DNR, was in the practice of monitoring the radio waves to determine where military activity was likely to take place. He was acutely attuned to the different accents of the people around him: "Russia does not acknowledge its participation in the war. But if you listen to their conversations over the radio, you will hear they are speaking pure Russian, the kind that no one in this part of Ukraine speaks." From his perspective, their accents were evidence that the movement for greater independence was foreign born. This, too, justified the military defense that was underway.

Other markers of difference included their discussions of navigation: "And they are obviously foreign because they are using the phone navigation and asking about addresses, the kind of information that locals would omit in conversations among themselves. They ask addresses that any local would know, like the street address of the mall." These imposters were sub-human because of the gratuitous, Rambo-esque shooting sprees they carried out without any regard for the safety of others. He called it "Aleppo-ization," referencing the war in Syria because they shot so indiscriminately. The mercenaries were also a lesser class from the perspective that they were operating for pay, not out of ideological conviction.

Visual

The people who waged this war could also be distinguished as other visually. Artem described how the phenotypic markers that could be tracked were crucial: "Those guys were obviously not locals. They had these beards. You know, with wide cheekbones? Our faces are mostly oval, and they had such round skulls, such wide faces. People in our town rarely have beards." He was especially upset because they had apparently disrupted a public prayer vigil by surrounding the people who were praying and challenging what they were doing. Although the color of their skin is not mentioned, this man is using a racial typology to distinguish an "us" and "them."

Among the enemy others were mercenaries who played a crucial role in the initial stages of the war. This was a time in which official Russian forces were working behind the scenes, and Chechen and other forces were fighting in their stead. Victoria witnessed this as follows: "They're rolling around outside, carrying AA [anti-artillery] guns, big guns, there were KAMAZ [large, heavy-duty trucks made in the Kama Auto Plant] trucks driving around with tons of Chechens in them, about 100 to 200 people. They were driving them, simply a horde, like an animal herd. Really, a herd. And that was it." She and her husband decided to leave. Figuring the forces as animal herds also exemplifies practical orientalism. If in sci-fi terms, the boundaries between human and nonhuman animal were breaking down, this disintegration of boundaries is especially significant because it was less civilized beings, lesser beings, that were taking over. This folds into everyday war because it was a way of participating in the logic of conflict in the midst of a crisis surrounding who was in charge and who belonged.

Victoria was not alone in registering the mercenaries as "animals." From her perspective, the group that rolled in was not fully human. The fear for their safety was magnified by stereotypes about Chechens left over from Russia's historic conflict with the breakaway republic of Chechnya. As a result of Russia's colonial domination of Chechnya and the Chechens' violent resistance, Chechens are, in the minds of many locals, equated with "savages" and "terrorists."

These processes of dehumanization went both ways. The people trying to leave the conflict zone also felt dehumanized into a "herd." As Bohdan described one of the checkpoints: "A large number of people turns into a herd. All humanity disappears there along with compassion for children, for elderly people. Well, people lose this." Getting through the checkpoints often meant standing out in the cold or the heat. Weathering the elements while unable to move freely led some people to liken their situation to being in a "concentration camp," another sign of feeling dehumanized.

Perhaps the most poignant description of the internal hierarchy that I heard was a mother whose young son watched his native Luhansk being taken over. He had a front row seat from the window in their high-rise apartment. For him, she said, it was like one of his video games. Straddling the unreal and real, he would tirelessly call out their adversaries from his windowed perch: "ours!" "not ours!" "ours," "not ours!" The game lost its flavor for him when they reached Kherson and it was only "ours" around, but the danger of the "game" was very real.

Getting in and Getting out: A Gendered Aporia

A crucial part of getting in or out of the zone was traversing the checkpoints punctuating the line of demarcation. We may recall that these posts were instituted on the Ukrainian side to prevent "terrorists" from entering the government-controlled parts of the country and on the DNR and LNR sides to control the flow of threatening *banderovtsi* and "Nazis" from Ukraine.

In this weird sci-fi world, femininity itself was described as having mutated. As Darina, a woman who returned to the Donetsk People's Republic with her teenage son for a visit, complained: "And when we were entering [DNR], we stopped [at the checkpoint] and a woman with too much makeup [on] and [finger] nails on her gun approached us. People said these were fingers, I said: no, these are giant TALONS, and she was so painted herself, in some unusual camouflage, with a beastly expression on her face . . . She seemed to be the leader, the ataman. I recalled at once the fairy tale about the Snow Queen: this person reminded me of something from that story, but it wasn't funny at all, it was scary." It is telling that Darina recalls a fairy tale in which the central conflict is between good and evil, and a main plot line is leaving the cold emotionless world to recover the world of tears and caring. The use of "talons" for nails and "beastly" for the expression on the woman's face point to a practical orientalism in which the guard embodied the kind of otherness that must be resisted or at least blocked from spreading. The excessive, badly applied makeup made it possible to liken her countenance to a scene from a horror movie. She said her distaste for the guard was so obvious that her son told her to lower her eyes lest she offend the woman with her stare and incur her wrath.

The discomfort she describes suggests that from her perspective at least, guards who jump gender barriers are like aliens or mutants. Although a number of people described female guards in this way, the narrators were all women, pointing to deeper concerns about losing their femininity in a time of war. Based on the buffer zone's weak rule of law, it is a reasonable conjecture that a masculinized persona could have been protective. In the eyes of other women, however, this produced a persona that was too masculine. Her drag was so over the top, it qualified as alien. The anxiety surrounding people perceived as half-man, half-woman reveals a somatic layer of gender distress, not necessarily in the guards, but in the people who observed them. Regardless of what the guards were aiming to accomplish (respect? preventing physical harm?), in the words of the IDPs who noticed what they called "creatures," a profound disruption appeared to be taking place.

Like Darina, Natalya struggled to find an apt description: "At the entrance to Gorlovka, there is a DNR roadblock, where there are these . . . men, women . . . I don't know what I should call them." In these statements, the apparently "bestial" quality of the women seems to reflect the bestial quality at least believed to inhere in the DNR itself.

It is precisely the in-between quality of the guards' gender identity that was disquieting. The importance of clear classifications for stabilizing lived worlds has been studied by anthropologist Mary Douglas. In *Purity and Danger*, she notes that the violation of established categories is perceived not so much as wrong or incorrect as dangerous (Douglas 1966). Women who became like men were perceived to have undermined the most intimate and relied-upon order.

Practical orientalism enables us to surface how traumatic experiences were shot through with awareness of difference. One limitation of the concept's use here is that it does not enable us to disaggregate the full variety of individuals. We risk reinforcing the dichotomy between us and them. Another limitation is that practical orientalism assumes official discourses are translated into everyday practices until they inflect the visual, olfactory, and emotional experience of difference (Herzfeld, 1997). What if this translation is not top down but more multidirectional? Finally, practical orientalism is concerned with the habitual, everyday ways that cultural difference is enacted and practiced through the body and senses. In the conflict over Donbas, this was hardly a stable, uniform or habitual process because the previously familiar social landscape became so strange.

Still, practical orientalism takes us farther toward understanding the lives of people forcibly displaced by the war in Donbas than liminality. The forced migrants who describe their experiences of a sci-fi reality in this chapter were anything but socially and structurally ambiguous: they were becoming acutely aware of their marked difference in the process of being forced out of their homes by violence. And many were excessively legible by virtue of harboring pro-Ukrainian sentiments or participating in pro-Maidan politics. Far from an "anti-structure" or "realm of pure possibilities" (Turner 1967: 97), then, military violence registered in embodied experiences and was reflected in both forced migration and growing disdain for the people who either harbored separatist sentiments or advanced their interests.

"None of This Will Be Resolved Any Time Soon"

Once settled in government-controlled parts of Ukraine, the people who had fled Donbas often spoke about being not only psychologically but physically changed by their experiences. One woman described how when she went back, people she had associated with for years no longer recognized her: something was very different about her. Several people described how the effects of the military conflict were still being worked out of their system through their teeth, which were falling out at an alarming rate, necessitating dentures.

The work of unraveling trauma is important to peace and reconciliation (Berkman 2004; Berents 2015; Crespo and Fernandez-Lansac 2016). Empathy and re-humanization are known to be beneficial (Licklider 1995; Halpern and Weinstein 2004). What often went unspoken in government-controlled parts of

Ukraine was that the people in nongovernment-controlled areas had legitimate aspirations for freedom, prosperity, and independence. This was a topic about which the professionals who built practices around care ethics were most articulate. I often heard it expressed that the end to the military hostilities is not the same as the arrival of peace. As Denys, a mental health professional, suggested, "If people think that with the end of shooting peace will start, they are mistaken and they are not ready to listen." Rather, the path out of terrifying strangeness, to his way of thinking, must be found in the recognition of common humanity.

Working against the vocabulary of herds and zombies, another professional I call Anna also tried to model recognition of common humanity: "They [the people of Donbas] also want normal living conditions. They want the same things you want. It's just that we've been separated, but we lack intelligence to throw away all that tinsel and realize that we're similar. We've got similar faces, we are of the same blood, of the same species, and . . . it is nonsense to separate. [The military conflict] will continue until we, Ukrainians, realize that we're of the same blood. That there are no monsters there, and until they realize that we're normal people here, we'll have this situation in Ukraine." Indeed, negative peace (the mere absence of conflict) doesn't allow for relationships to be fully restored or new institutions to meet the needs of the population to be built.

With other scholars of peace, however, I recognize the binary of positive and negative peace creates too stark a contrast. The journey through the sci-fi world of mutants and the escape from zombified friends and families points to collective suffering that made the forcibly displaced rethink who they were and where they belonged. This is to say encountering the military conflict produced a crisis of meaning that was partially managed by constructing the pro-separatist contingent in their midst as other.

Professionals I spoke with argued the embodied nature of this process would require a protracted healing period. One of the things psychologists like Anna and Denys tried to do was inform the rest of the medical community. As Anna put it: "It is very typical for IDPs to go from one doctor to the next. They go from the cardiologist to the neurologist and onward. They are thinking that their symptoms are physical. Doctors need training in order to be able to refer patients [to an appropriate kind of care] when they find that nothing is physically wrong. Not every doctor will recognize this." Unfortunately, the hallmarks of trauma were everywhere to be found, especially in the inability to adapt, fearful reactions to ordinary noises, sleeplessness, anger, and depression. These experiences cannot be neatly tied up. It is more a matter of learning to live with the ways that the war came to live inside them, and learning to live with the losses. The loss I have been most concerned with in this chapter has to do with people's altered way of being in the world. The homes, schools, and roads in the DNR and LNR can be repaired. The people who lived through their destruction, however, adopted a different way of thinking, feeling, and relating to themselves and one another.

This chapter has aimed to capture the sense of everyday sci-fi that pervaded the conflict zone where people's lived truth, as the saying goes, seemed stranger than fiction. The significance of the ethically motivated caring around the conflict zone—one of this book's through-lines—becomes more meaningful, I think, against the backdrop of loss and fragmentation. What can be gained by dwelling at the intersection of embodied trauma and embodied difference is a deeper appreciation of everyday war that establishes and enforces social boundaries.

Stated slightly differently, the everyday war readers have encountered in other chapters enabling people like Larysa to give her only son and people like Oleksandra to provision her sniper father with night vision goggles makes increasing sense at the intersection of embodied trauma and embodied othering. Buying tactical gloves and sending one's only son to war made more sense if the people of Donetsk or Luhansk were damaged, under a spell, zombified, bestial, or foreign. In this chapter, we witness the process of developing an embodied sense of difference from the people in nongovernment-controlled territories. Calling loved ones "zombies" was a rhetorical act of everyday war because zombification suggests that they are not fully human. I have therefore argued that trauma to body and mind catalyzed entry into a "sci-fi" world expressed through practical forms of orientalism.

The frame of mind tracked here is one in which the world seemed fantastical and had a science-fictional quality. While the cold world of the Snow Queen was left behind and challenges like "savages," "herds," and "creatures" were successfully confronted, the people that fled carry the memories of upsetting experiences with them. It may someday be possible to go back physically, but everything, it seems, has changed.

THE VOLUNTEER BODY COLLECTORS OF UKRAINE

Outsourcing Undertaking and Smuggling
Pediatric Insulin

"Maggots. And the smell. You can't forget the smell of a body that's been laying in a field for over a month," wrote Taras. He led a unit of men that was part of the Black Tulips, a group of volunteers engaged in crossing enemy lines to recover the remains of soldiers left behind by the retreating Ukrainian army. The Black Tulips adopted their name from the eponymous flights filled with dead Soviet soldiers being returned from Afghanistan in the 1980s. This chapter considers the Black Tulips' work and argues they exemplify the recalibration of personal values and priorities that was occurring as a result of war. Despite strict limitations placed on accessing the separatist-controlled territories, the volunteer body collectors were able to fulfill what they felt to be deep moral obligations in nongovernment-controlled territory, offering the bereaved peace of mind if not peace itself.[1] In this context, dead bodies carry political meaning, and the stories of their retrieval reveal something about personal transformation and how the war prompted people to care for others and take responsibility in ways they had not before.

I began puzzling through the politics of death surrounding fallen soldiers when I encountered stories about the Black Tulips on Radio Liberty/Radio Free Europe. Based on the number of interviews I had conducted between 2015 and 2017, I suspected I already knew someone who was involved with them in some way. It turned out that Kyrylo, who was quoted in the introduction and chapter 7 of this book, had worked with them. Kyrylo was the man who so aptly described the geography of risk using the colors of a stoplight. Kyrylo also put me in touch with Taras, who had worked as a Black Tulip. I should reiterate here that in this chapter, considering the sensitivity of this material, I assign pseudonyms to people who already went by pseudonyms and leave out the names of the specific places where they lived and worked. Kyrylo and Taras read and approved this chapter prior to its publication.

The Black Tulips

The Black Tulips began driving into separatist-controlled territory to retrieve bodily remains in September 2014. With little more than vests to identify them as noncombatants and masks to reduce the smell, these volunteers crossed battle lines, circumnavigated landmines, and sifted through shallow graves to do their retrieval work. The group delivered the soldiers' bodies—or pieces of them—to military authorities and morgues in Ukrainian government-controlled territory. Recovering the bodies was nothing short of macabre. In addition to being charred or dismembered by artillery fire, abandoned remains were often partially eaten by insects and wild animals. By the time they were reached, the corpses had of course begun to decompose. Recovering the bodies was no small task: in their eleven months of work between September 2014 and July 2015, the Black Tulips brought back 609 bags of various weights and sizes, filled with human remains.[2] Since the majority of the remains were not whole bodies but pieces, the Black Tulips were not in a position to state exactly how many people this represents.

The Black Tulips were able to carry out this mission because they took a staunchly neutral stance. They did not just pass through separatist-controlled territory to get the bodies. Separatists, some of them infamous, sat in the passenger seats of their vans to guide them to the rotting remains. They formed relationships of a sort. With time, the separatists requested that their side's dead be transported as well. The work of the Black Tulips therefore takes us deeper into the interpersonal peace that characterized the early stages of the conflict over Donbas.

The Tulips were inspired to become involved in September 2014 after the battle of Ilovaisk, when Ukrainian forces experienced a terrible defeat and many bodies were left behind. The Ukrainian military was so outgunned that it was all they could do to retreat with those who were still alive. Yaroslav Zhilkin is credited with first organizing the Black Tulips. He was a forty-three-year-old businessman when he first stepped into this gruesome world, and his main qualification was his participation in a club that recovered remains from Soviet battle sites, especially from World War II. Using metal detectors and other tools they purchased with their own savings, they spent weekends combing over battle sites that the Soviet government had ignored. Their objective was to find the remains of Red Army soldiers so they could be identified, honored, and given a dignified burial.

The group's connection to the world wars was more significant than one might imagine. The Black Tulip member I spoke with stressed that the group had earned credibility because of its excavations of World War II sites. In former Soviet areas, World War II is known as the Great Patriotic War and recalls the catastrophic sacrifices of those who helped defeat Nazi Germany. Over a period of decades, the Black Tulips had become well-known not just in Ukraine, but throughout the countries of the former Soviet Union for bringing dignity to the heroes of that war, even though the remains they recovered were mostly just bone fragments, medals, and epaulets. When the conflict over Donbas broke out, they were already highly esteemed. Without this reputation, they told me, it is unlikely they would have been permitted to recover the bodies at all. While the recovery of corpses from the war in Donbas represents some continuity with combing through battle sites of the world wars, the discontinuities are more significant. The missions to nongovernment controlled areas entailed taking gargantuan risks. The emotional toll to oneself and one's family were not trivial. There is also the fact that the government should have compensated them for their service. The Ukrainian Ministry of Defense, however, had effectively "outsourced" undertaking to whomever would take up this charge.

A Sacred Task: A Short History of Moving the Dead

From time immemorial, recovering soldiers' remains has been a hallowed duty. Many countries spare no effort or expense to recover the bodies of the people who give their lives for their country (Lindsay 2013). Facilitating, or at least not obstructing, the return of human remains is also a matter of humanitarian law. The Geneva Conventions, considered the cornerstone of international humanitarian law, seek to limit the effects of armed conflict. The Conventions, which have been ratified by all UN member states, lay out the specific standards for treatment of persons who have not participated or are no longer participating in hostilities. This includes prisoners, the shipwrecked, medical workers, civilians, and the dead. The conventions are considered "customary law," which means they apply whether or not a country has gone through the steps of signing and ratifying the treaties, making them binding on all states and parties to a conflict.

Moral thinking about the war dead runs deeper still, having been expressed in Homer's *Iliad* from around 800 BCE. In Homer's view, the gods stipulated that the decent burial of slain warriors is "the due" of the dead, casting it with strong moral overtones. Homer's *Iliad* (book 16, lines 569–683) contains a condemnation of any mutilation of the bodies of opponents and a denunciation of any refusal to return a body as immoral (*Iliad*, book 24, 569–683). The earliest historical record of a country bringing its fallen soldiers home across political borders was made by the famous Greek historian Thucydides. He described such an event taking place during the Peloponnesian Wars between Greece and Sparta (fifth century BCE). According to Thucydides's account, the remains of the dead were taken across political boundaries to Athens, where they were laid out with flowers in tents that had been set up so that family and friends could mourn them. After the period of mourning, so crucial to the grieving process as a whole, the bodies were placed in coffins and solemnly buried.

Subsequently, the practice faded in importance until the American Civil War, when bringing rank-and-file soldiers home became an issue. As one soldier during the American Civil War wrote, "It is dreadful to contemplate being killed on the field of battle without a kind hand to hide one's remains from the eye of the world or the gnawing of animals or buzzards."[3] President Abraham Lincoln responded to the increasingly widespread sentiment that the retrieval of remains is the only morally correct course of action by signing a bill to establish new national cemeteries. With time, the practice spread and came to be seen as a sacred duty to those who make what has been called the ultimate sacrifice. Envision for a moment your own remains lying in a ditch, being picked at by birds of prey and "gnawed" by animals. This profoundly unsettling prospect was within the realm of possibility for the men and women serving in Ukraine's armed services after some military encounters. What did it mean that this task—sacred in the eyes of so many—was left to volunteers? Grasping how the task of body collection could be left to volunteers, and how volunteers had risked their lives to take up this charge, stands to enhance our comprehension of the centrality of civilians in contemporary conflicts. This chapter therefore takes readers through steps toward finding answers.

Dead Body Politics

How, then, might we best think about the dead who were left behind by the retreating Ukrainian army in Donbas? Did leaving bodies behind at sites of battle constitute acts of commission or omission? What Kyrylo had to say was illuminating. From his perspective, with the conflict over Donbas, Ukrainian society had reached a moment in which it had to rethink how it dealt with dead bodies.[4] When the conflict broke out, Kyrylo argued, his country had not yet freed itself from the Soviet values that placed the collective above the individual. The many remains of soldiers who fought in the Great Patriotic War lying unburied and uncared for speaks to the culture surrounding death. The rank-and-file soldiers were viewed as a homogenous mass, not individual subjects with personal histories and rights. By contrast, Kyrylo said, a human rights approach calls for treating the dead as you would the living. The conflict over Donbas, Kyrylo felt, had provoked Ukrainians to shift their perspective and begin to think differently about the value of human life, a topic we return to in a moment.

Wanting to avoid a monocausal explanation, I probed Kyrylo a bit more as to why, as a practical matter, the Ukrainian military did not do more to recover these remains. He believed the Ukrainian authorities faced a Sophie's choice. With the Ukrainian military in shambles, they had to prioritize either helmets and vests for the living or coffins and refrigerated trucks for the dead. They chose the former until it was possible to also add the latter. This view certainly nests well in the factual reality that, as discussed in chapters 1 and 2, the military had been allowed to fall into disrepair on the (now obviously empty) promise that their territorial integrity would not be violated and that the United States would defend them militarily if their territorial integrity and sovereignty were breached. To summarize what Kyrylo argued, then, Ukraine's Soviet cultural legacy and the impoverished state of its military were contributing factors as to why the Ukrainian government was so slow to take up the recovery of fallen soldiers.

Many researchers of war and displacement turn to Mbembe's influential work on the relationship between death and politics to understand the role of political power in the often-avoidable deaths of millions of people. Inspired by Giorgio Agamben's 1995 book *Homo Sacer*, Mbembe's *necropolitics* describes politics in which sovereign power works not so much through managing a population's biological life force, Michel Foucault's contention (1988; 1983; 1979), as through the ability to determine which lives can be treated as disposable. Mbembe's aim was to help explain the prevalence of politically organized suffering and death. In his words, "the capacity to define who matters and who does not, who is disposable and who is not" (Mbembe 2003, 27) is an exercise of sovereignty. Viewed through the lens of necropolitics, the "instrumentalization" of human lives and the discarding and destruction of physical bodies whether already dead or still alive can be viewed as a core function of sovereignty (Mbembe 2003, 14).

One of the problems with using this explanation to understand Ukraine, however, is that in treating the soldiers' bodies as disposable, the Ukrainian government was not singling out any particular group. By definition, necropolitics operate according to an exclusionary logic (think apartheid or the death camps of the Third Reich for the most paradigmatic examples). In contrast, the Ukrainian government extended equal opportunities to those who died in battle. Moreover, four years into the conflict, the Ministry of Defense stepped up its efforts to help its military and civilian population, including issuing identification to soldiers, inaugurating a database for the dead and missing, and creating a Department of Civil-Military Cooperation (CIMIC) to help the civilian population in areas affected by military conflict.[5] Trying to understand the politics of these corpses solely through necropolitics steers us away from what people on the ground cared about most. Based on my conversations with individuals who had lived or worked behind enemy lines, what was most salient was the ability to fulfill moral imperatives in spite of state failures and party politics.

Whilst a rich body of literature exists on the relationship between death and power, what has received less attention is the relationship between death and care, the topic I turn to next.

The Recovery Mission

When the head of the Black Tulips put out a call for subgroups to assist with recovery missions, Taras was among those who responded. He was well qualified to help, having worked in a professional capacity in a field that was directly applicable to managing the hazards in the non-controlled territories. When I asked him to describe a memorable mission, he thought about it for a while before relating a story that expresses how his work was animated by ethically motivated caring. I invite readers to think about the goings-on around corpses as another dimension of ethically motivated caring and part of a much larger process in which norms and values were being recalibrated. My aim is to show the meanings that were being made by people working in the midst of human death. The politics of corpses, I found, was less about power (although clearly it could potentially be that, too) than about practices of care. In describing their missions, Black Tulips also describe the (re)construction of values and meanings. In effect, they enact their morals and ethics in the midst of witnessing a plethora of amoral acts. What is moral and ethical in these stories is necessarily partial and deeply situated. In the rest of the chapter, we consider the tension between harm and grace behind the front line.

To fully appreciate his story, it helps to know the recovery missions were organized into shifts of approximately ten days. In teams of five to eight people, volunteers traveled to the front lines from all over Ukraine. The base camp from which they launched retrieval operations was no more than a tent camp in an abandoned fruit orchard. The shift work did not allow for much sleep, and any rest they got had to be stolen from the elements because the old tents were peppered with holes and easily became soaked through with rain. The "facilities" were, as one might imagine, out in the open. When winter approached, the military gave them permission to use a partially destroyed home in an abandoned village near the line of demarcation. To hear Taras describe it, the scene appeared post-apocalyptic, but they pooled their efforts to repair the dwelling and make it as livable as they could. It served their purpose all the way until the work was terminated by the authorities of the DNR and LNR in 2016.

The working conditions were challenging to say the least. They had to bring their own food, mostly dry rations that would not spoil without refrigeration, and this was only sometimes supplemented by military supplies. Plus, the decrepit, domestically manufactured minivans they drove had what Taras referred to as temper tantrums, breaking down whenever and wherever they pleased. In Taras's group, the guys withstood it all, but he told me this was not the case for some other teams. Haunted by terrible sights and smells, it was difficult to return home, they said, having traversed this land of the unburied dead. Nightmares and sightings of ghosts could follow these missions.

It was late October or early November 2015 when Taras's group of seven men gathered in the office where they had previously discussed expeditions to search for World War II remains. This time was different because they had agreed to work as Black Tulips. After reviewing their itinerary and identifying the location they would be surveying, they piled into the van. Just as Taras was about to tell the driver to push off, however, two women peering at the closed and shuttered office caught his eye. The way they were looking around made it clear they were upset. So Taras got out of the van and asked them if he could help. The younger of the two women told him they needed someone from [the subgroup] of the Black Tulips [name withheld] that Taras led. They told him they had heard about the work they were doing through social media channels.

Taras invited them into the office, where they told him that they were searching for the older woman's son, also the brother of the younger woman. The comrades of the man who was presumed dead had informed them of the location where they believed he may have died. But that was all they could offer. With tears streaming down her face, the mother recounted being bounced around from one military office to another in search of information about her son. This purgatorial search came to a stop when one of the military authorities advised her to wait: no one would be searching for the fallen soldiers until relations with the separatists improved. It was as if respect for her loss had gone missing with the body (and dignity) of her son.

Taras jotted down the location where the son and brother was believed to have been killed. The mother and daughter pair described him, elaborating on his distinguishing features, until Taras had a full picture. Perhaps the most unique feature was that (if his arm was still attached to his body) they would find a tattoo depicting a mythical creature on his right forearm. They exchanged phone numbers, Taras returned to the minivan, and the team headed out.

On their way to the base camp, Taras related what he had learned from the two women. Taras also briefed the guys on topics like how to handle themselves in the event of a firefight. From what I gathered, the time in the van was mission-critical. Taras reviewed how to behave around the dead bodies and gave them detailed precautions for working around potentially explosive material. Interaction with the separatists, with whom they disagreed politically, was also covered: conversation was to be kept to an absolute minimum; they would need to conduct themselves with utmost diplomacy while having their documents and personal belongings inspected by the separatist forces.

Having put a certain number of kilometers behind them, they arrived at the base camp a little before midnight. There they were met by Yaroslav Zhilkin, the Black Tulips' progenitor. He happened to be leading the recovery mission that Taras's group would be replacing. Zhilkin's team was made up of people from Kyiv that they already knew well from previous expeditions. In earlier times, they had combed the battlefields of both world wars together. After a warm reunion, Zhilkin's team pulled Taras's crew into the tent, where they were fed a big dinner. Over coffee, Zhilkin's group shared their experiences crossing various posts and interacting with the separatists. Taras maintains the word "separatists" should be in scare quotes because his encounters with these individuals led him to believe this was far too charitable a term for people who had been terrorizing the residents of Donbas. The word "separatists" implies they had potentially legitimate political goals—exactly what Taras believed they lacked. While the term separatist may not be ideal, it is preferable to the "terrorist" label then used by the Ukrainian government.

The two teams talked late into the night, with Zhilkin providing more advanced instructions on the finer points of exhumations on uncontrolled territory. Finally, it was time to rest. They got up just a few hours later, however, because it was time to meet the Ukrainian serviceman who would accompany them on their next leg of the journey. So they quickly pulled themselves together, filled the tank with gas, and loaded up their dry rations. With the serviceman on board, they set out for the "ground zero" block post. It should be explained that the zero block post was the one closest to the line of demarcation between the warring parties. It marked the end of Ukrainian government-controlled territory. The atmosphere in the van that morning was so tense they scarcely said a word the whole way. They proceeded without stopping through the Ukrainian zero post, where the guards seemed surprised to see anyone at all, and just waved them through. The oncoming traffic, by contrast, was prodigious. People and cars heading into the government-controlled territory filled the road.

After a few kilometers, however, the landscape emptied precipitously. When they pulled up to the separatist-controlled block post, one of the DNR fighters motioned for them to park. They pulled over and killed the engine. It was here that the reality of what they were about to undertake hit them: looking to the right and to the left, they saw Ukrainian army vehicles that had been practically incinerated after venturing into the separatist-controlled territory just a few weeks before. The ground was festooned with all kinds of shot-up equipment and twisted metal debris, and the grass was charred to ash. After a few minutes, an armed man in camouflage came up to them and asked them to open the trunk of the van for inspection. They obliged. He also reviewed the men's identity documents. During this entire time, the group sat in frozen silence, the tension mounting. One of the guys made a small joke about the situation, but it fell flat.

After these formalities the commander, who was an infamous separatist, told them they could get on with their mission. But access was complicated: traveling through this territory required a chain of handlers, and because of landmines and the possibility of sniper fire, a wrong turn on one of the gutted roads could easily prove fatal. They had been assigned a guide, who met them on the road deeper into the separatist-controlled territory. Taras described him as looking like a walk-on character in an amateur play. In a country where men tend to be impeccably groomed, he had long disheveled hair, and his facial features seemed to have been conquered by a large and unkempt beard. He wore a long, dilapidated trench coat over his camouflage, which, Taras noted, was of the old Soviet variety. The whole assemblage was topped off by a woolen beret. Slung over one shoulder was a Soviet-era rifle to match. It was more of a prop than a weapon: Taras told me they eventually learned the sight on the rifle was broken and it shot badly. The guide also carried a bag with a homemade sandwich and rags to clean his rifle and its cartridges. He seated himself on the passenger side and introduced himself using his code name. Then they pressed on, periodically phoning the commander for approval to proceed onward. Kilometer after kilometer, they were confronted by mangled and burned equipment, empty towns and villages.

Arriving at the designated field, they began cautiously searching a section of the field where long grasses met the forest. About 350 meters from where they started, they discovered four bodies. Judging by the way they lay in an even row, with about three meters between them, they had been moved there. Taras speculated that whoever had moved them had helped themselves to any valuables they could find. The men's bags, disgorged of their contents, lay scattered. Casings from the mortar shelling were everywhere. The group got to work taking pictures of the location, the bodies, and the scattered belongings using a cell phone camera. Then they started their examination, writing down their description of the bodies, the clothing, tattoos, dentures, and contents of pockets. Taras reflected, "I have to give the boys credit. To see a corpse for the first time, and one that had been lying there for a month, with an abundance of insect larvae and a terrible smell, and force oneself to carry out a body search without losing the contents of one's stomach." When it came time to inspect the body of the third fighter, they saw he was tall, with a strong physique. He was dressed in army camouflage with a flak jacket on top. Taras stuck to the protocol, directing the sequence for the guys to follow. When they reached the inner pockets, they found an aluminum flask with a cloth cover. Knowing from their experiences searching World War II battlefields that flasks can be inscribed, they removed the fabric cover and their hopes were realized. The initials of the first and last names and patronymic were scratched on the back of the flask. "The three letters just exploded in my brain. They corresponded to the initials of the fighter the women were searching for. Hardly believing our luck, I asked M., who was searching the body, to push up the sleeve on the right forearm. There was the tattoo! The mythical creature, exactly as they had described." The remains and personal belongings of the victims were packed in body bags and loaded into the van. Most of us, I believe, can only guess at the enormity of having four badly decomposed soldiers to transport. Taras said the formalities at the separatists' block post went smoothly enough on the way out, but they had to put up with humiliating comments like "ukrop" toward the dead. To explain, "ykrop" is to Ukrainians what "Kike" is to Jews. Although there have been efforts to reappropriate the word (lit. "dill"), it is intended as an insult.

After reporting back on their first day, those who had recovered their appetites ate dinner. According to the rules, it was strictly prohibited for them to contact the relatives of the dead. Therefore, they could not even think about informing the mother that they had located a body they suspected was her son.

Taras recalled that his cell phone must have rung around 10 p.m. It was, predictably, the mother Taras had met prior to the mission. Prohibited from telling her about their find, however, Taras made vague references to rain that had ostensibly delayed them. I do not have any insight into why he set himself up in that particular way, but at this point in his story, he sprang into action, seeking out the deceased soldier's platoon commander through the servicemen on the nearby military base in the hopes that the commander could inform the mother. Although he was able to reach the commander by cell phone, the commander said he could not assist because he was on duty at a different post. His military protocol explains why he took a call from Taras, but was not allowed to dial one to the soldier's mother.

The mother called repeatedly, and Taras repeatedly followed the rules and made excuses. By the fourth call, however, he could no longer stand to hear her suffer. And frustrated by the military's inability to help, he told her what the team had found. After listening to his description of the tattoo, the flask, and other features, the mother replied, "That's him," thanked Taras, and hung up. The tsunami of mixed emotions, Taras told me, was enough to make him feel like banging his head against the wall.

When the family's knowledge was disclosed at the evening debriefing, the head of the mission lost his temper at Taras. Taras knew he had it coming. He said he was sorry, but ultimately, he had followed his conscience instead of the rules and did not regret sharing his information with the mother. Taras bucked the protocol because in this situation, the communication protocol seemed arbitrary and violated his ethics and his purpose for being on the mission. If, as philosopher Paul Ricoeur proposed, ethics have most fundamentally to do with how one lives well *with* others and *for* others (1994), Taras's choice to speak was intended to relieve the suffering of the bereaved family. It is this kind of ethical thinking, I suggest, that repairs the social fabric. With the remains of their son and brother found, the mother and daughter could finally grieve. Taras and people like him risked their lives to restore the dignity of the dead and ease the living's emotional burdens. Words like "ordinary" and "everyday" seem out of place when describing the volunteer body collectors.

Deeply moved by the work he was doing, I asked Taras what motivated him. After all, he had risked his life, born witness to others' violent deaths, and weathered extreme discomfort. It was one of those anthropologically inelegant questions, however, because from his perspective there should be no question. He replied that he did what every person in his or her right mind was doing: trying to defend the country against an existential threat. He said he found meaning in doing what he could and it was preferable to remaining idle. He seemed to traverse both geographies of emotion described in chapter 7 because he had to minimize the danger of landmines, sniper attacks, and other risks to do his job at the same time that he was ethically motivated to care about dead people he did not know and their families.

The ethics of the volunteer body collectors is not an isolated occurrence. In his ethnography of death in Japanese society, Mathew Marr notes that in Japan a respectful burial could not take place without being connected to a patriline. He adopted the term *necrosociality* to describe social innovation surrounding burial in Japan where people have devised ways to offer an honorable burial that is untethered to familial patrilines and the state. He uses *necrosociality* to describe an ongoing "relationship" to the dead. In the process of sustaining care, all kinds of connections among diverse groups of the living were also forged. Marr contends that through their concern for dead strangers, the Japanese people concerned found new common interests (Marr 2019, 1). The larger significance of these relations is that they compensate for the failure of social safety nets resulting from the workings of neoliberal capitalism in Japan (Marr 2019). The Black Tulips' work can be described as *necrosocial* in the sense that it establishes new relationships, substantiating that individuals affected by war care for one another creatively when previous ways of life have been disrupted.

Bodies . . . and Pediatric Insulin

Kyrylo's work can take us more deeply into some of these connections. He headed an organization that provided assistance, primarily in the form of medical support, to disabled children. This effort started in 2010, and when the conflict over Donbas began, he and his colleagues added operations to deliver meals and medicines to the front lines in two towns [names withheld]. One day on business at an orphanage in this area, Kyrylo got to talking with a nurse. She told him the children faced a terrifying predicament. Insulin had been free in peaceful times, but the supply chain was broken as a result of the war and strict controls on everything passing into the DNR. This was an especially pressing problem because neither Ukraine nor Russia actually manufactured insulin for children. It hadn't occurred to the de facto leaders of DNR or LNR to identify a new source. Simple workarounds like the postal service were out because there *was* no mail to the DNR or LNR. How, then, to get insulin, which needs to be refrigerated, to the children who needed it to stay alive?

What else needs to be refrigerated? Dead bodies. It was brilliant. An agreement was made whereby body collectors would bring insulin into the DNR when they traveled to get human remains out. Kyrylo rushed out and purchased his own body bags. The insulin was then loaded into the unused bags and slid into the back of the trucks destined to retrieve the remains of dead soldiers. Recalling the revelation that insulin and the dead could move in opposite directions, Kyrylo chuckled that at the time, he had felt like a drug dealer. As a matter of fact, he *was* dealing in illicit drugs in the eyes of the separatist authorities. But the thing was, when the guards at the checkpoints opened the back of the trucks to inspect the cargo, the smell was so unpleasant that they closed the vehicles back up rather than unzip the bags. It turned out that in this context, insulin and the dead made perfect partners. This "kula ring" lasted from spring 2015 until the fall of the same year. The Melanesian circular trade rings studied by Bronislaw Malinowski, known as kula, connected thousands of people traveling hundreds of miles by canoe with the purpose of exchanging decorative arm bands, necklaces, etc. made from shells. As Malinowski pointed out, items were traded across many islands in what constituted a gift economy (1922). At the risk of oversimplifying, he was striving to show the tremendous risks undertaken were hardly frivolous and indeed rational. Like these rings, the circular trade of bodies and insulin, also more about social obligations than monetary value, connected thousands of people. The corpses and insulin circuit came to an end in November or December, Kyrylo recalls, when the separatist authorities had worked out an arrangement for obtaining insulin via Russia.

Kyrylo estimated that more than one hundred children would have died had it not been for the smuggling operation over a six-month period. He recommended I look at the website of his organization for more information. When I visited and did not see any text explaining their activities, I was initially perplexed. There were only pictures. I scrolled and scrolled through the images of people, the vast majority of them children, holding cardboard boxes with insulin. Then it hit me. The smiling faces had been made possible by the circular exchange. As a practical matter, the images documented that the funds Kyrylo's organization obtained from charitable sources and private donors were being spent as directed: the medicines had reached their intended beneficiaries, not a black market. The story these images tell, however, also portends more. The flow of insulin to and bodies from the separatist-controlled territories illustrates the relationship that became evident between violent conflict and ever-evolving practices of care. In places where societies were being actively torn apart by the military conflict, social connections were rebuilt with the traffic in corpses and insulin.

Both the care for corpses and the care for children upend the traditional account of what qualifies as moral reasoning. As articulated by prominent philosophers like John Rawls, the highest moral development entails arriving at a state of detachment and separation in which decisions are made based on a rational, autonomous, and disembodied self (Hekman 1995) unencumbered by culture, emotion, or embodied experience. In *A Theory of Justice*, Rawls treats morality based on love and connection as inferior because it is contingent (1971, 26). Many researchers of ethics turn to Gilligan's work on care because it challenged the idea that there is linear development from lesser to greater moral reasoning (Gilligan et al. 1983, 1990). Subsequent writers on the topic (Ruddick 1989; Tronto 1993; Hekman 1995; Hankivsky 2004; Vaittinen at al. 2019) agree (although this necessarily glosses over the finer points of their arguments) that detachment and separation are not necessarily the best hallmarks for judging mature moral selfhood. It is therefore worthwhile to hold a space for ethics of care that can coexist with the abstract ethics of justice. Taras's treatment of dead bodies and the grieving mother exemplifies ethics that enact care. Similarly, Kyrylo's "drug smuggling" of pediatric insulin unfurls love for the future generations of the enemy's society: children. Their ethics gesture toward what Das called the "eventual everyday" (2012) because they model a world in which every life matters. The responsibilities they have been taking in the present help form future society based on respect for the dignity of the person, regardless of political sides.

What motivated Kyrylo? Before he was a humanitarian, he had been in business. He confided to me over the phone after I had returned to the United States that in the past, he had habitually thought in terms of efficiency and cost-benefit ratios. This meant that when he was planning a humanitarian delivery of some sort, he would postpone a trip if it meant he could work in multiple stops and save money. He confessed he thought the same way when he found out about the volunteers' body retrieval. He reported thinking to himself, "why transport the remains of one or two soldiers (as often happened) if they could be dealt with in bulk?" Then it so happened that on one occasion when he was planning a humanitarian mission to deliver food and medicine to a man (in a city that will remain unnamed here), it snowed. The resulting driving delays would add time and fuel costs. He decided to postpone the trip by a couple of days. When he pulled up to the man's private home in a small village, parked, and knocked on the front door, no one answered. He circled around to the back and tried again with the same result. Then a neighbor who heard the knocking came out. She explained that the man had committed suicide the day before. He had long suffered from depression, and when the food and medicine did not arrive as anticipated, he lost hope and took his own life.

Kyrylo was devastated. This experience was instrumental in what he described as "changing my mind about life." He said that whereas in the past he operated according to a business mindset, he experienced a significant shift in personal values beginning with the suicide because he began to see the problem with treating people in bulk, rather than in a way that ensured each and every life counted. Having testified to the destructive effects of war, and having borne witness to the work of groups like the Black Tulips, he embraced the core value that each and every life should be treated with the utmost care. There are also political impulses to be uncovered in all this.

Necroactivism

The necrosocial practices of care we have been exploring are closely related to the notion of *necroactivism*, developed by Noam Leshem, who takes an interest in the agency surrounding negotiations about the placement of human remains in the Israel-Palestine conflict (2015, 34). He suggests that tracking the forms of activism that center on the dead counters the unnecessarily negative picture conjured by writings on the necropolitical (Leshem 2015, 42). The kind of "resistant necropolitics from below" that Leshem wants to uncover are evident in Zhilkin's call for families of the deceased to make a case to the European Court of Human Rights regarding the treatment of their missing sons and daughters. In making this case, Zhilkin contrasted Ukraine's treatment of its dead soldiers with the efforts made by the United States, pointing out that when two American soldiers were missing, more than eight thousand troops and an entire team of paid forensic experts were sent to recover them (Miller 2014). Of course, the United States approached its dead with vastly more power, experience, and resources than a deeply indebted country facing an existential crisis like Ukraine. Another necroactivist practice by Zhilkin was challenging the death toll by publicizing the operations of his team, which recovered approximately four times the official death toll (Miller 2014). The International Commission on Missing Persons supported his contention that there was "systematic" undercounting on the part of the Ukrainian Ministry of Defense.[6] Zhilkin attempted to raise awareness so a more accurate death toll could facilitate a better accounting of the human costs of the war. There was also activism in establishing a Union of People's Memory to honor the dead and explain conditions at the front for the uninitiated. The union occupies a permanent exhibit space in Kyiv with dioramas depicting scenes from the front. Necroactivism illuminates additional facets of the relationship between death and care.

Interpersonal Peace

What are the implications of the volunteer body collectors' work for peace? Taras described how at first the separatist assigned to keep tabs on them in his second-hand gear seemed to be trying to create the impression that he was a seasoned warrior. Eventually, they all relaxed somewhat. Taras recounted: "In the early days of meeting him, it was clear that he was wary and could not decide how to relate to us. When we searched an area, he would withdraw to the side and, as it were, keep watch. When we laid out our simple dry rations to have lunch in the field, he walked off for a smoke and most likely remained hungry all day. Then, a few days later, I invited him to eat with us. He refused at first, but the guys insisted and he joined. . . . Over time, we learned that in peacetime he was a math teacher. . . . He explained his wariness by the fact that during his briefing, we had been presented [to him] as terrible Bandera and spies. Eventually he became so used to us that he could throw his weapons in the minibus and completely surrender to tinkering with the engine." I quote at length to show how interpersonal peace seeped into the interstices between opposing sides. The reason this particular separatist had resembled a walk-on in an amateur play was because he had trouble staying in character. As much as Taras lacked respect for the so-called separatists, his description of this man humanizes him: he gets hungry and feels lost at times. We can imagine the man buying his own gear at an internet website, or perhaps a secondhand store. He stopped accompanying them, they heard, because he went home to his wife in Russia for a break. Perhaps he will return to teaching school someday, or tell his children wild stories about his picnics with the "ukrops" and "banderovtsi."

The scene in the field Taras describes affords us an opportunity to reflect on one of the most significant criticisms of the concept of everyday peace, which is that it is a very limited form of peace (Mac Ginty 2014, 557). It is indeed clear that the various ways in which the volunteer body collectors forged interpersonal peace cannot necessarily be transformed into anything larger. In fact, all of the efforts to create interpersonal peace described in this book lacked the power to do anything to end the conflict itself. But that kind of criticism completely distorts the significance of everyday peace, which lies in its ability not to change the behavior and thinking of elites, but to make life more bearable for people affected by conflict (Heitmeyer 2009, 114; Sorabji 2008, 98). Interacting with his group's assigned separatist gradually led Taras to see something of a paper tiger instead of a staunch enemy. The machinations around the international peace process are less consequential here than the ability to deal with the separatists (something beyond the capacity of the official military). This ability enabled the volunteer body collectors to do things the official military could not: restore dignity to remains and provide closure to families. To criticize interpersonal or "everyday" peace efforts on the grounds they only effect a "limited" kind of peace is to return the focus to elites and to place the highest value on geopolitics.

The activities of the volunteer body collectors therefore provide a basis for countering the criticism that everyday peace is an inadequate form of peace (Heitmeyer 2009, 114; Sorabji 2008, 98). The volunteer body collectors of eastern Ukraine (and the interpersonal peace forged within friendships described in chapter 3) demonstrate the value of everyday peace at the interpersonal level. This chapter has connected everyday peace with care ethics and the ability to fulfill moral obligations.

What did it mean that the sacred task of tending to the dead was left to volunteers? For Taras and other body collectors, it was about providing peace of mind to bereaved loved ones and dignity to the dead. For Kyrylo, it was about extending the lives of children on the other side of enemy lines. In keeping with the invitation to think differently about military conflict articulated at the beginning of this book, this chapter has shown how (extraordinary) people were able to fulfill moral obligations across the line of demarcation. The bodies-to-insulin circuit explained in this chapter is indicative of something more far-reaching than a relationship that evolved between corpses and children. This circulation provides evidence that the state's inattention to people in and around the zone of conflict elicited ethically motivated caring.

I suggest that ethically motivated caring continues alongside, in spite of, and in response to conflict. The narratives and experiences of the people affected by the war went beyond hoping for an end to the conflict. Their stories also engaged questions of responsibility and connection. Part of what is at stake here is whether ample latitude can be created within studies of war, conflict, and population displacement to capture reassertions of human dignity and resilience. Volunteers like the ones described here provided threads of civility for knitting Ukrainians together across the line of demarcation and across politics. Whether or not this will still be possible after the 2022 Russian invasion of Ukraine remains to be seen. Although fragile and temporary, their work forged an interpersonal web that made life on the front lines less bleak.

Postscript: CIMIC

In 2018, Ukraine began issuing dog tags and passed a resolution to establish a register for the missing, as well as procedures for exhuming the dead.[7] The register will help write soldiers who gave their lives for their country in the early days of the conflict back into the history of the war. In 2018 a new unit within the Ministry of Defense, the Upravlinnya tsyvil'no-viys'kovoho spivrobitnytstva Zbroynykh Syl Ukrayiny or CIMIC (Office of Civil-Military Cooperation of the Armed Forces of Ukraine), was created. Their operations were regulated by Ukrainian Decree 998-r of the Cabinet of Ministers "On measures to perpetuate the memory of the defenders of Ukraine for the period up to 2020" as part of the humanitarian project Evacuation 200.

The civil-military cooperation was based on the model of NATO and intended to enable the armed forces (in this case of Ukraine) to collaborate with other military formations, law enforcement agencies, local authorities, public associations, organizations, and citizens where armed forces are deployed. While it is unfortunate this did not happen sooner, it represented a step in a positive direction.

CONCLUDING THOUGHTS

During my research, the conflict over the Donbas region of Ukraine was never declared a war. But the military activity there began seriously injuring, forcibly displacing, and taking lives, including those of civilians in 2014. This book set out to provide a better conceptual vocabulary for describing what happens to civilians in a time of war, without that war being declared, and without relying on what has been called "the suffering slot," by which is meant viewing survivors of conflict primarily as traumatized victims. Agreeing with Lauren Berlant that it is more worthwhile to track the formation of the "new ordinaries" (Berlant 2011) in a crisis-filled present, I focused on the mutual care people were able to foster in this difficult environment. The book points to the productive potential that inheres when there are ethics of care inherent in worlds also filled with violence, and everyday peace in the midst of war. The central premise is that military violence in Donbas and the absence of an adequate social safety net prompted people to repair society through their own efforts. A whole constellation of creative practices emerged from individuals acknowledging one another's human vulnerability and connectedness both within and outside the confines of kin relations.

The book shows the multiple ways the geopolitical conflict was woven into the fabric of interpersonal relationships. Some relationships were like undeclared dead. But practices of interpersonal peace could also knit people together in spite of political divides. The ethically motivated care people extended to one another was conducive to interpersonal peace. As such, we may think of interpersonal peace as a possible outcome under the larger rubric of care.

The way this care transpired, however, was not always or exclusively peaceful. Nor was it conducive to the ultimate goal of peace, reconciliation. The interpersonal peace that was forged could only bracket out war, not end it. And people found themselves engaged in many forms of what I called everyday war, providing sustenance to volunteer soldiers and arming them too when their emotional well-being depended on it. To answer the question I posed at the beginning of the book, people forged peace in the face of indiscriminate violence through myriad practices of ethically motivated caring. But this ethically motivated care could also be divisive, as readers saw in the embodied and practical forms of orientalism that demonized or looked down upon people who saw politics differently. The kind of peace this produced was one that did not fundamentally challenge or transcend the political terms in which the military conflict was being carried out. As such, interpersonal peace was bit of a handmaiden to continued conflict. At this writing, official talks and peace formulas have not led to peace. As forged from care, then, interpersonal peace can only provide a temporary and unfinished sanctuary.

The Russian Invasion in 2022

As this book was entering the final stages of the production process, Russia invaded Ukraine, and what had previously been deemed a "conflict" with domestic and international dimensions was officially called "war." According to the United Nations High Commissioner for Refugees, there were 5.5 million refugees by the end of April 2022 (UNHCR 2022). The International Organization for Migration estimated there were 7.1 million people internally displaced by that same time (IOM 2022). The death toll, although difficult to calculate under present conditions, was estimated to be approximately 3,000 Ukrainians according to the United Nations Office of the High Commissioner for Human Rights (UN OHCHR 2022). Readers of this book will have insight into how resilience in the face of unthinkable loss and hardship have actually been a staple feature of life in Ukraine since the first Russian tanks rolled into Crimea and Donbas in 2014. Thus the chapters provide deeper historical perspective and a useful theoretical framework for understanding the conflict leading up to Russia's February 2022 invasion of Ukraine.

The introduction was written when the idea that there had to be two legitimate "sides" to the conflict over Donbas was the predominant interpretation. Since February 2022, narratives suggesting there are two sides have increasingly been rejected in favor of stating unequivocally that Russia's invasion constitutes unwarranted, unprovoked, and unilateral aggression.

Ukrainians' robust response to Russian aggression since the 2022 Russian invasion is consistent with and in many ways amplifies the book's core insights. The "everyday war" described in this book has only intensified. This book has explored myriad examples of everyday war, from delivering groceries and antibacterial ointment to the front, to holding bake sales to support volunteer battalions, to pledging one's future children to the fight. Now it is even more clear that the way noncombatant civilians actively participate in war is of consequence. In February and March 2022, activities included making homemade Molotov cocktails (sometimes called Banderite smoothies), assembling roadblocks (sometimes called hedgehogs), and destroying road signs to disorient Russian forces.

I developed the term "everyday war" because its partner term "everyday peace" was a luxury many people in Ukraine could not afford. Rather, they found themselves entangled in a war that has no real or metaphorical sidelines. Everyday war is distinguished from war itself by its objective, which is not to destroy an enemy but rather to preserve human connections and affirm national belonging. The objectives of connecting and preserving are abundantly clear in the food prepared for fighters in recent weeks (Lucas 2022) and the rifles shouldered for neighborhood patrols watching out for Russian saboteurs and tanks in residential neighborhoods.

An important part of everyday war is the disruption to personal relationships. This book has described how the conflict over Donbas has disrupted friend, family, and romantic relationships. Breaking with the tendency to focus on individual trauma or geopolitical turmoil, I argued in favor of thinking about harm to personal relationships as an additional and connecting analytic layer. The injuries to interpersonal relationships are also a significant component of the 2022 Russian invasion of Ukraine. I hope other scholars of the ongoing war will join me in seeking ways to theorize when, how, and why political tensions are refracted through families and friendships. So far, journalism on the recent invasion has only touched upon how Russian-Ukrainian families in particular are divided by the conflict (Lucas 2022; Tondo and Rice-Oxley 2022). This is more than a human interest story, however, because the destruction of personal relationships between people who are pro-Ukrainian and pro-Russian shapes choices about where to direct resources, armaments, attention, and human beings themselves. The relational "casualties" of conflict are far from epiphenomenal: relational "wounds" will also affect how Ukrainian society rebuilds itself in the wake of this war.

Discussion of the disruption to relationships would be incomplete without also considering the ways families repurposed for war in what I call "tactical kinship." In chapter five of this book, I used the example of a young woman, Oleksandra, who spent her time provisioning her father with military equipment that the official Ukrainian military had not been able to supply. It started with footwear and continued with night vision goggles, camouflage, and tactical gloves. She knew he would use them for killing and chose to do what she could to support him. These are the care ethics that Ukrainians utilize every day now. With the 2022 invasion, tactical kinship has become even more significant as millions of families reorganize their daily lives around war. It extends beyond sending sons to defend the country or provisioning kin in the nongovernment controlled parts of the country. Family members literally defended one another in besieged cities like Kharkiv, Mariupol, Irpin, and Bucha. Choices about who to befriend and who to marry will continue to be filtered through the calculus of war.

In a way, tactical kinship was enshrined in state policy in 2022 with the mandate that males between the ages of 18 and 60 stay to defend their country rather than take refuge outside it. War unquestionably affects men and women differently. In allowing the women (as well as children and the elderly) to seek humanitarian protection outside Ukraine, the government legislated the gendered division of labor we also saw being asserted by social workers in chapter four. They hoped returning to previous roles would help veterans' families reknit themselves after absences due to military service. To be fair, the Ukrainian government has been noting women's contribution to the territorial defense and acknowledges some 15 percent of the military forces are female (Bloom and Moskalenko 2022). At the same time, female conscripts are not necessarily treated equally: often it is their physical appearance that is stressed in news reports, and in July 2021 they were forced to march in high heels (Guy and Lapin 2021). Gender norms and values, then, remain an integral if complicated part of Ukraine's defensive efforts.

In this book, I discussed how families that were physically separated as a result of war often stayed that way. At the very least, coming back together is rarely the straightforward process one might hope. New ways of being (and new families) formed in displacement, and trauma became increasingly layered and complex, which can complicate relationships. Whatever happens to the millions of families physically separated by Russia's invasion, we can think of family units as integral to the territorial defense.

In writing this book, I sought to move the study of forced migration beyond its negativity bias of focusing primarily on what has been called the "suffering slot." If everyday war is about forging and maintaining human connections in the midst of loss, it is nowhere clearer than in the practices of caring for the dead. Chapter 8 explored how volunteer body collectors crossed enemy lines to bring home dead soldiers and civilians. They helped families they did not know and would never have otherwise met to grieve their losses in the interest of healing and national unity. I argued that these practices were "necrosocial," constituting a positive and fundamentally peaceful antidote to necropolitics, in which some people are relegated to live deathlike lives. The February 2022 invasion thwarted these necrosocial efforts when the miserable security situation made collecting the dead impossible, and bodies were left in the streets, crumpled and burned, for days and weeks at a time (BBC 2022).

Many of the people affected by conflict that I spoke with between 2015 and 2017 described a world so altered by violence that it felt like living in a science fiction drama. In chapter 7, I showed how the familiar had become strange, and existing meaning-making schemes were inadequate. People described their new realities through their embodied experiences and personal possessions. The 2022 invasion, which has reduced towns and cities to rubble, has expanded that tendency. With the invasion of 2022, there is also a flagrant and widespread disregard for humanitarian law and human rights on the part of the invading Russian forces. Evidence of war crimes in multiple locations elicits unspeakable horror. There is also the very real possibility of lasting Europe-wide environmental damage from the nuclear waste disturbed at the Chernobyl nuclear exclusion zone (Jacobo 2022).

During my research, I saw the distinctly social consequences of embodied trauma and political difference: people in the conflict zone felt that they had become alien others to Russia's supporters and began to see Russians as lesser humans. The distinction between who is "ours" and who is "not ours" has become sharper since the 2022 invasion. Where embodied trauma and new social divisions overlapped, I found a kind of proto-othering in the discomfort that arose between people on different political sides. Since February 2022, these experiences have escalated far beyond anything that could be accurately described as "proto" or even "othering." The practical forms of orientalism I described, a surprise at the time, seem mild in comparison to today, and a canary in a veritable coal mine of hatred. Several of the people interviewed for chapter 7 recently reported feeling a level of hatred for Russians that they did not previously know was possible. Even dispassionate scholars began speaking of the loathing they had for Russia and Russians.

This book has aimed to shed light on the subjective experience of war and demonstrate concretely how even a place with military conflict in residential areas can be a place where ethics thrive. The ethical is obvious not only in formal principles or ethical laws (many of which have been trampled) but in local, quotidian, and only seemingly small choices about creating a livable world in a war zone. Given the stakes in this conflict, the choices that noncombatant Ukrainians make have consequences for peace and prosperity in the world as a whole. Close consideration of the subjective experience of war in previous chapters revealed that binary distinctions between combatant and noncombatant, battlefield and residential neighborhood, personal and political are artificial. The 2022 invasion of Ukraine may demonstrate that even more powerfully.

INTERTEXT
"I Realize that Nothing Will Be the Same Again"

The second and concluding intertext that follows has been culled from the sixty-five interviews with people who were in some way exposed to the conflict in Donbas and had an opportunity to reflect on it from the relative safety of the government-controlled parts of Ukraine. As argued in the chapters above, experiences of war and displacement sometimes result in difficulties seriating events. This intertext utilizes a form that replicates the nonlinear, nonchronological content of many interviews.

> I do not want to live with those people anymore, to breathe the same oxygen as them.
> My sense of time split into the time before war and the time after.
> War influenced everyone, even those who don't care about the war.
> Perhaps one can never be healed from the effects of seeing war, but one can learn to think differently and see the world with different eyes.
> And plans, you know, plans are not so long-term.
> I was hesitant to do anything here. Now I think we'll change the wallpaper.
> Those shots hurt me, they hurt my soul.
> I keep our house cozy, I decide what towels to buy.
> You can learn to understand that war is evil.
> I realize that nothing will be the same again.

Maybe we can have some calm, like a light version of war: "War Lite."

Me and my family have decided that we're apolitical. My task is to help, to care.

My life has taught me not to make plans for the future.

You appreciate small things, really small things.

It's more like Japanese philosophy: my body is my home, where my body is, there is my home.

I couldn't live without helping people.

I'm kind of . . . a leap, you know, of imagination. I want, you know, to fly.

Appendix: Pseudonyms of Interviewees

PSEUDONYM	MIGRATION, EMPLOYMENT STATUS	AGE	GENDER	INTERVIEW
Aleksey	IDP	60	M	164
Alina	IDP humanitarian worker	35	F	46
Anna	Non-IDP mental health service provider	N/A	F	154
Artem	IDP	29	M	13
Bohdan	IDP	37	M	150
Danilo	IDP	33	M	89
Daria	Non-IDP humanitarian, social worker	N/A	F	118
Darina	IDP	35	F	140
Denys	Non-IDP mental health service provider	N/A	M	161
Eduard	Veteran, business owner	N/A	M	183
Father Nikolai	Non-IDP priest, humanitarian worker	N/A	M	64
Galya	IDP	42	F	95
Ivan	IDP	22	M	142
Kira	IDP	41	F	85
Konstantin	IDP	N/A	M	162
Ksenia	Non-IDP social worker	N/A	F	120
Kyrylo	Non-IDP humanitarian worker	N/A	M	1
Larysa	IDP	39	F	20
Lidiya	IDP	32	F	31
Liuba	IDP	31	F	99
Lola	IDP	40	F	29
Maria	Non-IDP mental health service provider	N/A	F	153
Masha	IDP	39	F	97
Mikaela	IDP	30	F	9
Mila	IDP	51	F	30
Mirabelle	IDP	27	F	98
Mykola	IDP	28	M	7
Natalya	IDP	41	F	33
Natasha	IDP	55	F	112
Oleg	IDP	47	M	147
Oleksandra	IDP	21	F	27
Olena	IDP humanitarian worker	37	F	68

(continued)

PSEUDONYM	MIGRATION, EMPLOYMENT STATUS	AGE	GENDER	INTERVIEW
Pasha	IDP	57	M	155
Pastor Sergei	Non-IDP pastor, humanitarian, social worker	N/A	M	139
Raina	IDP humanitarian, social worker	N/A	F	152
Sasha	IDP	40	M	145
Sofia	IDP	31	F	149
Svetlana	IDP	40	F	172
Tamara	IDP	22	M	143
Taras	Non-IDP humanitarian worker	N/A	M	181
Vera	IDP	32	F	171
Victoria	IDP	41	F	84
Vladimir	IDP	43	M	93
Xristina	IDP	25	F	86
Yuliya	IDP	50	F	75
Yuri	Veteran, business owner	N/A	M	184
Zoya	IDP	63	F	166

Notes

INTRODUCTION

1. See for example Sasse and Lackner 2018; Onuch et al. 2018; and Harris 2020.

2. A version of this was published at the Savage Minds website: https://savageminds .org/author/greta/.

3. For example, Sara Ruddick suggested that the moral reasoning associated with mothering could provide a "standpoint from which to criticize the destructiveness of war and begin to reinvent peace" (1989, 12). In her account, this "maternal" thinking is not only tied to women, but to any responsible adult for whom taking responsibility for others is significant. A few decades old, care ethics have produced a large literature. Some have tried replacing the term care with "relational ethics" or "ethics of love," but as Held notes, they keep coming back to the generic term "care" because it can encompass both values and practices (Held 2006, 9).

4. Especially the strains of peace and conflict research interested in the local turn (Randazzo 2016; Julian et al. 2019) and postliberal peace-building (Richmond 2010, 2011; Mac Ginty 2014; Berents 2015).

1. "NOW WE HAVE FUNERAL AFTER FUNERAL"

1. https://cxid.info/126599_.html, accessed January 4, 2019.

2. "Esli by ne dobrovol'cheskie batal'yony, razmezhevanie s rossiiskimi terroristami prokhodilo by gde-to po Dnepru—Anton Gerashchenko" [If it had not been for the volunteer battalions, the line of demarcation with Russian terrorists would be somewhere on the Dnipro River], Censor, posted November 9, 2014, http://censor.net.ua/n311039.

3. Social suffering aims to capture how power, whether political, economic, or institutional, configures abjectivity, which is ultimately as much a social experience as it is an individual one (Kleinman, Das, and Lock 1997, ix).

4. http://www.the-monitor.org/en-gb/reports/2019/landmine-monitor-2019.aspx.

2. WELCOME TO CAFÉ PATRIOT!

1. https://www.history.com/news/vietnam-war-veterans-treatment, accessed July 12, 2017.

3. INTERPERSONAL PEACE

1. https://en.wikipedia.org/wiki/Second_Battle_of_Donetsk_Airport#/media/File:Rui ns_of_Donetsk_International_airport_(38),_16_January_2015.jpg., accessed June 5, 2016.

4. HOME FRONTS

1. https://www.unfpa.org/news/men-ukraine-hold-fast-gender-norms-landmark-study -finds, accessed October 2, 2019.

2. Her idea about the divorce rate rising was not (at the time of writing) reflected in data from the State Statistics Service of Ukraine. Still, concern about what would happen to an already high divorce rate as a result of the war was widespread. Whether or

not she was factually correct is both difficult to determine (statistics were unreliable) and perhaps beside the point because the topic here is the concerns people raised.

3. There are documented correlations between what happens on literal battlefields and what transpires subsequently within intimate partnerships. Some argue that a hyper- or militarized form of masculinity, in which resorting to violence is a normal way to resolve disputes, is at fault.

4. Whereas 65 percent of the IDPs from Donbas I interviewed reported a loss of friends, 15 percent experienced war-related family discord.

5. Banderovtsi or "Banderas" is a term that pro-Russian people have used against Ukrainians to associate them with the forces of Stepan Bandera, who led the Organization of Ukrainian Nationalists that were known to engage in atrocities such as the murder of Jewish and Polish civilians. The slur equates contemporary nationalists with the nationalists who collaborated with the Nazi regime.

6. Of the forty-five interviews I conducted with people from the east, twenty were married, fifteen were single, seven were divorced, and three were widowed. Of the people who were divorced, only one divorce had taken place as a result of the conflict. Of the forty-five people who fled the conflict zone, approximately half—twenty-two people—had physically moved away from nuclear family members, typically parents but sometimes siblings, and were dealing with the consequences.

5. BOOTS, GLOVES, AND TACTICAL KINSHIP

1. Specifically, the Donbas, Dnipro 1, and Azov battalions were crucial in the Ilovaisk battle and Right Sector in the Donetsk airport battle. The Azov battalion launched a counteroffensive east and northeast of Mariupol in February 2015.

6. PRAYING TO BE KILLED AT ONCE

1. The critical language that has been used to understand the lives of people living in abjection has often fallen short. For example, the concept of structural violence often occludes many aspects of how individuals subject to such violence view their situations. Johannes Galtung's focus on people's inability to reach their "potential" under these conditions is tone deaf to experiences of loss and survival. More subtle than a direct imposition of power or hegemony, the idea of symbolic violence is concerned with the legitimization of power on the basis of largely unspoken justifications and beliefs (Bourdieu 1992). This term is an improvement but still incomplete as a lens for understanding the lived experience of the conflict zone, even though he does aptly identify the ways in which people often unwittingly assent to power differences.

2. This chapter therefore works against the tendency for researchers interested in emotion, with notable exceptions of course, to avoid the historical dimension and lodge their work entirely in the present noted by William Reddy (2001, 47 and 113) and Nitzan Shoshan (2014).

7. EVERYDAY SCI-FI AND PRACTICAL ORIENTALISM

1. Philosopher Edmund Husserl who first developed the term "other" wanted a word to refer to the way people related intersubjectively. Othering, then, refers to the reductive process of labeling and categorizing.

8. THE VOLUNTEER BODY COLLECTORS OF UKRAINE

1. This chapter contributes to other anthropologies of death and dead body politics. Anthropologists have long been interested in the "making and unmaking of persons and relationships" (Kaufman and Morgan 2005, 318). But anthropological investigations have

seen a major shift from cataloging practices empirically to considering analytically how death is an eminently social event (Mueggler 2001; Briggs 2004; Taussig 1984). Looking at eastern Europe, Verdery showed how dead bodies have "lives" of their own and participate in the reinvigoration of politics. Examining the dynamics surrounding exhumation and reburial, she argues, reveals the transformation of norms and values (1999, 19).

2. https://www.kyivpost.com/article/content/war-against-ukraine/black-tulip-volunteers-halt-work-recovering-bodies-of-soldiers-in-eastern-ukraine-393810.html.

3. https://www.historynet.com/rest-in-peace-bringing-home-u-s-war-dead.htm. This article originally appeared in the Winter 2013 issue (Vol. 25, No. 2) of The Quarterly Journal of Military History with the headline: "These Hideous Weapons." Accessed November 10, 2017.

4. As he also pointed out, the Orthodox church stipulates that the dead must remain whole and be kissed.

5. See https://www.cimic-coe.org/news/tag/ukraine/?page=0.

6. "Ukraine's Forgotten Missing and Disappeared," https://www.icmp.int/news/ukraines-forgotten-missing-and-disappeared/.

7. In July 2018, Ukraine's parliament, the Verkhovna Rada passed a bill (5435) to provide for the creation of a single register for people who have disappeared and set up a procedure for searching for remains, extracting bodies, and exhuming human remains.

References

Agamben, Giorgio. 2005. 1995 (1998). *Homo Sacer: Sovereign Power and Bare Life*. Translated by Daniel Heller-Roazen. Stanford, CA: Stanford University Press. https://ebookcentral-proquest-com.proxy.lib.umich.edu/lib/umichigan/detail.action?docID=4862150.

——. *State of Exception*. Translated by Kevin Attell. Chicago: University of Chicago Press. https://ebookcentral-proquest-com.proxy.lib.umich.edu/lib/umichigan/detail.action?docID=547685.

Åhäll, Laura. 2018. "Feeling Everyday IR: Embodied, Affective, Militarizing Movement as Choreography of War." *Cooperation and Conflict* 54, no. 2: 1–18. https://doi.org/10.1177/0010836718807501.

Ahmed, Sarah. 2004. *The Cultural Politics of Emotions*. New York: Routledge. https://ebookcentral-proquest-com.proxy.lib.umich.edu/lib/umichigan/detail.action?docID=1767554.

Alekseyeva, Elena Sergevna. 2016. "O Nastupatel'noy Strategii Rossii v Usloviyakh Sovremennoy Informatsionnoy Voyny" [On the offensive strategy of Russia under the conditions of the contemporary information war]. *Journal of Public Administration* 4: 7–24. No DOI or permalink.

Amnesty International. 2014. "Ukraine: Abuses and War Crimes by the Aider Volunteer Battalion in the North Luhansk Region." Accessed June 19, 2019. https://www.amnesty.org/en/documents/EUR50/040/2014/en/.

Anderson, Benedict. 1991. *Imagined Communities: Reflections on the Origin and Spread of Nationalism*. London: Verso. https://doi.org/10.1093/fmls/cqp012.

Baker, Catherine, Victoria Basham, Sarah Bulmer, Harriet Gray, and Alexandra Hyde. 2016. "Encounters with the Military: toward a Feminist Ethics of Critique?" *International Feminist Journal of Politics* 18, no. 1: 140–154. https://doi.org/10.1080/14616742.2015.1106102.

Balibar, Etienne. 2001. "Frontières du monde, frontières de la politique." In *Nous, citoyens d'Europe? Les frontières, l'État, le peuple*, 163–181. Paris: La Découverte. https://doi.org/10.1177/03058298010300030916.

Barrington, Lowell W., and Erik S. Herron. 2004. "One Ukraine or Many? Regionalism in Ukraine and its Political Consequences." *Nationalities Papers* 32: 53–86. https://doi.org/10.1080/0090599042000186179.

Baumann, Mario. 2020. "'Propaganda Fights' and 'Disinformation Campaigns': the discourse on information warfare in Russia-West relations." *Contemporary Politics* 26, no. 3: 288–307, https://doi.org/10.1080/13569775.2020.1728612.

BBC. 2022. "Bucha Killings: Satellite Image of Bodies Site Contradicts Russian Claims." March 11, 2022 https://www.bbc.com/news/60981238.

Belkin, Aaron. 2012. *Bring Me Men: Military Masculinity and the Benign Façade of Empire 1898–2001*. London: Hurst & Co. No DOI.

Benezer, Gadi, and Roger Zetter. 2014. "Searching for Directions: Conceptual and Methodological Challenges in Researching Refugee Journeys." *Journal of Refugee Studies* 28, no. 3: 297–318. https://doi.org/10.1093/jrs/feu022.

Berents, Helen. 2015. "An Embodied Everyday Peace in the Midst of Violence." *Peacebuilding* 3, no. 2: 1–14. https://doi.org/10.1080/21647259.2015.1052632.

———. 2018. *Young People and Everyday Peace: Exclusion, Insecurity and Peacebuilding in Colombia.* Routledge Studies in Latin American Politics 22. Routledge, United States of America. https://doi.org/10.4324/9781315150215.

Berkman, Jodi. 2004. "Rehumanizing the Other: Empathy and Reconciliation." *Human Rights Quarterly* 26, no. 3: 561–583. https://doi.org/10.1353/hrq.2004.0036.

Berlant, Lauren. 2011. 1991. *The Anatomy of National Fantasy: Hawthorne, Utopia, and Everyday Life.* Chicago: University of Chicago Press. No DOI. https://search.lib .umich.edu/catalog/record/990024614590106381.

———. *Cruel Optimism.* Durham, NC: Duke University Press. https://doi.org/10.1215 /9780822394716.

Bessire, Lucas. 2011. "Apocalyptic Futures: The Violent Transformation of Moral Human Life among Ayoreo-Speaking People of the Paraguayan Gran Chaco." *American Ethnologist* 38, no. 4: 743–757. https://doi.org/10.1111/j.1548-1425.2011.01334.x.

Bjorkdahl, Annika, Martin Hall, and Ted Svensson. 2019. "Everyday international relations: Editors' introduction." *Cooperation and Conflict* 54, no. 2: 123–130. https:// doi.org/10.1177/0010836719845834.

Bloom, Mia, and Sophia Makarenko. 2022. "Ukraine's Women Fighters Reflect a Cultural Tradition of Feminist Independence." *The Conversation*, March 21. https:// theconversation.com/ukraines-women-fighters-reflect-a-cultural-tradition-of -feminist-independence-179529.

Bobrow-Strain, Aaron. 2007. *Intimate Enemies: Landowners, Power and Violence in Chiapas.* Durham, NC: Duke University Press. https://search.lib.umich.edu/catalog /record/990055798850106381.

Bourdieu, Pierre. 1992. *An Invitation to Reflexive Sociology.* Chicago: University of Chicago Press. https://babel.hathitrust.org/cgi/pt?id=hvd.32044051816445.

———. 1990. *The Logic of Practice.* Cambridge: Polity Press. https://search.lib.umich.edu /catalog/record/990020592240106381.

———. 1977. *Outline of a Theory of Practice.* Cambridge: Cambridge University Press. No DOI. https://search.lib.umich.edu/catalog/record/990000841630106381

Briggs, Charles L. 2004. "Theorizing Modernity Conspiratorially: Science, Scale, and the Political Economy of Public Discourse in Explanations of a Cholera Epidemic." *American Ethnologist* 31: 164–187. https://doi.org/10.1525/ae.2004.31.2.164.

Buckley, Cynthia, Ralph Clem, and Erik S. Herron. 2019. "An assessment of attributing public healthcare infrastructure damage in the Donbas five years after the Euromaidan: Implications for Ukrainian state legitimacy." *Eurasian Geography and Economics* 60, no. 1: 54–72. https://doi.org/10.1080/15387216.2019.1581634.

Bulakh, Tania. 2017. "'Strangers among Ours': State and Civil Responses to the Phenomenon of Internal Displacement in Ukraine." In *Migration and the Ukraine Crisis: A Two Country Perspective*, edited by Agnieszka Pikulicka-Wilczewska and Greta Uehling, 49–61. E-international Relations. https://search.lib.umich.edu/catalog/record /990152341020106381.

Bulmer, Sarah, and Maya Eichler. 2017. "Unmaking Militarized Masculinity: Veterans and the Project of Military-to-Civilian Transition." *Critical Military Studies* 3, no. 2: 161–181. https://doi.org/10.1080/23337486.2017.1320055.

Burkitt, Ian. 2014. *Emotions and Social Relations.* Los Angeles: Sage. https://doi.org/10 .4135/9781473915060.

Butler, Judith. 1999. *Gender Trouble: Feminism and the Subversion of Identity.* New York: Routledge. https://search.lib.umich.edu/catalog/record/990037090920106381.

——. 2006. *Precarious Life: The Powers of Mourning and Violence.* New York: Verso. https://search.lib.umich.edu/catalog/record/990039060220106381.

Butler, Judith, and Athena Athanasiou. 2013. *Dispossession: The Performative in the Political.* Malden, MA: Polity Press. https://ebookcentral-proquest-com.proxy.lib.umich.edu/lib/umichigan/detail.action?docID=1166844.

Carston, Janet. 2007. Introduction to *Ghosts of Memory: Essays on Remembrance and Relatedness,* edited by Janet Carston, 1–35. Malden, MA: Blackwell. https://doi.org/10.1002/9780470692301.

Castillejo Cuellar, Alejandro. 2005. "Unraveling Silence: Violence, Memory and the Limits of Anthropology's Craft." *Dialectical Anthropology* 29, no. 2: 159–180. https://doi.org/10.1007/s10624-005-5117-3.

Cockburn, Cynthia. 2010. "Gender Relations as Causal in Militarization and War." *International Feminist Journal of Politics* 12, no. 2: 139–157. https://doi.org/10.1080/14616741003665169.

Cohn, Carol. 1987. "Sex and Death in the Rational World of Defense Intellectuals." *Signs* 12, no. 4: 687–718. https://www.jstor.org/stable/3174209.

——. 2013. "Women and Wars: toward a Conceptual Framework." In *Women and Wars,* edited by Carol Cohn, 1–35. Cambridge, UK: Polity. https://search.lib.umich.edu/catalog/record/990121842860106381.

Crenshaw, Kimberlé. 1989. "Demarginalizing the Intersection of Race and Sex: A Black Feminist Critique of Antidiscrimination Doctrine, Feminist Theory and Antiracist Politics." *University of Chicago Legal Forum* 1, Article 8. https://doi.org/10.4324/9780429500480-5.

Crespo, Maria, and Violeta Fernandez-Lansac. 2016. "Memory and Narrative of Traumatic Events: A Literature Review." *Psychological Trauma: Theory, Research, Practice and Policy* 8, no. 2: 149–156. https://doi.org/10.1037/tra0000041.

Daniel, E. Valentine. 1996. *Charred Lullabies: Chapters in an Anthropology of Violence.* Princeton, NJ: Princeton University Press. https://ebookcentral-proquest-com.proxy.lib.umich.edu/lib/umichigan/detail.action?docID=581578.

Das, Veena. 2000. "The Act of Witnessing: Violence, Poisonous Knowledge, and Subjectivity." In *Violence and Subjectivity,* edited by Veena Das, Arthur Kleinman, Mamphela Ramphele, and Pamela Reynolds, 205–225. Berkeley: University of California Press.

——. 1995. *Critical Events: An Anthropological Perspective on Contemporary India.* Delhi: Oxford University Press. https://search.lib.umich.edu/catalog/record/99004 1199680106381.

——. 2007. *Life and Words: Violence and the Descent into the Ordinary.* Berkeley: University of California Press. https://ebookcentral-proquest-com.proxy.lib.umich.edu/lib/umichigan/detail.action?docID=275766.

——. 2012. "Ordinary Ethics." In *A Companion to Moral Anthropology,* edited by Didier Fassin, 133–149. Hoboken, NJ: John Wiley and Sons, Inc. https://doi.org/10.1002/9781118290620.

Davies, Thom, Arshad Isakjee, and Surindar Dhesi. 2017. "Violent Inaction: The Necropolitical Experience of Refugees in Europe." *Antipode* 49, no. 5: 1263–1284. https://doi.org/10.1111/anti.12325.

De Certeau, Michel. 1984. *The Practice of Everyday Life.* Translated by Steven Rendall. Berkeley: University of California Press. https://search.lib.umich.edu/catalog/record/990159921090106381.

Deleuze, Gilles, and Feliz Guattari. 1987. *A Thousand Plateaus: Capitalism and Schizophrenia.* London: Athlone Press. https://search.lib.umich.edu/catalog/record/990008 450390106381.

Desai, Amit, and Evan Killick. 2010. Introduction to *The Ways of Friendship*, edited by Amit Desai and Evan Killick, 1–19. Oxford: Berghahn Books. https://ebookcentral -proquest-com.proxy.lib.umich.edu/lib/umichigan/detail.action?docID=583667.

Dowler, Lorraine. 2012. "Gender, Militarization, and Sovereignty." *Geography Compass* 6, no. 8: 490–499. https://doi.org/10.1111/j.1749-8198.2012.00509.x.

Douglas, Mary. 1966. *Purity and Danger: An Analysis of Concepts of Pollution and Taboo.* New York: Routledge. https://ebookcentral-proquest-com.proxy.lib.umich.edu/lib /umichigan/detail.action?docID=1223047.

Dragneva, Rilka, and Kataryna Wolczuk. 2015. *Ukraine between the EU and Russia: The Integration Challenge.* New York: Palgrave Macmillan. https://doi.org/10.1111/jcms .12567.

Duffield, Mark. 2007. *Development, Security and Unending War: Governing the World of Peoples.* Cambridge: Polity Press. https://doi.org/10.3917/polaf.125.0215.

Duncanson, Claire. 2015. "Hegemonic Masculinity and the Possibility of Change in Gender Relations." *Men and Masculinities* 18, no. 2: 231–248. https://doi.org/10.1177 /1097184X15584912.

Duriesmith, David, and Noor Huda Ismail. 2019. "Militarized Masculinities beyond Methodological Nationalism: Charting the Multiple Masculinities of an Indonesian Jihadi." *International Theory* 11, no. 2: 139–159. https://doi.org/10.1017/S175297 1919000034.

Dutta, Urmitapa, Andrea Kashimana Andzenge, and Kayla Walking. 2016. "The Everyday Peace Project: An Innovative Approach to Peace Pedagogy." *Journal of Peace Education* 13, no. 1: 79–104. https://doi.org/10.1080/17400201.2016.1151773.

Dyvik, Synne. 2016. "Of Bats and Bodies: Methods for Reading and Writing Embodiment." *Critical Military Studies* 2, no. 1: 56–69. https://doi.org/10.1080/23337486 .2016.1184471.

Enloe, Cynthia. 2007. *Globalization and Militarism: Feminists Make the Link.* Lanham: Rowman & Littlefield Publishers. https://search.lib.umich.edu/catalog/record /990055390480106381.

——. 2000. *Maneuvers: The Intellectual Politics of Militarizing Women's Lives.* Berkeley: University of California Press. http://proxy.lib.umich.edu/login?url=https://search .ebscohost.com/login.aspx?direct=true&db=nlebk&AN=42263&site=ehost -live&scope=site.

——. 2005. "What if Patriarchy *Is* 'the Big Picture'? An Afterward." In *Gender, Conflict and Peacekeeping*, edited by Dyan Mazurana, Angela Raven-Roberts, and Jane Parpart, 280–283. Lanham, MD: Rowman and Littlefield. https://search.lib.umich .edu/catalog/record/990049615220106381.

EPRS. 2015. European Parliamentary Research Service Blog. Retrieved from https:// epthinktank.eu/ 2015/11/17/understanding-propaganda-and-disinformation/.

Farish, Matthew. 2013. "Militarization." *The Ashgate Research Companion to Critical Geopolitics*, edited by Klaus Dodds, Merje Kuus, and Joanne Sharp, 247–262. New York: Routledge. https://doi.org/10.1111/tesg.12058.

Fattal, Alexander l. 2019. "Target Intimacy: Notes on the Convergence of the Militarization and Marketization of Love in Colombia." *Current Anthropology* 60, no. 19: S49–S61. https://doi.org/10.1086/699911.

Fassin, Didier. 2012. "Introduction: Toward a Critical Moral Anthropology." In *A Companion to Moral Anthropology*, edited by Didier Fassin, 1–17. Hoboken, NJ: John Wiley & Sons. https://doi.org/10.1002/9781118290620.

Feldman, Alan. 1991. *Formations of Violence: The Narrative of the Body and Political Terror in Northern Ireland.* Chicago: Chicago University Press. https://ebookcentral -proquest-com.proxy.lib.umich.edu/lib/umichigan/detail.action?docID=665704.

Foucault, Michel. 1979. *Birth of Biopolitics: Lectures at the College de France, 1978.* Michel Senellart, ed. Translated by Graham Burchell. New York: St. Martin's Press. https://search.lib.umich.edu/catalog/record/990058062190106381.

——. 1983. "The Subject and Power." In *Michel Foucault: Beyond Structuralism and Hermeneutics,* 2nd ed, edited by H. L. Dreyfus and P. Rabinow, 208–228. Chicago: University of Chicago Press. https://search.lib.umich.edu/catalog/record/99004547 1030106381.

——. 1988. "Technologies of the Self." In *Technologies of the Self: A Seminar with Michel Foucault,* edited by L. H. Martin, L. H. Gutman, and P. H. Hutton, 16–49. Amherst: University of Massachusetts Press. https://search.lib.umich.edu/catalog /record/990008434250106381.

Gadamer, Hans-Georg. 1999. "Friendship and Solidarity." *Research in Phenomenology* 39: 3–12. https://doi.org/10.1163/156916408X389604.

Gal, Susan, and Gail Kligman. 2000. *The Politics of Gender after Socialism.* Princeton, NJ: Princeton University Press. https://hdl-handle-net.proxy.lib.umich.edu /2027/heb.04390.

Galeotti, Mark. The CSS Blog Network, Center for Security Studies, ETH Zürich. January 11, 2016. Retrieved from http://isnblog. ethz.ch/security/russias-new-national -security-strategy-familiar-themes-gaudy-rhetoric-2.

——. 2016a. "Hybrid, Ambiguous, and Non-linear? How New is Russia's 'New Way of War'?." *Small Wars and Insurgencies* 27, no. 2: 282–301. https://doi.org/10.1080 /09592318.2015.1129170.

Galtung, Johannes. 1969. "Violence, Peace, and Peace Research." *Journal of Peace Research* 6, no. 3: 167–191. https://doi.org/10.1177/002234336900600301.

Gavriely-Nuri, Dalia. 2013. *The Normalization of War in Israeli Discourse.* Lanham: Lexington Books. http://proxy.lib.umich.edu/login?url=https://search.ebscohost.com /login.aspx?direct=true&db=e000xna&AN=521720&site=ehost-live&scope=site.

Gilligan, Carol. 1983. *In a Different Voice: Psychological Theory and Women's Development.* Cambridge, MA: Harvard University Press. https://search.lib.umich.edu /catalog/record/990003067190106381.

Gilligan, Carol, Annie Rogers, and Lyn Brown. 1990. Epilogue to *Making Connections: The relational worlds of adolescent girls at Emma Willard School,* edited by Carol Gilligan, Nona Lyons, and Trudy Hanmer, 314–334. Cambridge, MA: Harvard University Press. https://psycnet.apa.org/record/1990-97676-000.

Goffman, Erving. 1959. *The Presentation of Self in Everyday Life.* New York: Double Day. https://search.lib.umich.edu/catalog/record/990067670350106381.

Gonzales, Roberto, and Leo Chavez. 2012. "Awakening to a Nightmare: Abjectivity and Illegality in the Lives of Undocumented 1.5-Generation Latino Immigrants in the United States." *Current Anthropology* 53, no. 3: 255–281. https://doi.org/10.1086 /665414.

Gorenburg, Dmitry. 2014. "Ukrainian Military Capabilities." *Russian Military Reform* blog 22, December 2014, http://wp.me/pBeNm-q8.

Gourevitch, Philip. 1998. *We Wish to Inform You That Tomorrow We Will Be Killed with Our Families.* New York: Farrar, Straus and Giroux. https://search.lib.umich.edu /catalog/record/990045708060106381.

Gregory, Derek. 2010. "War and Peace." *Transactions of the Institute of British Geographers* 35, no. 2: 154–186. https://doi.org/10.1111/j.1475-5661.2010.00381.x.

Griffiths, Paul E., and Andrea Scarantino. 2009. "Emotions in the Wild: The Situated Perspective on Emotion." In *Cambridge Handbook of Situated Cognition,* edited by P. Robbins and M. Aydede, 437–453. Cambridge: Cambridge University Press. https:// search.lib.umich.edu/catalog/record/990059155090106381.

Grossman, Eric. 2018. "Russia's Frozen Conflicts and the Donbas." *Parameters* 48, no. 2: 51–62. https://link.gale.com/apps/doc/A563359215/AONE?u=umuser&sid=bookma rk-AONE&xid=8858f1ab.

Guy, Jack, and Denis Lapin. 2021. "Ukrainian Army's Decision to Make Female Soldiers March in High Heels Sparks Backlash." CNN. https://www.cnn.com/2021/07 /05/europe/ukraine-female-soldiers-heels-scli-intl/index.html#:~:text=(CNN) %20Ukraine's%20Ministry%20of%20Defense,an%20outcry%20from%20local %20lawmakers.

Haldrup, Michael, Lasse Koefoed, and Kirsten Simonsen. 2006. "Practical Orientalism— Bodies, Everyday Life and the Construction of Otherness." *Geografiska Annaler: Series B, Human Geography* 88, no. 2: 173–184. https://doi.org/10.1111/j.0435-3684 .2006.00213.x.

Halpern, Jodi, and Harvey M. Weinstein. 2004. "Rehumanizing the Other: Empathy and Reconciliation," *Human Rights Quarterly* 26: 561–583. https://doi.org/10.1353/hrq .2004.0036.

Han, Clara. 2004. "The Work of Indebtedness: The Traumatic Present in Late Capitalist Chile." *Cultural Medical Psychiatry* 28, no. 2: 169–187. https://doi.org/10.1023 /B:MEDI.0000034409.70790.66.

Harari, Yuval Noah. 2004. *Renaissance Military Memoirs: War, History and Identity 1450– 1600.* Woodbridge, UK: Boydell. https://search.lib.umich.edu/catalog/record/9900 49131360106381.

Hankivsky, Olena. 2004. *Social Policy and the Ethics of Care.* Vancouver: UBC Press. https://ebookcentral-proquest-com.proxy.lib.umich.edu/lib/umichigan/detail .action?docID=3412039.

Harris, Erika. 2020. "What is the Role of Nationalism and Ethnicity in the Russia-Ukraine Crisis." *Europe Asia Studies* 72, no. 4: 593–613. https://doi.org/10.1080/09668136 .2019.1708865.

Hautzinger, Sarah, and Jean Scandlyn. 2013. *Beyond Post-Traumatic Stress: Homefront Struggles with the Wars on Terror.* Walnut Creek, CA: Left Coast Press. http://proxy .lib.umich.edu/login?url=https://search.ebscohost.com/login.aspx?direct =true&db=e000xna&AN=598430&site=ehost-live&scope=site.

Hedstrom, Jenny. 2018. "Militarization in Five Vignettes." *Critical Military Studies* 5, no. 2: 189–190. https://doi.org/10.1080/23337486.2018.1483631.

Hegel, Georg Wilhelm Friedrich. (1807) 1977. *The Phenomenology of Spirit.* Translated by with introduction and commentary by Michael Inwood. Oxford, UK: Clarendon Press. https://search.lib.umich.edu/catalog/record/990161896590106381.

Heitmeyer, Carrie. 2009. "'There Is Peace Here': Managing Communal Relations in a Town in Central Gujarat." *Journal of South Asian Development* 4, no. 1: 103–120. https:// doi.org/10.1177/097317410900400107.

Hekman, Susan J. 1995. *Moral Voices, Moral Selves: Carol Gilligan and Feminist Moral Theory.* University Park: University of Pennsylvania Press. https://search.lib.umich .edu/catalog/record/990045561360106381.

Held, Virginia. 2006. *The Ethics of Care: Personal, Political, and Global.* Oxford, UK: Oxford University Press. https://search.lib.umich.edu/catalog/record/990050892870106381.

Herron, Erik S. 2020. *Normalizing Corruption: Failures of Accountability in Ukraine.* Ann Arbor: University of Michigan Press. https://doi.org/10.3998/mpub.11596348.

Herzfeld, Michael. 2005. *Cultural Intimacy: Social Poetics in the Nation-State,* New York: Routledge. https://ebookcentral-proquest-com.proxy.lib.umich.edu/lib/umichigan /detail.action?docID=1689007.

Higate, Paul, and Marsha Henry. 2011. "Militarizing Spaces: A Geographical Explora- tion of Cyprus." In *Reconstructing Conflict, Integrating War and Post-war Geog-*

raphies, edited by Stuart Kirsch and Colin Flint, 133–157. Surrey: Ashgate. https://search.lib.umich.edu/catalog/record/990105027520106381.

Hinton Devon E., and Alexander Hinton. 2015. "Introduction: An Anthropology of the Effects of Genocide and Mass Memory, Symptom, and Recovery," In *Genocide and Mass Violence: Memory, Symptom, and Recovery*. 1–42 Cambridge: Cambridge University Press.

Hoffman, Frank G. 2007. *Conflict in the 21st Century: The Rise of Hybrid Wars*. Arlington: Potomac Institute for Policy Studies. Accessed August 9, 2018. https://potomacins titute.org/reports/19-reports/1163-conflict-in-the-21st-century-the-rise-of-hyb rid-wars.

Holtzman, Jon. 2016. *Killing Your Neighbors: Friendship and Violence in Northern Kenya and Beyond*. Oakland, CA. University of California Press. http://proxy.lib.umich .edu/login?url=https://search.ebscohost.com/login.aspx?direct=true&db=e000 xna&AN=1357207&site=ehost-live&scope=site.

Hunt, Krista, and Kim Rygiel. 2006. "(En)Gendered War Stories and Camouflaged Politics." In *(En)gendering the War on Terror: War Stories and Camouflaged Politics*, edited by Krista Hunt and Kim Rygiel, 1–26. Burlington, VT: Ashgate. https://doi.org/10.4324/9781315564371.

Huysmans, Jef. 2008. "The Jargon of Exceptions-On Schmitt, Agamben and the Absences of Political Society." *International Political Sociology* 2, 165–183. https://doi.org/10.1111/j.1749-5687.2008.00042.x.

International Criminal Court. 2018. "Report on Preliminary Examination Activities." Office of the Prosecutor General. Netherlands: The Hague. Accessed June 6, 2020. https://www.icc-cpi.int/itemsDocuments/181205-rep-otp-PE-ENG.pdf.

International Organization for Migration. 2022. "7.1 Million People Displaced by the War in Ukraine: IOM Survey." https://www.iom.int/news/71-million-people-displaced -war-ukraine-iom-survey#:~:text=Geneva%20%E2%80%93%20Over%207.1%20 million%20people,Organization%20for%20Migration%20(IOM).

Jackson, Michael. 2004. "The Prose of Suffering and the Practice of Silence." *Spiritus: A Journal of Christian Spirituality* 4, no. 1: 44–59. https://doi.org/10.1353/scs.2004.0011.

Jacobo, Julia. 2022. "Experts Predict Lasting Environmental Damage from Russia's Invasion of Ukraine." https://abcnews.go.com/International/experts-lasting-envir onmental-damage-russias-invasion-ukraine/story?id=83347671.

Jaeger, Jeff, Katie Lindblom, Kelly Parker-Guilbert, and Lori Zoellner. 2014. "Trauma Narratives: It's What You Say, Not How You Say It?" *Psycho-Trauma* 6, no. 5: 473–481. https://doi.org/10.1037/a0035239.

Jaitner, Margarita. 2015. "Russian Information Warfare: Lessons from Ukraine." In *Cyber Warfare in Perspective: Russian Aggression against Ukraine*, edited by Kenneth Geers, 87–94. Tallinn: NATO Cooperative Cyber Defense Center of Excellence.

Käihkö, Ilmari. 2018. "A Nation-in-the-Making, in Arms: Control of Force, Strategy, and the Ukrainian Volunteer Battalions." *Defense Studies* 18, no. 2: 147–166. https://doi.org/10.1080/14702436.2018.1461013.

Kaldor, Mary. 2013. "In Defense of New Wars." *Stability* 2, no. 1: 1–16. https://doi.org/10.5334/sta.at.

——. 2006. *New and Old Wars: Organized Violence in a Global Era*. Cambridge UK: Polity Press. https://doi.org/10.2307/40203425.

Kaufman, Sharon, and Lynn Morgan. 2005. "The Anthropology of the Beginnings and Ends of Life." *Annual Review of Anthropology* 34: 317–341. https://doi.org/10.1146/annurev.anthro.34.081804.120452.

Keane, Webb. 2015. *Ethical Life: Its Natural and Social Histories*. Princeton, NJ: Princeton University Press. https://doi-org.proxy.lib.umich.edu/10.1515/9781400873593.

———. 2014. "Rotting Bodies: The Clash of Stances toward Materiality and Its Ethical Affordances." *Cultural Anthropology* 55 (S10): S312–S321. https://doi.org/10.1086/678290.

Kidd-Nakai, Akari. 2015. "Architecture, Affect and Architectural Practice." PhD diss, Victoria University of Wellington. No DOI.

Kidron, Carol. 2009. "Toward an Ethnography of Silence: The Lived Presence of the Past in the Everyday Life of Holocaust Trauma Survivors and their Descendants in Israel." *Current Anthropology* 50, no. 1: 5–27. https://doi.org/10.1086/595623.

Klein, Margerete. 2015. "Ukraine's Volunteer Battalions—Advantages and Challenges." Swedish Defense Research Agency Report RUFS Briefing No. 27, April. No link, No DOI.

Kleinman, Arthur. 2006. *What Really Matters: Living a Moral Life amidst Uncertainty and Danger.* New York: Oxford University Press. https://search.lib.umich.edu/catalog/record/990067671110106381.

Kleinman, Arthur, Veena Das, and Margaret Lock. 1997. *Social Suffering.* Berkeley and Los Angeles: University of California Press. https://search.lib.umich.edu/catalog/record/990039523180106381.

Krakhmalova, Kateryna. 2019. "Internally Displaced Persons in Pursuit for Access to Justice: Ukraine." *International Migration* 57: 309–322. https://doi.org/10.1111/imig.12500.

Kubicek, Paul. 2000. "Regional Polarisation in Ukraine: Public Opinion, Voting and Legislative Behaviour." *Europe-Asia Studies* 52: 273–294. https://doi.org/10.1080/09668130050006790.

Kudelia, Serhiy. 2014. "The House that Yanukovych Built," *Journal of Democracy* 25, no. 3: 19–34. https://doi.org/10.1353/jod.2014.0039.

Kuznetsova, Irina, Oksana Mikheieva, Gulnara Gulyieva, Rilka Dragneva, and Vlad Mykhnenko. 2018. "The Social Consequences of Population Displacement in Ukraine: The Risks of Marginalization and Social Exclusion." Accessed February 3, 2020. https://www.researchgate.net/publication/331703553_The_social_consequences_of_population_displacement_in_Ukraine_the_risks_of_marginalization_and_social_exclusion.

Kuromiya, Hiroaki. 1998. *Freedom and Terror in the Donbas: A Ukrainian-Russian Borderland 1870s–1990s.* Cambridge: Cambridge University Press. https://search.lib.umich.edu/catalog/record/990040248140106381.

Kuzio, Taras. 2017. *Putin's War against Ukraine: Revolution, Nationalism, and Crime.* Toronto: Chair of Ukrainian Studies University of Toronto. Self-published: No DOI.

Lambek, Michael. 2010. "Toward an Ethics of the Act." In *Ordinary Ethics: Anthropology, Language and Action,* edited by Michael Lambek, 1–39. New York: Fordham University Press. https://ebookcentral-proquest-com.proxy.lib.umich.edu/lib/umichigan/detail.action?docID=3239541.

Lattimore, Richmond, trans. 1951. *The Iliad of Homer.* Translated by Alexander Pope. Chicago: University of Chicago Press. Homer. N.d. Iliad, Book XXIV, 1–76 and XVI, 569–683. https://hdl.handle.net/2027/osu.32435016519761?urlappend=%3Bseq=7%3Bownerid=116396726-11.

Lederach, John Paul. 2005. *The Moral Imagination: The Art and Soul of Building Peace.* New York: Oxford. https://ebookcentral-proquest-com.proxy.lib.umich.edu/lib/umichigan/detail.action?docID=3052023.

LeFranc, Sandrine. 2011. "A Critique of 'Bottom-up' Peacebuilding: Do Peaceful Individuals Make Peaceful Societies?" *Peacebuilding, Memory and Reconciliation.* https://doi.org/halshs-00646986f.

Leshem, Noam. 2015. "'Over Our Dead Bodies': Placing Necropolitical Activism." *Political Geography* 45: 34–44. https://doi.org/10.1016/j.polgeo.2014.09.003.

Licklider, Roy. 1995. "The Consequences of Negotiated Settlements in Civil Wars, 1945–1993." *American Political Science Review* 89, no. 3: 681–690. https://doi.org/10.2307/2082982.

Lindsay, Drew. 2013. "Rest in Peace? Bringing Home U.S. War Dead" *HistoryNet*, Winter 2013. https://www.historynet.com/rest-in-peace-bringing-home-u-s-war-dead.htm.

Lucas, Ryan. 2022. "Ukrainian-Russian families are being torn apart by Russia's invasion" National Public Radio, 7 March 2022, https://www.npr.org/2022/03/06/1084800742/relationships-across-the-ukraine-russia-border-feel-the-strain-of-war.

Lutz, Caroline. 2002. "Making War at Home in the United States: Militarization and the Current Crisis." *American Anthropologist* 104, no. 3: 723–735. https://doi.org/10.1525/aa.2002.104.3.723.

Mac Ginty, Roger. 2014. "Everyday Peace: Bottom-up and Local Agency in Conflict-Affected Societies." *Security Dialogue* 45, no. 6: 548–564. https://doi.org/10.1177/0967010614550899.

——. 2010. "Hybrid Peace: The Interaction between Top-Down and Bottom-Up Peace." *Security Dialogue* 41, no. 4: 391–412. https://doi.org/10.1177/0967010610374312.

——. 2008. "Indigenous Peace-Making Versus the Liberal Peace." *Cooperation and Conflict* 43, no. 2: 139–163. https://doi.org/10.1177/0010836708089080.

Mac Ginty, Roger, and Pamina Firchow. 2016. "Top-down and Bottom-up Narratives of Peace and Conflict." *Politics* 36, no. 3: 308–323. https://doi.org/10.1177/0263395715622967.

Malinowski, Bronislaw. 1922. *Argonauts of the Western Pacific: An Account of Native Enterprise and Adventure in the Archipelagos of Melanesian New Guinea.* London: Routledge & Kegan Paul. https://babel.hathitrust.org/cgi/pt?id=uc1.32106000760451&view=1up&seq=7.

Malkki, Liisa. 1996. *Purity and Exile: Violence, Memory, and National Cosmology among Hutu Refugees in Tanzania.* Chicago: University of Chicago Press. https://search.lib.umich.edu/catalog/record/990030038530106381.

Malyarenko, Tatyana, and Stefan Wolff. 2018. "The Logic of Competitive Influence Seeking: Russia, Ukraine, and the Conflict in Donbas," *Post-Soviet Affairs* 34, no. 4: 191–212. https://doi.org/10.1080/1060586X.2018.1425083.

Marr, Mathew. 2019. "The Ohaka (Grave) Project: Post-Secular Social Service Delivery and Resistant Necropolitics in San'ya Tokyo." *Ethnography* (May): 1–23. https://doi.org/10.1177/1466138119845393.

Mbembe, Achille. 2003. "Necropolitics." *Public Culture* 15, no. 1: 11–40. https://doi.org/10.1215/08992363-15-1-11.

McClintock, Anne. 1993. "Family Feuds: Gender, Nationalism and the Family." *Feminist Review* 44 (Summer): 61–80. https://doi.org/10.2307/1395196.

Merleau-Ponty, Michel. 1962. *Phenomenology of Perception.* Translated by Colin Smith. London: Routledge and Kegan Paul. https://search.lib.umich.edu/catalog/record/990044615780106381.

——. 1968. *The Visible and the Invisible.* Translated by Alphonso Lingis. Evanston, IL: Northwestern University Press. https://search.lib.umich.edu/catalog/record/990013849270106381.

Miller, Christopher. 2014. "The Body Collector from Ukraine." *Mashable*, November 3, 2014. https://mashable.com/2014/11/03/the-ukrainian-body-collector/.

Mirovich Media. 2017. "Ресторан во Львове, куда лучше не ходить россиянам" [The restaurant in Lviv where it is better for Russians not to go] *Livejournal* [in Russian]. Accessed April 15, 2019. https://maxim-nm.livejournal.com/351606.html.

Mitchell, Audra. 2011. *Lost in Transformation: Violent Peace and Peaceful Conflict in Northern Ireland*. Basingstoke: Palgrave. https://search.lib.umich.edu/catalog /record/990099978880106381.

Mitrokhin, Nikolay. 2015. "Infiltration, Instruktion, Invasion: Russlands Krieg in der Ukraine," *Osteuropa* 64, no. 8: 3–16. https://mgetit.lib.umich.edu/go/7366466.

Mosse, George. 1985. *Nationalism and Sexuality: Respectability and Abnormal Sexuality in Europe*. New York: Howard Fertig. https://search.lib.umich.edu/catalog/record /990004640930106381.

Mueggler, Erik. 2001. *The Age of Wild Ghosts: Memory, Violence, and Place in Southwest China*. Berkeley: University of California Press. http://proxy.lib.umich.edu/login ?url=https://search.ebscohost.com/login.aspx?direct=true&db=e000xna&AN =65753&site=ehost-live&scope=site.

Mukomel, Vladimir. 2017. "Migration of Ukrainians to Russia in 2014–2015: Discourses and Perceptions of the Local Population." In *Migration and the Ukraine Crisis: A Two Country Perspective*, edited by Agneiszka Pikulicka-Wilczewska and Greta Uehling, 105–115. *E-international Relations*. https://search.lib.umich.edu/catalog /record/990152341020106381.

Mykhnenko, Vlad. 2020. "Causes and Consequences of the War in Eastern Ukraine: An Economic Geography Perspective," *Europe-Asia Studies* 72, no. 3: 528–560. https://doi.org/10.1080/09668136.2019.1684447.

NATO. 2018. "Brussels Summit Declaration." Retrieved from https://www.nato.int/cps /en/natohq/ official_texts_156624.htm.

Navaro-Yashin, Yael. 2012. *The Make Believe Space: Affective Geography in a Postwar Polity*. Durham, NC: Duke University Press. https://doi.org/10.1215/9780822395133.

Nieczypor, Krzysztof. 2019. "*In the Shadow of War. Ukraine's Policy towards Internally Displaced Persons*" January 31, www.osw.waw.pl/en/publikacje/osw-commentary /2019-01-16/shadow-war-ukraines-policy-towards-internally-displaced.

Nielsen, Cynthia R. 2017. "Gadamer and Scholz on Solidarity: Disclosing, Avowing, and Performing Solidaristic Ties with Human and Natural Others." *Journal of the British Society for Phenomenology* 48, no. 3: 240–256. https://doi.org/10.1080/00071773 .2017.1303117.

Nordstrom, Caroline, and Antonius C. G. M. Robben, eds. 1996. *Fieldwork under Fire: Contemporary Studies of Violence and Culture*. Berkeley: University of California Press. http://proxy.lib.umich.edu/login?url=https://search.ebscohost.com/login .aspx?direct=true&db=nlebk&AN=11688&site=ehost-live&scope=site.

OCHA. 2020. "Humanitarian Needs Overview." https://reliefweb.int/report/ukraine /ukraine-humanitarian-needs-overview-2020-january-2020.

OHCHR (Office of the United Nations High Commissioner for Human Rights). 2017. "Report on the Human Rights Situation in Ukraine, 16 February to 15 May 2017." https://reliefweb.int/report/ukraine/report-human-rights-situation-ukraine-16 -february-15-may-2017-ahrc34crp5-enruuk.2018. "Report of the Special Rapporteur on Torture and Other Cruel, Inhuman or Degrading Treatment or Punishment on his Visit to Ukraine." Accessed June 24, 2019.

——. 2018. "Report of the Special Rapporteur on Torture and Other Cruel, Inhuman or Degrading Treatment or Punishment on his Visit to Ukraine." Accessed June 24, 2019.

——. 2022. "Ukraine Civilian Casualty Update. April 21, 2022." https://www.ohchr.org /en/news/2022/04/ukraine-civilian-casualty-update-21-april-2022#:~:text =OHCHR%20notes%20the%20report%20of,killed%2C%20including%20 women%20and%20children.

Onuch, Olga, Henry Hale, and Gwendolyn Sasse. 2018. "Studying Identity in Ukraine." *Post-Soviet Affairs* 34, no. 2–3: 79–83. https://doi.org/10.1080/1060586X.2018.1451241.

Pavluchkovich, Kristina. 2017. "«Патріот» - ресторан, де можна відчути, що таке війна" [Patriot is a restaurant where you can feel/tell what war is]. *Forpost* [in Ukrainian]. July 12. Accessed April 15, 2019. http://forpost.lviv.ua/txt/suspilstvo/5013-patriot -restoran-de-mozhna-vidchuty-shcho-take-viina.

Peterson, Spike V. 2010. "Gendered Identities, Ideologies, and Practices in the Context of War and Militarism." In *Gender, War, and Militarism,* edited by Laura Sjoberg and Sandra Via, 17–29. Santa Barbara: Praeger. https://search.lib.umich.edu/catalog /record/990027304490106381.

Peterson, Spike V., and A. Sisson Runyan. 1999. *Global Gender Issues: Dilemmas in World Politics.* Boulder: Westview Press. https://search.lib.umich.edu/catalog/record /990088587810106381.

Pifer, Steven. 2019. "Why care about Ukraine and the Budapest Memorandum?" Thursday December 5, Brookings. https://www.brookings.edu/blog/order-from-chaos /2019/12/05/why-care-about-ukraine-and-the-budapest-memorandum/.

Pillen, Alex. 2016. "Language, Translation, Trauma." *Annual Review of Anthropology* 45: 95–111. https://doi.org/10.1146/annurev-anthro-102215-100232.

Polyakova, Alina. 2018. "Weapons of the Weak: Russia and AI-Driven Asymmetric Warfare. Thursday, November 15, 2018, Brookings. https://www.brookings.edu/research /weapons-of-the-weak-russia-and-ai-driven-asymmetric-warfare/.

Pupavac, Vanessa. 2002. "Pathologizing Populations and Colonizing Minds: International Psychosocial Programs in Kosovo." *Alternatives* 27: 489–511. https://doi.org /10.1177/030437540202700404.

Puggioni, Raffaela. 2014. "Against Camps' Violence: Some Voices on Italian Holding Centers." *Political Studies* 62, no. 4: 945–960. https://doi.org/10.1111/1467-9248.12051.

Puglisi, Rosaria. 2015. "Heroes of Villains? Volunteer Battalions in Post-Maidan Ukraine." *Istituo Affari Internazionali Working Paper.* Accessed July 2016. https://www.iai.it /en/pubblicazioni/heroes-or-villains.

Puig de la Bellacasa, Maria. 2017. *Matters of Care: Speculative Ethics in More than Human Worlds.* Minneapolis: University of Minnesota Press. https://muse-jhu-edu.proxy .lib.umich.edu/book/50528.

Putin, Vladimir. 2014. "Transcript: Vladimir Putin's April 17 Q&A." *Washington Post,* April 17, 2014. Accessed November 1, 2016. https://www.washingtonpost.com /world/transcript-vladimirputins-april-17-qanda/2014/04/17/ff77b4a2-c635-11e3 -8b9a-8e0977a24aeb_story.html.

Ramadan, Adam. 2013. "Spatialising the Refugee Camp." *Transactions—Institute of British Geographers* 38, no. 1: 65–77. https://doi.org/10.1111/j.1475-5661.2012 .00509.x.

Randazzo, Elisa. 2016. "The Paradoxes of the 'Everyday': Scrutinizing the Local Turn in Peace Building." *Third World Quarterly* 37, no. 8: 1351–1370. https://doi.org/10 .1080/01436597.2015.1120154.

Rawls, John. 1971. *A Theory of Justice.* Cambridge, MA: The Belknap Press of Harvard University Press. https://doi-org.proxy.lib.umich.edu/10.2307/j.ctvkjb25m.

Reddy, William. 2001. *The Navigation of Feeling: A Framework for the History of Emotions.* Cambridge: Cambridge University Press. http://proxy.lib.umich.edu/login ?url=https://search.ebscohost.com/login.aspx?direct=true&db=e000xna&AN =112574&site=ehost-live&scope=site.

Reeves, Madeleine. 2014. *Border Work: Culture and Society after Socialism.* Ithaca, NY: Cornell University Press. https://ebookcentral-proquest-com.proxy.lib.umich .edu/lib/umichigan/detail.action?docID=3138578.

RFE/RL RadioFree Europe/ Radio Liberty. 2017. *Cargo-200: The Road Home.* Accessed April 3, 2019. https://www.youtube.com/watch?v=mMpGDWWAMy8.

Richmond, Oliver. 2014. "The dilemmas of a hybrid peace: Negative or positive?" *Cooperation and Conflict* 50, no. 1: 50–68. https://doi.org/10.1177/00108367145 37053.

——. 2011. *A Post-liberal Peace.* London: Routledge. https://ebookcentral-proquest -com.proxy.lib.umich.edu/lib/umichigan/detail.action?docID=1020305.

——. 2010 "Resistance and the Post-Liberal Peace." *Millennium—Journal of International Studies* 38, no. 3: 665–692. https://doi.org/10.1177/0305829810365017.

Ricoeur, Paul. 1994. *Oneself as Another.* Translated by Kathleen Blamey. Chicago: University of Chicago Press. https://search.lib.umich.edu/catalog/record/9900258152 20106381.

Ring, Laura. 2006. *Zenana: Everyday Peace in a Karachi Apartment Building.* Bloomington: Indiana University Press. https://search.lib.umich.edu/catalog/record /990053979910106381.

Robbins, Joel. 2013. "Beyond the Suffering Slot: toward an Anthropology of the Good." *Journal of the Royal Anthropological Institute* 19, no. 3: 447–462. https://doi.org /10.1111/1467-9655.12044.

Rose, Nicholas. 1998. *Inventing Ourselves: Psychology, Power and Personhood.* Cambridge: Cambridge University Press. https://search.lib.umich.edu/catalog/record /990030855900106381.

Rosenwein, Barbara H. 2006. *Emotional Communities in the Early Middle Ages.* Ithaca, NY: Cornell University Press. https://search.lib.umich.edu/catalog/record/9900523 43380106381.

Ross, Stephen. 2017. "The Secret Agency of Dispossession." *Etudes Britannique Contemporaines* 53: 1–18. https://doi.org/10.4000/ebc.3739.

Rubin, Steven Jay. 2018. "'Saving Private Ryan at 20: How Spielberg's Vivid D-Day Story Changed War Movies Forever." *Los Angeles Times.* July 24. Accessed July 25, 2018. https://www.latimes.com/entertainment/movies/la-ca-mn-saving-private-ryan -20-story.html.

Ruddick, Sara. 1989. *Maternal Thinking: toward a Politics of Peace.* Boston, MA: Beacon Press. https://search.lib.umich.edu/catalog/record/990044123510106381.

Said, Edward. 1997. *Covering Islam. How the Media and the Experts Determine How We See the Rest of the World.* Vintage Books, New York. https://search.lib.umich.edu /catalog/record/990031657860106381.

——. 1995. *Orientalism. Western Conceptions of the Orient.* Penguin Books, London. https://ebookcentral-proquest-com.proxy.lib.umich.edu/lib/umichigan/detail .action?docID=5337468.

Sanders, Deborah. 2017. "'The War We Want; The War That We Get': Ukraine's Military Reform and the Conflict in the East." *The Journal of Slavic Military Studies* 30, no. 1: 30–49. https://doi.org/10.1080/13518046.2017.1271652.

Sasse, Gwendolyn, and Alice Lackner. 2018. "War and Identity: The Case of the Donbas in Ukraine." *Post-Soviet Affairs* 34, no. 2–3: 139–157. https://doi.org/10.1080 /1060586X.2018.1452209.

Scarry, Elaine. 1988. *The Body in Pain: The Making and Unmaking of the World.* Oxford, UK: Oxford University Press. https://search.lib.umich.edu/catalog/record/9900 45765580106381.

Schaeuble, Michaela. 2014. *Narrating Victimhood.* New York: Berghahn Books. http:// proxy.lib.umich.edu/login?url=https://search.ebscohost.com/login.aspx?direct =true&db=e000xna&AN=638345&site=ehost-live&scope=site.

Schmitt, Carl. 2005. *Political Theology: Four Chapters on the Concept of Sovereignty,* Translated by George Schwab. Chicago: The University of Chicago Press. https:// search.lib.umich.edu/catalog/record/990044317970106381.

Schweitzer, R., M. Brough, and L. Vromans. 2011. "Mental Health of Newly Arrived Burmese Refugees in Australia: Contributions of Pre-Migration and Post-Migration Experiences." *Australian and New Zealand Journal of Psychiatry* 45, no. 4: 299–307. https://doi.org/10.3109/00048674.2010.543412.

Semenenko, Viktoriia. 2018. "Ensuring Equal Regional Employment Conditions as a Mechanism to Overcome the Problems of Employment of IDPS." *Journal of Geography, Politics and Society* 8, no. 1: 44–48. https://doi.org/10.4467/24512249JG .18.005.8157.

Shim, David. 2016. "Between the International and the Everyday: Geopolitics and Imaginaries of Home." *International Studies Review* 18, no. 4: 597–613. https://doi.org /10.1093/isr/viw025.

Shlapentokh, Vladimir. 1984. "Social Values in the Soviet Union: Major Trends in the Post-Stalin Period." Final Report to the National Council for Soviet and East European Research. Accessed July 15, 2017. https://www.ucis.pitt.edu/nceeer/1984 -626-13-Shlapentokh.pdf.

Shoshan, Nitzan. 2014. "Managing Hate: Political Delinquency and Affective Governance in Germany," *Cultural Anthropology* 29, no. 1: 150–172. https://doi.org/10 .14506/ca29.1.09.

Simonsen, Kirsten. 2008. "Practice, Narrative and the 'Multicultural City' A Copenhagen Case. *European Urban and Regional Studies* 15, no. 2: 145–158. https://doi .org/10.1177/0969776407087547.

Sjoberg, Laura, and Sandra Via. 2010. Introduction to *Gender War, and Militarism,* edited by Laura Sjoberg and Sandra Via, 1–16. Santa Barbara: Praeger. https:// search.lib.umich.edu/catalog/record/990088587810106381.

Skoggard, Ian, and Alisse Waterston. 2015. "Introduction: Toward an Anthropology of Affect and Evocative Ethnography." *Anthropology of Consciousness* 26, no. 2: 109–120. https://doi.org/10.1111/anoc.12041.

Smiley, Christopher. 2016. "Disneyland of War." Accessed February 22, 2019. https:// www.youtube.com/watch?v=USnNFkFkdEk.

Smith, Sir R. 2006. *The Utility of Force: The Art of War in the Modern World.* Harmondsworth: Penguin. https://search.lib.umich.edu/catalog/record/990050736900106381.

Solomon, Ty, and Brent Steele. 2017. "Micro-moves in International Relations Theory." *European Journal of International Relations* 23, no. 2: 267–291. https://doi.org /10.1177/1354066116634442.

Sorabji, Cornelia. 2008. "Bosnian Neighbourhoods Revisited: Tolerance, Commitment and Komsiluk." In *On the Margins of Religion,* edited by Frances Pine and João de Pina-Cabral, 97–113. New York: Berghan Books. https://ebookcentral-proquest -com.proxy.lib.umich.edu/lib/umichigan/detail.action?docID=544290.

State Committee on Statistics 2001.

Sorokin, Oleksiy. 2019. "Waiting for Peace: Russia, domestic opposition frustrates Zelensky's plans in Donbas," *Kyiv Post,* October 25, 2019. https://www.kyivpost.com/ukraine -politics/russian-shooting-stalls-zelenskys-hopes-for-peace-plan-in-donbas.html.

Stebelsky, Ihor. 2018. "A Tale of Two Regions: Geopolitics, Identities, Narratives, and Conflict in Kharkiv and the Donbas," *Eurasian Geography and Economics* 59, no. 1: 28–50. https://doi.org/10.1080/15387216.2018.1428904.

Sylvester, Christine. 2013. "Experiencing War: An Introduction." In *Experiencing War,* edited by Christine Sylvester, 1–7. New York: Routledge. https://search.lib.umich .edu/catalog/record/990093623470106381.

——. 2011. "Pathways to Experiencing War." In *Experiencing War,* edited by Cathleen Sylvester, 118–130. Abingdon: Routledge. https://search.lib.umich.edu/catalog /record/990093623470106381.

Synovitz, Ron. 2014. "Explainer: The Budapest Memorandum and its Relevance to Crimea." RadioFreeEurope/Radio Liberty, February 28, 2014. https://www.rferl.org/a/ukraine-explainer-budapest-memorandum/25280502.html.

Taussig, Michael. 1984. "Culture of Terror—Space of Death: Roger Casement's Putumayo Report and the Explanation of Torture." *Comparative Studies in Society and History* 26, no. 3: 467–497. https://doi.org/10.1017/S0010417500011105.

Tondo, Lorenzo and Mark Rice-Oxley. 2022. "'They Don't Believe It's Real': How War Has Split Ukrainian-Russian Families." *The Guardian*, March 18, 2022, https://www.theguardian.com/world/2022/mar/18/ukraine-russia-families-divided-over-war.

Torres, Nicole, and Andrew Gurevich. 2018. "Introduction: Militarization of Consciousness." *Anthropology of Consciousness* 29, no. 2: 137–144. https://doi.org/10.1111/anoc.12101.

Trouillot, Michel-Rolph. 2003. *Global Transformations: Anthropology and the Modern World*. New York: Palgrave Macmillan. https://doi.org/10.1353/jhs.2013.0046.

Tronto, Joan C. 1993. *Moral Boundaries: A Political Argument for an Ethic of Care*. New York: Routledge. https://search.lib.umich.edu/catalog/record/990045452150106381.

Turbine, Vikki. 2012. "Locating Women's Human Rights in Post-Soviet Provincial Russia." *Europe Asia Studies* 64, no. 10: 1847–1869. https://doi.org/10.1080/09668136.2012.681245.

Turner, Victor. 1967. *The Forest of Symbols: Aspects of Ndembu Ritual*. New York: Cornell University Press. https://search.lib.umich.edu/catalog/record/990045242220106381.

Tyner, James A. 2016. "Hate-Crimes as Racial Violence: A Critique of the Exceptional." *Social and Cultural Geography* 17, no. 8: 1060–1078. https://doi.org/10.1080/14649365.2016.1152392.

Uehling, Greta. 2020. "Working through Warfare in Ukraine: Rethinking Militarization in a Ukrainian Theme Café." *International Feminist Journal of Politics* 22, no. 3: 335–358. DOI: 10.1080/14616742.2019.1678393.

Umland, Andreas. 2014. "In Defense of Conspirology: A Rejoinder to Serhiy Kudelia's Anti-Political Analysis of the Hybrid War in Eastern Ukraine," *PONARS Eurasia*, September 30. www.ponarseurasia.org/article/defense-conspirology-rejoinder-serhiy-kudelias-anti-political-analysis-hybrid-war-eastern.

United Nations Economic and Social Council. 1998. "Guiding Principles on Internal Displacement." E/CN.4/1998/53/Add. 2. February 11, 1998. Accessed May 14, 2020. https://documents-dds-ny.un.org/doc/UNDOC/GEN/G98/104/93/PDF/G9810493.pdf?OpenElement.

United Nations High Commissioner for Refugees. 2022. "Ukraine Refugee Situation." https://data2.unhcr.org/en/situations/ukraine.

United Nations Population Fund. 2018. "Men in Ukraine still hold fast to gender norms, landmark study finds." Accessed December 21, 2018. https://www.unfpa.org/news/men-ukraine-hold-fast-gender-norms-landmark-study-finds.

United Nations Security Council Press Release. 2003. "Women Suffer Disproportionately during and after War, Security Council Told during Day Long Debate on Women, Peace and Security." Accessed November 2, 2015. https://www.un.org/press/en/2003/sc7908.doc.htm.

Vaittinen, Tiina, Amanda Donahoe, Rahel Kunz, Silja Bára Ómarsdóttir, and Sanam Roohi. 2019. "Care as Everyday Peacebuilding." *Peacebuilding* 7, no. 2: 194–209. https://doi.org/10.1080/21647259.2019.1588453.

van der Kolk, Bessel, and Rita Fisler. 1995. "Dissociation and the Fragmentary Nature of Traumatic Memories: Overview and Exploratory Study." *Journal of Traumatic Stress* 8, no. 4: 505–525. https://doi.org/10.1080/21647259.2019.1588453.

van der Kolk, Bessel, and Onno van der Hart. 1995. "The Intrusive Past: The Flexibility of Memory and the Engraving of Trauma." In Caruth Cathy, ed. 1995. *Trauma: Explorations in Memory.* 158–182 Baltimore, MD and London: Johns Hopkins University Press. https://search.lib.umich.edu/catalog/record/990030024210106381.

Van Gennup, Arnold. (1909) 2004. *The Rites of Passage.* Translated by Monika B. Vizedom and Gabrielle L. Caffee. Introduction by Solon Kimball. New York: Routledge. https://search.lib.umich.edu/catalog/record/990044210540106381.

Van Leeuwen, Mathijs, Willemijn Verkoren, and Freerk Boedeltje. 2012. "Thinking beyond the Liberal Peace: from Utopia to Heterotopia." *Acta Politica* 47, no. 3: 292–316. https://doi.org/10.1057/ap.2012.1.

Verdery, Katherine. 1999. *The Political Lives of Dead Bodies: Reburial and Postsocialist Change.* New York: Columbia University Press. https://search.lib.umich.edu/catalog/record/990040244370106381.

Wall, Tyler. 2011. "Philanthropic Soldiers, Practical Orientalism, and the Occupation of Iraq," *Identities: Global Studies in Culture and Power* 18, no. 5: 481–501. https://doi.org/10.1080/1070289X.2011.671710.

Wanner, Catherine. 2010. *Burden of Dreams: History and Identity in Post-Soviet Ukraine.* Pennsylvania: Penn State University Press.

Wetherell, Margaret. 2012. *Affect and Emotion: A New Social Science Understanding.* London: Sage.

Wezeman, Siemon T., and Alexandra Kuimova. 2018. "Ukraine and Black Sea Security." *SIPRI Background Paper,* December 2018. https://www.sipri.org/sites/default/files/2018-12/bp_1812_black_sea_ukraine_0.pdf.

Willen, Sarah S. 2007. "Toward a Critical Phenomenology of 'Illegality': State Power, Criminalization, and Abjectivity among Undocumented Migrant Workers in Tel Aviv, Israel." *International Migration* 45: 8–38. https://doi.org/10.1111/j.1468-2435.2007.00409.x.

Williams, Philippa. 2015. *Everyday Peace?: Politics, Citizenship and Muslim Lives in India.* Hoboken, NJ: John Wiley & Sons. https://search.lib.umich.edu/catalog/record/990139670770106381.

Wilkinson, Cai. 2018. "Mother Russia in Queer Peril: The Gender Logic of the Hypermasculine State." In *Revisiting Gendered States: Feminist Imaginings of the State in International Relations,* edited by S. Parashar, J. A. Tickner, and J. True, 105–121. New York: Oxford University Press. https://search.lib.umich.edu/catalog/record/990161295290106381.

Wilson, Andrew. 2016. "The Donbas in 2014: Explaining Civil Conflict Perhaps, but not Civil War," *Europe-Asia Studies* 68, no. 4: 631–652. https://doi.org/10.1080/09668136.2016.1176994.

——. 2002. *The Ukrainians: Unexpected Nation.* New Haven: Yale University Press. http://proxy.lib.umich.edu/login?url=https://search.ebscohost.com/login.aspx?direct=true&db=e000xna&AN=1074228&site=ehost-live&scope=site.

Woodward, Rachel. 2018. "From Military Geography to Militarism's Geographies: Disciplinary Engagements with the Geographies of Militarism and Military Activities." *Progress in Human Geography* 29, no. 6: 718–740. https://doi.org/10.1191/0309132505ph579oa.

Yakubova, Larysa. 2015. "Etnonatsional'na spetsyfika Donbasu" [Ethnonational Specifics of the Donbas]. *Rehional'na istoriya Ukrayiny [Regional History of Ukraine]* 9: 229–244. No DOI or permalink.

Yurchak, Alexei. 2006. *Everything was Forever, Until It Was No More: The Last Soviet Generation.* Princeton, NJ: Princeton University Press. https://hdl-handle-net.proxy.lib.umich.edu/2027/heb.32326.

Yuval-Davis, Nira. 1997. *Gender & Nation*. London, Thousand Oaks: Sage. https://search.lib.umich.edu/catalog/record/990031832160106381.

Zhukov, Yuri M. 2016. "Trading Hard Hats for Combat Helmets: The Economics of Rebellion in Eastern Ukraine," *Journal of Comparative Economics* 44, no. 1: 1–15. https://doi.org/10.1016/j.jce.2015.10.010.

Index

suffering (*continued*)
161; humanitarian crisis and, 29; military violence resulting in, 113; sci-fi awareness and, 139; social suffering, 28, 167n3; tolerance for, 116; verbal reconstructions of, 125–126. *See also* trauma
suffering "slot", 28, 158, 161
Svetlana (interviewee), 16, 53–56, 74, 127
symbolic violence, 168n1

tactical kinship, 92–93, 94–99, 96*f,* 160–161
Tamara (interviewee), 75, 87
Taras (interviewee), 141–142, 146–151, 153, 155–156
terrorism: ATO (Antiterrorist Operation), 19, 42, 48, 53; separatists viewed as terrorists, 21, 26, 31, 136, 148
Thucydides, 144
Torres, Nicole and Andrew Gurevich, 38
trauma: agency and, 121; crisis ordinariness and, 113, 121; dissociation and, 126; embodiment of, 124–129, 162; forced displacement and, 28, 138–140; practical orientalism and, 125, 126; sci-fi awareness and, 125–126; silence and, 125–126
Treaty on the Non-Proliferation of Nuclear Weapons, 25
Two Rabbits (café), 99

Ukrainian language, 21–22
Union of People's Memory (Kyiv), 155
United Nations: on Donbas conflict, 31; Geneva Conventions and, 143; Guiding Principles on Internal Displacement, 27–28; High Commissioner for Human Rights, 159; High Commissioner for Refugees, 159; peace-building by, 56; Population Fund, 78

values, 9, 20, 40, 87, 144, 146, 154, 161, 167n3, 169n1
Van Leeuwen, Mathijs, 57
Vera (interviewee), 71
Verdery, Katherine, 169n1
victims, xi, 28, 62, 150, 158
Victoria (interviewee), 68–69, 136
Vietnam War, 38
violence: masculinity and, 43–45, 167n3; normalization of, 40, 93, 113, 117, 119;

structural, 112, 119, 168n1; symbolic, 168n1. *See also* militarization; trauma
visual forms of practical orientalism, 135–136
Vladimir (interviewee), 88–89
Volodya (interviewee), 128
volunteer body collectors, 13, 17, 141–157; dead body politics and, 144–146; history of moving the dead, 143–144; interpersonal peace and, 155–156; neutrality of, 142; pediatric insulin deliveries by, 152–155, 156–157; recovery mission of, 146–152; sovereignty and, 145

Wanner, Catherine, 133
war, hybrid, 2, 3, 24, 31; peace processes and, 57, 70; "undeclared," 31, 38, 47. *See also* everyday war; militarization
Weinstein, Harvey M., 52
Williams, Philippa, 54
Willis, Paul, 112, 121
Wilson, Andrew, 21
women: agency and, 57; family-nation relationship and, 76–77, 102; friendships and, 69; humanitarian crisis and, 31; practical orientalism and, 137–138; Russia's invasion of Ukraine (2022) and, 161. *See also* femininity; gender

Xristina (interviewee), 72

Yakubova, Larysa, 20
Yanukovych, Victor, 18–19, 22, 23–24, 69; clan, of, 24
"ykrop," 150, 156
Yuliya (interviewee), 9, 15, 68–69, 127–128
Yurchak, Alexei, 133
Yuri Antonov (interviewee), 33–34, 36–37, 41–45, 47, 49–50
Yuval-Davis, Nira, 102

Zaporozhian Cossack heritage, 20
Zhenia (interviewee), 127
Zhilkin, Yaroslav, 142, 148, 154–155
Zhukov, Yuri M., 23
zombies and zombification, 11, 17, 58, 71–73, 87, 91, 125, 139–140
Zoya (interviewee), 21

CPSIA information can be obtained
at www.ICGtesting.com
Printed in the USA
LVHW041328060123
736516LV00003B/365

9 781501 768484